Shadow on the White House

MODERN WAR STUDIES

Theodore A. Wilson
General Editor

Raymond A. Callahan
J. Garry Clifford
Jacob W. Kipp
Jay Luvaas
Allan R. Millett
Series Editors

Shadow on the White House
Presidents and the Vietnam War, 1945–1975

Edited by David L. Anderson

 University Press of Kansas

Published by the University Press of Kansas (Lawrence, Kansas 66049), which was
organized by the Kansas Board of Regents and is operated and funded by Emporia
State University, Fort Hays State University, Kansas State University, Pittsburg State
University, the University of Kansas, and Wichita State University

Library of Congress Cataloging-in-Publication Data

Shadow on the White House : presidents and the Vietnam War, 1945–1975
  / David L. Anderson, editor.
      p.   cm. — (Modern war studies)
    Includes bibliographical references and index.
    ISBN 0-7006-0582-7 (hardcover) — ISBN 0-7006-0583-5 (pbk.)
    1. Vietnamese Conflict, 1961–1975—United States.   2. United
States—Foreign relations—Vietnam.   3. Vietnam—Foreign relations—
United States.   4. United States—Politics and government—1945–
I. Anderson, David L., 1945-   . II. Series.
DS558.S43   1993
959.704'3373—dc20   92-35898

British Library Cataloguing in Publication Data is available.

Printed in the United States of America
10 9 8 7 6 5 4 3 2

The paper used in this publication meets the minimum requirements of the American
National Standard for Permanence of Paper for Printed Library Materials
Z39.48-1984.

Contents

1

Presidential Leadership and U.S. Intervention in Southeast Asia: The Buck Stops—and Starts—Here

David L. Anderson

Protesters outside the Pentagon in October 1967 carried huge posters with a portrait of President Lyndon B. Johnson and an accusing caption, "WAR CRIMINAL." In the opinion of many critics, the massively destructive conflagration raging in Southeast Asia was "Johnson's War." Two years later, President Richard M. Nixon asked the "silent majority" to support his continued pursuit of victory in Vietnam, and opponents christened the conflict "Nixon's War." Conducted without a congressional declaration of war, the Vietnam War was manifestly a presidential war. Justice Abe Fortas, one of Johnson's closest associates, observed that "Johnson pursued the Vietnam War because of Eisenhower's position and Kennedy's position."[1] Could the U.S. military intervention in Vietnam also be called Kennedy's War or Eisenhower's War or even Truman's War? From 1945, when Harry S. Truman's administration began searching for an American response to the clash in Indochina between French colonialism and Vietminh communism, through 1975, when Gerald R. Ford and his aides tried unsuccessfully to solicit additional aid for South Vietnam from a reluctant Congress, presidents struggled with the war in Vietnam. For three decades the conflict cast a continuing shadow on the White House.

The assumption connecting the chapters in this volume is that each president placed his personal stamp on the Vietnam issue. Each made substantive decisions or conscious choices from among clearly delineated options that shaped U.S. policy beyond his own term in office. The level of personal involvement in Southeast Asian questions varied considerably from the minimal attention of Truman to the weighty preoccupation of Johnson and Nixon. In all cases, however, the president exhibited a particular decision-

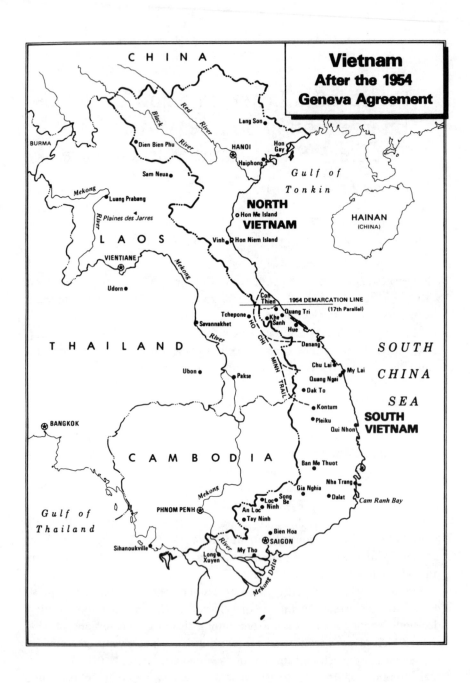

**Vietnam
After the 1954
Geneva Agreement**

CHINA

BURMA

Lang Son

Black River
Red River

HANOI
Hon Gay
Haiphong

Gulf of Tonkin

Dien Bien Phu

Sam Neua

Mekong River

Luang Prabang

Plaines des Jarres

NORTH VIETNAM
Hon Me Island

HAINAN
(CHINA)

LAOS

VIENTIANE

Vinh
Hon Niem Island

Udorn

Mekong River

Con Thien
Quang Tri
Khe Sanh

1954 DEMARCATION LINE
(17th Parallel)

Tchepone

Savannakhet

Hue

HO CHI MINH TRAIL

Danang

THAILAND

River

SOUTH CHINA SEA

Chu Lai
My Lai
Quang Ngai

Ubon

Pakse

Dak To

Kontum

Pleiku
Qui Nhon

SOUTH VIETNAM

BANGKOK

CAMBODIA

Ban Me Thuot

Nha Trang

Mekong

Gia Nghia
Song Be
Loc Ninh
An Loc
Tay Ninh

Dalat
Cam Ranh Bay

Gulf of Thailand

PHNOM PENH

Bien Hoa
SAIGON

Sihanoukville

River
Long Xuyen
My Tho

Mekong Delta

making style and set priorities or objectives for his administration that translated into specific actions. Even when a president delegated policy formulation to others or took a less direct role in Vietnam deliberations because of other demands of his office, it was still the president's team at work.

The contributors to this book seek to clarify some of the interconnections between the modern presidency and the nation's frustrating, tragic, and humiliating failure in Southeast Asia. Their case studies focus on the personality, politics, priorities, and actions of the presidents. They also consider the institution of the presidency and especially the often-noted expansion of presidential power in foreign policy formulation since World War II. Although many studies of modern executive power begin with Franklin D. Roosevelt, this book starts with Truman. The connecting theme is consideration of the reasons and ways that presidents committed U.S. money, manpower, and prestige in Indochina in opposition to the socialist revolution there—a decision faced by Truman, Eisenhower, Kennedy, Johnson, Nixon, and Ford, but not by Roosevelt.

By the end of World War II, the office of president of the United States was probably the single most powerful political position in the world. Despite constitutional provisions that balanced the authority of the president with that of Congress and the courts, chief executives beginning with George Washington have enlarged the powers of their office. Even among the generation that authored the Constitution, such critics of centralized authority as Thomas Jefferson and James Madison often exercised forceful leadership when they acquired the office. Andrew Jackson, Abraham Lincoln, Theodore Roosevelt, Woodrow Wilson, Franklin Roosevelt, and other presidents assumed a broad definition of presidential prerogatives. This steady growth of executive influence affected both domestic and foreign policy, but it quickened markedly in the international arena during the twentieth century as the United States joined in two world wars. At the moment of Allied victory over Germany and Japan in 1945, the maturing of presidential power and U.S. world power came together.

This linkage between presidential leadership and U.S. global supremacy had a host of implications for the United States both at home and abroad. Some of these issues were constants in the history of the presidency, and others were products of the idiosyncrasies of each president and of the particular circumstances of the world after World War II. The Cold War with the Soviet Union, the American economic stake in the vitality of world capitalism, and the global instability created by nationalist revolutions in the developing nations placed great demands on the U.S. government for forceful leadership. The growing U.S. involvement in Vietnam after 1945 was both a result of and an influence on this already volatile mixture of forces. It was an incessant challenge to the presidents and their stewardship of the national interest.

How much emphasis should be given to the office of president and to its occupant when analyzing public policy? Clearly, the Constitution established a unitary executive, that is, it placed the authority of the office in the hands of a single person. In *Federalist* Number 70, Alexander Hamilton defended this arrangement as conducive to "energy in the executive," which is "a leading character in the definition of good government." He went on to enumerate the virtues of the single executive: "decision, activity, secrecy, and dispatch."[2] Over the decades, however, this single office grew into a branch of government comprising thousands of persons. In response to the Great Depression and World War II, Franklin Roosevelt greatly expanded executive agencies, and that proliferation continued after the war. All this growth challenged the concept of the unitary executive, and, as one political scientist has put it, a modern president makes policy the way a restaurant customer makes dinner when he orders a meal. He selects from a menu presented to him and accepts the food as the establishment has prepared it.[3]

Unlike the restaurant patron, however, the president of the United States controls the kitchen help.[4] He shapes and directs his advisory staff and through it the expansive executive bureaucracy. Both constitutional principle and contemporary practice make the presidency central to American political life. Since the Roosevelt administration, presidents with their aides have been able to initiate public policy and in many respects to set the national agenda. This pivotal role has given the president high visibility, and in the public eye the presidency is a one-person job. The importance of the office makes the identity and character of its occupant a matter of significance in the formation of government policy.[5]

In no area of public life has the identification of presidents with particular policies been more apparent than in foreign affairs. In the early republic there were, for example, Washington's Neutrality Proclamation, Jefferson's Embargo, and the Monroe Doctrine. Contemporaries called the War of 1812 "Mr. Madison's War," and critics of the war with Mexico in 1846–1848 christened it "Mr. Polk's War." Later came Theodore Roosevelt's Corollary to the Monroe Doctrine, Taft's Dollar Diplomacy, and Wilson's Fourteen Points. The public and historians have linked Franklin Roosevelt's name with many initiatives, such as the Good Neighbor Policy, Lend-Lease, and even the controversial Back Door to War argument that he purposely allowed the Japanese attack on Pearl Harbor. After World War II, presidential "doctrines" mushroomed, with the term being applied to foreign policy pronouncements by Truman, Eisenhower, Nixon, Carter, and Reagan.[6]

This presidential preeminence had its roots both in the "energy" of the chief executive admired by Hamilton and in the vagaries of the constitutional balance of power in the area of foreign affairs. Article Two of the Constitution explicitly vests "executive Power" in the president but provides no precise definition of that authority. Presidents may make treaties and appoint ambassadors with the concurrence of the Senate and may receive emissaries of other governments. The one clear and unqualified power of the office in foreign affairs is the designation of the president as commander in chief of the army, navy, and militia when called to federal service. Conversely, the Constitution leaves a number of foreign policy powers to Congress. It is the legislative branch that regulates foreign commerce and monetary exchange, defines violations of international law, funds the army and navy, establishes military regulations, calls out the militia, and—most notably—declares war. The war power is the ultimate prerogative in foreign policy, and the Constitution clearly places it in Congress. The language of the document also allows the executive to make policy, however, including the use of military force as commander in chief. The history of American foreign policymaking has been a chronicle of conflict and confusion between the president and Congress.[7]

Some scholars have characterized this tug-of-war as a pendulum in which an assertive president or a series of them dominates the process for a period until the legislature eventually asserts itself and pushes the balance back to its side. Lincoln, for example, initiated military action in the Civil War without Congress even being in session and continued throughout the war to make military and diplomatic decisions that Capitol Hill had to accept as faits accomplis. His successor was impeached, however, and Andrew Johnson and several presidents after him were largely overshadowed by influential congressional leaders. Similarly, Wilson conducted U.S. policy during World War I almost as his personal crusade for collective security only to be repudiated by the Senate's rejection of the Versailles Treaty and League of Nations. This pendulum theory fails to acknowledge, however, that powers gained by the presidency have seldom been completely withdrawn by a resurgent Congress. For example, Washington successfully resisted congressional efforts to obtain copies of administration documents detailing John Jay's treaty mission to Britain. Presidents ever since have jealously protected this claim of "executive privilege" to confidential communication with their aides and officers. An extensive body of precedents has developed a pattern of executive authority in foreign relations that has been more of a staircase than a pendulum. That is, presidential power has steadily mounted with only periodic levelings of that power by Congress.[8]

With the advent of the Cold War, this historical pattern of executive ascendancy became more pronounced. In his so-called Truman Doctrine speech of March 1947, Truman appealed to the nation to close ranks with him in a struggle for freedom. Truman, Eisenhower, and their successors portrayed the challenge of Soviet totalitarianism and communist ideology as a global crisis that endangered the American "way of life"—an all-encompassing term that included the strategic, economic, and ideological well-being of the United States. The magnitude of this threat seemed so overwhelming that Congress and the American public looked to the commander in chief for reassurance, especially since the Soviet adversary was armed with nuclear weapons. Through new and powerful executive instruments—such as the National Security Council, the Central Intelligence Agency, and the Joint Chiefs of Staff—presidents initiated and managed foreign policy, often in a crisis atmosphere behind a veil of tight secrecy.[9]

As Robert J. McMahon demonstrates in Chapter 2, the Truman administration began the process of turning Vietnam into one of several Cold War battlegrounds. During World War II, Roosevelt had envisioned a phased independence process for the former French colonies in Indochina under a trusteeship plan. But U.S. officials never formalized this concept, and even before Roosevelt's death in 1945, Washington was backing away from the idea. Increasing friction with the Soviet Union over European issues prompted the administration to cultivate cooperation with France and to avoid conflict with Paris over the colonial issue. When Truman suddenly found himself in the White House, there was no explicit U.S. policy for Indochina. Before he left office, however, he had made, in the context of the Cold War, the first presidential decisions that involved the United States directly in the fate of Vietnam. The United States began aiding the French war effort against the communist-led Vietnamese independence movement known as the Vietminh.

Eisenhower accepted Truman's assessment that Vietnam was a vital nation in the United States' global strategy to contain communism. As David L. Anderson describes in Chapter 3, however, the new administration had to develop new tactics because of France's decision to end its costly war in Indochina. With Eisenhower directly involved in the decision-making process, the United States resisted military intervention in 1954 to save the floundering French effort, and scholars have credited the president with statesmanlike restraint. At the same time, however, the Eisenhower administration began to attempt to create a new nation in South Vietnam to hold the containment line against the Democratic Republic of Vietnam that had defeated the French and controlled the North. The instrument of this nation building was to be an autocratic politician named Ngo Dinh Diem. By the time Eisenhower left office in 1961, Diem's regime still survived in South Vietnam, but violent resistance to his rule was mounting. American intervention in Vietnamese politics had firmly cemented U.S. interests to Diem's dubious legitimacy and shaky leadership. In contrast to the seeming astuteness of 1954, Eisenhower's subsequent policies had sharply limited U.S. choices. His successors could give up on Diem and thereby discredit a decade of U.S. policy in the region, or they could persevere in the increasingly dangerous and costly support of South Vietnam as an American Cold War outpost.

Spurning what he viewed to be Eisenhower's defensive approach, Kennedy came to the White House determined to take the initiative in the global contest with the Soviet Union and People's Republic of China for influence in the so-called Third World of developing nations. The Peace Corps, Alliance for Progress, and a large increase in U.S. economic and military aid to South Vietnam were, according to Gary R. Hess, part of this effort. Despite the positive rhetoric from Kennedy and his energetic aides, they never resolved the central policy issue in Vietnam and other Third World areas: How far should the United States go in using its resources, influence, and prestige to ensure the survival of governments like Diem's that rest on a narrow popular base? Kennedy's policy was ambiguous, and that ambiguity was dramatically revealed when the White House allowed a plot to proceed that resulted in the death of Diem three weeks before Kennedy's own murder.

Taking the presidential oath after the assassinations of Kennedy and Diem, Johnson confronted both domestic and international challenges that could have debilitated U.S. policies. Instead, he quickly emerged as a chief executive who had an enormous impact on both the shape of the modern presidency and the conduct of the American war in Vietnam. To examine the multiple dimensions of this powerful politician, George C. Herring and Sandra C. Taylor investigate two key aspects of Johnson's character and leadership. Taylor uses racial and cultural concepts in her chapter, and Herring employs a military command analysis. Both find that the Vietnam War

thrust Johnson into roles for which he was ill suited, but his actions had profound consequences for the people of both the United States and Indochina.

Were his critics correct to label the Vietnam War "Lyndon Johnson's
War"? He was certainly a forceful leader who dominated his administration. He demanded loyalty from subordinates, searched for consensus on
controversial issues, and personalized all challenges to his policies. In these
ways he made the war his war. But, Herring contends, in other ways his style
and personality also made him a victim of the war. Johnson lacked diplomatic and military experience, and his blustering approach masked his own
insecurity in handling national security issues. His preoccupation with and
love for his domestic Great Society program also restricted the energy and
vision he had for international problems. In addition, this strange war—so
blithely labeled a "limited war"—confronted him, as it did other presidents,
with an incredibly complex and difficult military, political, and diplomatic
challenge. Johnson had deficiencies as a war manager. He was unwilling to
take control of the war or to permit establishment of the bureaucratic machinery needed to wage it effectively. The purpose of Herring's chapter is
not to extend the long-standing controversy over whether Johnson could or
should have won the war. Rather, it addresses one of the most basic questions of the war: How did such a dynamic leader of such a strong nation fail
so tragically both at home and abroad?

Taylor explores an equally fundamental question: How did the vast cultural and racial differences between the United States and Vietnam influence
U.S. conduct of the war? The question could be applied to almost any U.S.
policymaker, but she raises it about Johnson because of the complexity of
his personality and the devastating effect of his policies on the daily lives of
ordinary Vietnamese citizens. Johnson was a populist and a self-styled
champion of the common man. He was a regional, indeed provincial, politician who had risen to national leadership through a brilliant mastery of domestic politics with a corresponding absence of attention to international
affairs. He overcame the racist culture of his native South to become a pro-
moter of civil rights and economic advancement for poor Americans—
black, brown, and white. Yet this same defender of social justice personally
humiliated South Vietnamese leaders and unleashed upon the rural population of Vietnam a maelstrom of modern weaponry that killed thousands of
people and devastated the physical and cultural landscape for those who remained. Taylor probes into the mysteries of political psychology and offers
some provocative ideas about Johnson's leadership and limitations in articu-

lating U.S. purposes in Vietnam. Although she finds no "smoking guns," she raises serious questions about this architect of the Great Society.

By the time Nixon became president, the American nation and the presidency were both deeply mired in the Vietnam War. Johnson and earlier presidents had made Vietnam a president's war, and Nixon took up the tasks of defending the presidential prerogative of shaping wartime policy and of bringing the war to a successful conclusion. Nixon conceived of his role as similar to that of other wartime presidents such as Lincoln, Wilson, Roosevelt, and Truman. He assumed that the national emergency justified a sweeping exercise of executive power without detailed congressional or public review, a constitutional luxury of peacetime. Melvin Small examines how Nixon fought this two-front war—abroad against the Vietnamese communists and at home against those Americans who would limit his presidential powers. Jeffrey P. Kimball follows the same theme but addresses how Nixon arranged the Paris peace settlement of 1973 not only to provide an immediate U.S. exit from the military conflict but also to preserve his own reputation, the powers of his office, and the future influence of the United States in world affairs.

When Nixon took office in January 1969, he confronted a vigorous antiwar movement whose supporters included many on Capitol Hill, in the media, and among the general public. He was determined not to leave Vietnam without a "peace with honor" but was equally determined to end U.S. involvement before the next election. Confident of his ability to obtain that peace, Nixon believed he first had to neutralize the antiwar critics. That neutralization was initially attempted through reescalation by stealth, according to Small, and when that failed, through an unprecedented media management and suppression campaign and an associated assault on dissenters. Much of this innovative domestic containment program became part of the bill of charges against Nixon during the Watergate investigation. The critics of his policy initiatives exercised a powerful restraining influence on U.S. actions, Small contends, even when those critics were temporarily contained during periods of Nixon's first administration.

While Nixon campaigned for reelection in 1972, his national security adviser, Henry A. Kissinger, feverishly and secretly labored to fashion the promised "peace with honor." Kimball argues that Nixon's decisions during these critical months, which finally led to the agreement terminating U.S. military intervention in Vietnam, were deeply rooted in the president's past political and diplomatic experience and in his psychological traits. Nixon combined rational and irrational notions about the use of massive military power in the conduct of foreign affairs. In April he ordered extensive air raids throughout South and North Vietnam (Operation LINEBACKER) while Kissinger continued negotiations. After his election victory, Nixon suddenly broke off the talks in December and launched new B-52 bomber raids against Hanoi (LINEBACKER II). On January 2, 1973, both sides agreed to a final treaty that resembled in its essentials an agreement reached in October. Why did Nixon feel that the so-called Christmas bombing was necessary? In part, its purpose was to create conditions that would ensure South Vietnamese president Nguyen Van Thieu's acquiescence to the treaty. According to Kimball, the massive and dramatic bombing also offered Nixon and Kissinger several mostly symbolic advantages in American domestic politics and in their effort to maintain the credibility of American world hegemony.

When Ford succeeded Nixon in August 1974, the presidency was in crisis, and the killing continued in Indochina. Nixon's resignation in the face of imminent impeachment brought Ford, who had been appointed, not elected, vice-president, to the Oval Office. These unprecedented circumstances greatly restricted the new president's leadership as the nation faced critical international challenges, including increasing energy dependency, instability in the Middle East, and nuclear arms control negotiations. Meanwhile, the 1973 Paris agreement had not brought peace to Southeast Asia. Fighting still raged in the region, and the U.S.-backed governments in South Vietnam and Cambodia stood on the brink of collapse. With the assistance of Kissinger, who carried over from Nixon's team, Ford tried to contain the Indochina hostilities, to maintain the image of firm U.S. support for its allies, and especially to guard against congressional usurpation of executive authority in foreign policy. Although the communist-led forces finally emerged victorious after Ford took office, David Anderson suggests that Ford was able to hold the line with Congress on some key aspects of military and diplomatic decision making. Still, Ford's struggle with congressional leaders over how to respond to the demise of America's twenty-five years of intervention in Southeast Asia symbolized how the war had affected the American political structure.

As profound as the lessons of the Vietnam War were for U.S. foreign policy, the war's domestic consequences were equally significant. The good health of a democratic system depends on communication and understanding between a responsible electorate and its responsive representatives. The Vietnam War and the related Watergate scandal that toppled Nixon brought to a head a number of political pathologies. One of these was the ever-increasing dominance of the presidency within the federal government. This "imperial presidency" had its corollary in the frequent default of Congress to serve as a balance to the executive, especially in foreign affairs. A second devastating impact of Vietnam was the destruction of credibility within the political process. Not only did the public come to distrust its leaders, but presidents and other officials distrusted the public. Compounding the problems of executive-legislative balance and political credibility was the war's creation of various socioeconomic burdens. Problems such as inflation, unfulfilled Great Society reforms, and the generation gap were aggravated by the Vietnam War. These pathologies brought an end to the domestic consensus that had sustained U.S. Cold War policies since World War II and undergirded the federal government's authority structure since the time of Franklin Roosevelt. In 1961, Kennedy had echoed the long-standing liberal credo that the United States was willing to bear any burden and pay any price in defense of liberty. After Vietnam, the American public was skeptical of such appeals for sacrifice and of politicians who used such rhetoric.

Many critics of the Vietnam War consider it to be one of the starkest examples of the imperial presidency. Through World War II, presidents generally respected the constitutional stipulation that only Congress could declare war. In Korea, Truman committed U.S. forces to major combat without a formal congressional declaration. Eisenhower fought no presidential wars, but he vigorously and successfully opposed the Bricker Amendment, which attempted to place congressional restraints on executive freedom in foreign affairs. Without consulting Congress, Kennedy sanctioned a military move against Cuba's communist government, went to the nuclear brink over Soviet missiles in Cuba, and clandestinely involved the United States in the overthrow and assassination of President Diem. Johnson misled Congress into near unanimous passage of the Gulf of Tonkin Resolution in 1964, which, until 1970, was the only explicit legislative sanction for the extensive ground and air war conducted in Vietnam by both Johnson and Nixon.

As early as 1966, influential senators such as J. William Fulbright (D-Ark.) were questioning the White House's rationale and objectives in Vietnam, but Congress declined to check executive authority. There were almost continuous congressional hearings on various aspects of U.S. Indochina policy throughout the late 1960s, but appropriations for the war continued and no legislative limits were imposed. The reasons are complex and include fear of appearing to abandon the men who were fighting, reluctance to assume responsibility for a major shift in U.S. policy, and the power of some hawkish committee chairmen. Only after the ground war expanded to Cambodia in 1970 did Congress repeal the Gulf of Tonkin Resolution and pass

the Cooper-Church Amendment forbidding an expansion of the war without congressional approval. Following the Nixon administration's negotiated withdrawal of U.S. combat forces from Vietnam in 1973, Congress approved, over a presidential veto, the War Powers Resolution, which enabled
the legislature to countermand an extended overseas deployment of U.S.
military units.[10]

Although these congressional responses to the imperial presidency were
notable products of the Vietnam experience, they were far from a definitive
clarification of executive-legislative relations. On such issues as Watergate,
the ratification of the SALT II treaty with the Soviet Union, and aid to the
Nicaraguan Contras, Capitol Hill was assertive. On the other hand, the War
Powers Resolution and other post-Vietnam measures were not directly applied to Ronald Reagan's deployment of U.S. military forces in Lebanon,
Grenada, and the Persian Gulf or to George Bush's attack on Panama in
1989. In the 1990–1991 war against Iraq, Bush obtained congressional acquiescence to the use of force after he had already dispatched half a million
troops. Congress has yet to use the War Powers Resolution to overrule a
president's initiative.

Beyond the constitutional questions, the Vietnam War also created a
credibility gap in the U.S. political system. At the time of the Gulf of Tonkin
Resolution in August 1964, Congress, the press, and most of the American
public believed that U.S. support of South Vietnam was a justifiable and af-
fordable commitment. In November, the voters handed Johnson a sweeping
endorsement of his foreign and domestic performance. In the months that
followed, however, the magnitude and costs of the U.S. effort in Vietnam
grew and questions increased. Demands for explanations intensified. The
skepticism grew slowly at first, but it broke wide open in 1968 when the Vietnamese communists' Tet Offensive seemed to expose the lie of administration claims that peace was just around the corner. Johnson and his party
paid the political price at the polls that year, but the entire government was
under attack. Outside official circles, the press and a burgeoning antiwar
protest movement became the principal purveyors of the public's distrust.

Reading the first teletyped bulletins of the Tet Offensive, Walter Cronkite,
the highly respected CBS anchorman, exclaimed: "What the hell is going
on? I thought we were winning the war."[11] At the beginning of the Johnson
administration's escalation of U.S. involvement in Vietnam, the mass media
had relied primarily on official government sources of information. This so-
called establishment reporting largely prevailed until Tet, although congressional hearings and the efforts of a few intrepid reporters had begun to pro-

vide the press with some alternative viewpoints. After Tet, the media became increasingly critical of official explanations and played a key role in widening the credibility gap between the government and the public. Indeed, some postmortems on Vietnam, such as that of General William C. Westmoreland, the commander of U.S. forces in Vietnam from 1964 to 1968, have placed heavy blame on the press for America's loss of will to fight the war. More objective observers, however, have reasoned that the media did not create the credibility gap. The gap arose from the disparity between the U.S. government's wishes and expectations in Vietnam on the one hand and the actual obstacles and requirements inherent in meeting those objectives on the other. In 1971, the *New York Times* printed excerpts from the *Pentagon Papers*, a secret Defense Department history of Vietnam decision making that basically substantiated the media's perception of the shallowness of Washington's thinking about Indochina.[12]

Like the press, the antiwar movement—or simply "the movement," as the protesters called it—was a vehicle for popular dissent. A diverse assemblage of anti-imperialists, pacifists, and peace liberals, the movement lacked organization and cohesion, but its ad hoc nature attested to its spontaneous and genuinely popular origins. Thousands of Americans, many of the post–World War II baby-boom generation, marched in massive protest demonstrations. Never before in U.S. history had a popular movement of such magnitude emerged to serve a specific and limited political purpose. Equally unprecedented numbers of disaffected young men defied the long-cherished patriotic tradition of military obligation and deserted, evaded the draft, or committed other acts of resistance.

Although most Americans were not active participants in the movement, its existence and vitality destroyed any semblance of a national consensus on the war or on the processes of government. During the huge Moratorium Day March in Washington in November 1969, youths were heard chanting with regard to Richard ("Tricky-Dicky") Nixon:

> One, two, three, four
> Tricky-Dicky stop the war.
> Two, four, six, eight
> Organize to smash the state.

A middle-aged government bureaucrat standing on the curb observed: "It is quite remarkable. American students used to be the most apathetic in the world. . . . Who'd ever think they'd feel so strongly about anything to do something like this?"[13]

The movement gained both energy and controversy from its convergence with other social protests, especially the civil rights movement and the counterculture rebellion symbolized by the long-haired, dope-smoking, free-loving hippies. By the early 1970s, both election returns and public-opinion polls revealed the unpopularity of the war, but they also showed that many Americans were disturbed by the movement. The Johnson and Nixon administrations used surveillance, arrests, and other harassment to try to intimidate protesters. The presidents also sought to make the patriotism of the dissenters, not the morality of the war, the focus of the public's doubt. The nation's schizophrenia was dramatically apparent following the tragic deaths of four Kent State University students and the wounding of several others during an antiwar protest in May 1970. When Ohio National Guard bullets felled the students, some of whom were simply onlookers, many Americans responded with shocked dismay, but others came to the defense of the Ohio authorities and suggested that the students got what they deserved. The Vietnam War had violently rent the fabric of trust and accommodation that traditionally clothed the American polity.

The domestic consequences of the Vietnam War pervaded many areas of American life. The psychological costs of the conflict were difficult to quantify. Restriction of civil liberties left many citizens disenchanted and cynical. Families were at odds over their younger members' attitudes and actions toward the war and the military. The grisly toll of casualties in a struggle for vague objectives stunned sensibility. For the first time in the history of American warfare, some veterans returned from the battlefield to organize openly against the war effort. Within the military, drugs, "fragging" (murdering with a fragmentation grenade) of officers, and other serious problems humbled a once proud institution. Perhaps worst of all, many veterans returned home to face hostility or indifference, when in fact they were in desperate need of counseling or even a simple "thank you" to help them face the private, personal hells of their Vietnam memories.[14]

Two socioeconomic impacts of the war were clearly documented: inflation and the demise of Johnson's Great Society reform program. Although economists argued about whether inflation would have occurred even without the war, the impact of war spending on the nation was clear. Johnson's January 1966 budget message insisted that increases in both domestic and defense spending could be managed without increased taxes, but that assertion was already proving false. The inflation rate for 1966 was the highest since the Korean War. The United States spent an average of over $20 billion a year in Indochina from 1965 to 1972. Expenditures of that magnitude could have funded the urban renewal of most of America's largest cities.[15]

Urban development, aid to education, job training, and other worthwhile elements of Johnson's Great Society agenda, although approved in principle by Congress, went underfunded or in some cases unfunded throughout the 1960s. Johnson himself complained in his earthy style that his involvement with "that bitch of a war on the other side of the world" had lost him "the woman I really loved—the Great Society."[16] Senator Fulbright, who supported the Great Society and came to oppose the Vietnam War, contended that an "arrogance of power" had led America into a preoccupation with Vietnam and diverted the "nation from the sources of its strength, which are its domestic life." Many nations, he argued, "have been ruined by expending their energies in foreign adventures while allowing the domestic bases to deteriorate."[17]

In his analysis of the rise and fall of great powers, historian Paul Kennedy has compared the Vietnam War's impact on the United States to World War I's impact on Europe.[18] Vietnam produced a personal, psychological, and constitutional crisis in American civilization. After World War I, European nations experienced various forms of revolution and sweeping political change. America's post-Vietnam revolution was Watergate. This abuse of presidential power did not begin with the infamous break-in at the Democratic National Headquarters in 1972. Watergate began when Nixon ordered wiretaps on members of the executive branch and on newspeople in an attempt to plug leaks that he believed were endangering Kissinger's secret negotiations and exposing the clandestine bombing of Cambodia. Other wiretaps, break-ins, and various illegal activities followed—aimed at antiwar activists, political opponents, and others on Nixon's "enemies list." As these activities became known, the White House then engaged in a massive cover-up to obstruct the investigation into criminal conduct. Throughout the Watergate episode, there was the exaltation of presidential power, the obsession with secrecy and national security, and the mutual distrust between the president and the public that had become hallmarks of the Vietnam experience.[19]

The Vietnam War was an agonizing, bitter, and unprecedented military loss for the United States. It broke the hold of America's superpower complacency and made everything—including presidential authority—debatable. In the flush of victory after World War II, the American people had easily transferred the wartime crusade against totalitarianism into an undifferentiated Cold War anticommunism. The Cold War consensus gave the nation's political leadership great latitude and support, but Vietnam shattered the consensus. The public came to believe that the war was unwinnable without greater costs and, more importantly, that the moral and political burdens and consequences of the war were wrong. Revisionist historians who argue that the war could and should have been won reveal a profound disregard for the American public's feelings about the war.[20] American domestic values would not support the use of means disproportionate to the limited ends of U.S. objectives in Vietnam. The 1968 election revealed that the people wanted out. The war was lost not because the United States did too little, but because the costs and destruction were too much and too inhumane to justify.

In the early 1970s, the "silent majority," despite Nixon's assertion to the contrary, wanted an end to U.S. involvement in Vietnam, and only a minority of Americans remained committed to the old consensus. Indeed, "commitment" had become a suspicious concept. The split in American thought came to a climax with Watergate, the most serious constitutional and domestic trauma since the Civil War. Vietnam and Watergate brought on a crisis that challenged some of the basic tenets of American politics: the sharing of power between the president and Congress, the moral value of the Bill of Rights, and, perhaps most significantly, the timeless reality that foreign policy must always serve the domestic interests and internal welfare of the nation.

Notes

1. Quoted in Kenneth W. Thompson, "The Johnson Presidency and Foreign Policy: The Unresolved Conflict between National Interest and Collective Security," in Bernard J. Firestone and Robert C. Vogt, eds., *Lyndon Johnson and the Uses of Power* (New York: Greenwood, 1988), 291.

2. Alexander Hamilton, James Madison, and John Jay, *The Federalist Papers*, introduction by Clinton Rossiter (New York: New American Library, 1961), 423–24.

3. Robert L. Gallucci, *Neither Peace nor Honor: The Politics of U.S. Military Policy in Vietnam* (Baltimore: Johns Hopkins University Press, 1975), 7. See also George Reedy, *The Twilight of the Presidency* (New York: World, 1970); and Hugh Heclo, "Introduction: The Presidential Illusion," in Hugh Heclo and Lester M. Salamon, eds., *The Illusion of Presidential Government* (Boulder, Colo.: Westview Press, 1981), 1–20.

4. Fred I. Greenstein, "Nine Presidents in Search of a Modern Presidency," in Fred I. Greenstein, ed., *Leadership in the Modern Presidency* (Cambridge, Mass.: Harvard University Press, 1988), 351–52.

5. Clinton Rossiter, *The American Presidency*, 2d ed. (New York: Harcourt,

Brace & World, 1960), 43, 82–83, 141; Richard E. Neustadt, *Presidential Power and the Modern Presidents: The Politics of Leadership from Roosevelt to Reagan* (New York: Free Press, 1990), 183–85; James David Barber, *The Presidential Character: Predicting Performance in the White House*, 3d ed. (Englewood Cliffs, N.J.: Prentice-Hall, 1985), 1–4, 501.

6. See almost any survey of U.S. diplomatic history, such as Walter LaFeber, *The American Age: United States Foreign Policy at Home and Abroad since 1750* (New York: Norton, 1989); and Thomas G. Paterson, J. Garry Clifford, and Kenneth J. Hagan, *American Foreign Policy: A History*, 3d ed., 2 vols. (Lexington, Mass.: D. C. Heath, 1988 [vol. 2 revised 1991]).

7. Louis Henkin, *Foreign Affairs and the Constitution* (New York: Norton, 1975), 273–74.

8. Arthur M. Schlesinger, Jr., *The Imperial Presidency* (Boston: Houghton Mifflin, 1973); Patrick McGeever, "The Presidency and Congress," 34–35 (paper in author's possession).

9. Walter LaFeber, *America, Russia, and the Cold War, 1945–1990*, 6th ed. (New York: McGraw-Hill, 1991), 57, 68.

10. Paul M. Kattenburg, *The Vietnam Trauma in American Foreign Policy, 1945–75* (New Brunswick, N.J.: Transaction Books, 1980), 233–35, 275–76.

11. Quoted in Peter Braestrup, *Big Story* (New York: Anchor Books, 1978), 49.

12. William M. Hammond, *Public Affairs: The Military and the Media, 1962–1968* (Washington, D.C.: GPO, 1988); Neil Sheehan et al., *The Pentagon Papers as Published by the New York Times* (Chicago: Quadrangle Books, 1971); William C. Westmoreland, *A Soldier Reports* (New York: Doubleday, 1976).

13. Quoted in John Clark Pratt, comp., *Vietnam Voices: Perspectives on the War Years, 1941–1982* (New York: Penguin Books, 1984), 410. See also Charles DeBenedetti with Charles Chatfield, *An American Ordeal: The Antiwar Movement of the Vietnam Era* (Syracuse, N.Y.: Syracuse University Press, 1990).

14. Myra MacPherson, *Long Time Passing: Vietnam and the Haunted Generation* (Garden City, N.Y.: Doubleday, 1984).

15. Allen J. Matusow, *The Unraveling of America: A History of Liberalism in the 1960s* (New York: Harper & Row, 1984), 153–79; Georgetown University Center for Strategic Studies, *Economic Impact of the Vietnam War* (Washington, D.C., June 1967).

16. Quoted in Doris Kearns, *Lyndon Johnson and the American Dream* (New York: New American Library, 1977), 263.

17. J. William Fulbright, *The Arrogance of Power* (New York: Vintage, 1966), 20–21.

18. Paul Kennedy, *The Rise and Fall of the Great Powers: Economic Change and Military Conflict from 1500 to 2000* (New York: Vintage, 1989), 404–5.

19. Theodore H. White, *Breach of Faith: The Fall of Richard Nixon* (New York: Atheneum, 1975).

20. George C. Herring, "The 'Vietnam Syndrome' and American Foreign Policy," *Virginia Quarterly Review* 57 (Autumn 1981): 594–612; Walter LaFeber, "The Last War, the Next War, and the New Revisionists," *democracy* 1 (January 1981):

93–103. For a useful retrospective on the war, see "Lessons and Non-Lessons of the U.S. Experience in Vietnam," in Peter Braestrup, ed., *Vietnam as History: Ten Years after the Paris Peace Accords* (Washington, D.C.: Woodrow Wilson Center and University Press of America, 1984), 138–47.

2
Harry S. Truman and the Roots of U.S. Involvement in Indochina, 1945–1953

Robert J. McMahon

A unique set of historical circumstances forced Harry S. Truman to make as many pivotal decisions as any American president before or since. He authorized the use of two devastating atomic bombs on Japan, oversaw the transition from global conflict to global Cold War, sent American troops to fight another war in Korea, created the essential institutions of the modern national security state, initiated a vast increase in defense spending, committed an unprecedented quantity of U.S. resources to the reconstruction of war-torn Europe and Japan, led his nation into its first entangling alliance since the French treaty of 1778, and launched an ambitious global strategy for containing the power and influence of the Soviet Union. Few contemporaries, whether supporters or critics of the president, could have forecast that later generations would consider his commitment to aid and support a French colonial war in the remote reaches of Southeast Asia as of almost comparable importance. Not even the most farsighted among them could have imagined the heightened significance that subsequent developments would lend to a seemingly minor commitment in an area that appeared far removed from the nation's core strategic and economic interests.

Yet Truman's decision early in 1950 to begin providing modest levels of military and economic assistance to France in its struggle against a communist-led indigenous insurgency in Indochina now clearly stands as one of the most momentous of his presidency. It marked the first milestone in what became America's longest war, a twenty-five-year struggle to prevent communist forces from triumphing in Indochina. It was a struggle that ultimately claimed over 50,000 American lives, brought defeat and humiliation to the world's most powerful nation, shattered the domestic economy, divided the

Truman meets at the White House with French Premier René Pleven in January 1951 to reaffirm the fundamental unity between the United States and France. Secretary of State Dean Acheson and Secretary of Defense George C. Marshall look on. (National Park Service—Abbie Rowe, courtesy Harry S. Truman Library)

nation more profoundly than any event since the Civil War, and sparked an intensely emotional debate about the United States' place in the world.

The Truman administration's initial involvement in Indochina has, not surprisingly, drawn its share of historical interpreters. It has inspired a healthy amount of scholarly controversy as well. Scholars writing about this period while the war in Vietnam still raged tended either to downplay the importance of the initial U.S. commitment to the French or to ascribe that commitment to a combination of inadvertence and happenstance. They did not, for the most part, see the U.S. commitment to the French as stemming from a set of well-defined national security interests.[1] Over the past fifteen years, a spate of articles and monographs has forced a fundamental rethinking of that view. Despite often sharp disagreements about the relative weight of the ideological, economic, strategic, political, and psychological wellsprings of the U.S. commitment, recent scholarship posits a much more conscious, deliberate, and calculated policy. It depicts the Truman administration responding to a set of clearly articulated national security objectives. Those objectives led U.S. officials to link the Franco-Vietnamese struggle to broader regional and global foreign policy goals in a deepening Cold War.

Indochina became crucial to Truman administration planners by the late 1940s because of a perceived relationship between stability in Southeast Asia and economic recovery in Western Europe and Japan. U.S. intervention in Indochina formed part of a carefully conceived, if ultimately flawed, effort to preserve the economic resources of Southeast Asia for the West while denying them to the communist powers. It grew, in short, from America's overall Cold War strategy for containing Soviet power and influence, a strategy that led to a blurring of distinctions between core and periphery and elevated Southeast Asia into a national security concern of the first order.[2]

When Truman found the awesome joint responsibilities of president and commander in chief suddenly thrust upon him in April 1945, his understandable inclination was to continue the policies of his predecessor. Possessing neither the experience nor the self-assurance to question decisions made by a man who, even in death, overshadowed the insecure Missourian, Truman strove for continuity in the countless details of postwar planning. The new chief executive consequently leaned heavily on senior State and War Department officials for advice on national security matters, a trait that would characterize Truman's leadership style throughout his presidency. A simple and straightforward man who blended a parochial nationalist outlook with the convictions of a pragmatic internationalist, Truman gladly delegated most day-to-day diplomatic decisions to trusted advisers. During his early months in office, the new president deferred most often to Secretary of State James F. Byrnes, a former Senate colleague. Later, George C. Marshall and Dean Acheson would assume comparable roles within the administration. The policies that those advisers developed and implemented in his name—in Indochina and elsewhere—were entirely consistent with Truman's own assumptions about U.S. national security interests and global strategy. Accordingly, he gave an unusual degree of latitude to his senior diplomatic and defense appointees, confident that their policy recommendations would almost always comport with his own views of world affairs and yet spring from a much deeper reservoir of knowledge about particular issues. At the same time, Truman insisted that he remain the final decision maker.[3]

The future of French Indochina was but one of a bewildering galaxy of problems that required an early decision by the new president. At first glance, this particular problem appeared a good deal less complex than most. During his last months in office, Franklin D. Roosevelt had assured French authorities, as he had their British and Dutch counterparts, that Washington would not oppose the reimposition of European control over colonial territories occupied by Japan during the war. Certain that he was simply following a well-established policy for the Japanese-occupied areas of Southeast Asia, Truman quickly conveyed the same message to French, British, and Dutch officials.

Truman's reassurances were entirely consistent with those given earlier by Roosevelt; they were meant to signal continuity, not change. Nonetheless, Truman's straightforward recognition of the colonial powers' claims to territorial sovereignty in Southeast Asia obscured the more complex reality surrounding the U.S. stance toward colonialism. Roosevelt's various wartime plans and pronouncements regarding European colonies in general, and French Indochina in particular, were sufficiently contradictory that Truman actually inherited a much more ambiguous legacy than he could possibly have realized. The emergence in September 1945 of an independent Vietnamese nationalist regime, demanding international recognition and framing its case in terms of American wartime statements and promises, drove home the complexities and contradictions of the Roosevelt legacy.

During the early years of World War II, Roosevelt and other top officials declared with some regularity that the United States supported the principle of self-determination for all peoples. The president, who took the lead on this issue, often prodded European officials about the need to commit themselves to a timetable for eventual colonial independence. Much to the discomfiture of America's European allies, Roosevelt and Secretary of State Cordell Hull proposed that a trusteeship system be established in the postwar period through which different developed nations, acting as trustees, would prepare local elites to assume the responsibilities of self-government. Trusteeship represented a compromise solution to Roosevelt; he believed that it would guarantee future independence while avoiding the danger of a premature transfer of power to inexperienced indigenous rulers.[4]

Roosevelt's plans for the colonial world represented a nearly indistinguishable blend of American ideals and American interests. The president found the conditions under which so many subject peoples lived appallingly primitive. After passing through the British colony of Gambia in early 1942, for example, he railed against the poverty and disease he had witnessed everywhere, referring to the dependency as a "hellhole" and calling the experience "the most horrible thing I have ever seen in my life."[5] Although Roosevelt never visited Indochina, the lack of personal contact did not prevent the president from berating the colony's French overlords in equally harsh terms. In fact, he considered the French the least enlightened of all the colonial powers and often singled out for particular censure their sorry record in Indochina. Despite "nearly one hundred years" of French rule in Indochina, he complained on one occasion, "the people are worse off than they were at the beginning."[6]

Roosevelt's genuine humanitarian impulses coexisted with a more practical strain. The preservation of the colonial system stood as an impediment to the kind of world order most conducive to U.S. interests. Roosevelt was convinced that the imperial order, with its restrictive trading practices, economic exploitation, and political repression, would simply sow the seeds for future instability within the colonies and future conflicts among the great powers. The United States sought a more open world, one characterized by free trade and democratic principles. Only such a world, according to the president and his chief advisers, would ensure the peace, prosperity, stability, and security that the United States sought. Roosevelt's proselytizing on behalf of a more liberal approach to dependent areas thus bespoke an unsentimental calculation of national interests as much as it did a revulsion against imperialism's excesses.[7]

Before his death, Roosevelt significantly modified his approach to colonial questions. Late in 1944 he jettisoned trusteeship planning for Indochina and other areas, offering instead a promise not to interfere with the reimposition of colonial rule in Southeast Asia. This policy shift reflected the president's essential pragmatism in the face of a series of complex, cross-cutting interests. From its inception, his trusteeship formula had generated heated rebukes from the colonial powers. British Prime Minister Winston Churchill, Roosevelt's most important ally, made clear on numerous occasions his unbending opposition to U.S. tampering with European colonies. Free French leader General Charles de Gaulle was no less adamant in opposing U.S. plans. The Roosevelt administration feared that an aggressive advocacy of trusteeship, in the face of such angry and unified opposition, might create intolerable strains within the wartime alliance and might jeopardize postwar cooperation in Western Europe, the most vital region of all to the United States. Defense needs also militated against persisting in an anticolonial campaign. Planners in the War and Navy Departments insisted that U.S. national security required exclusive control over the Japanese-mandated islands in the Pacific. With the president's concurrence, they intended to establish a permanent U.S. military presence throughout the Pacific in order to add depth and flexibility to the nation's air and naval capability. That high-priority goal, according to military experts, could not be compromised by trusteeship principles that could easily be applied to strategic U.S.-occupied territory as well as to European colonies. Broader political, strategic, and military concerns, in short, necessitated a tactical retreat from earlier anticolonial pronouncements and plans.[8]

Ho Chi Minh's declaration of an independent Vietnamese state on September 2, 1945, brought to a head many of the contradictions embedded in the Roosevelt administration's colonial policy. Quoting liberally from the American Declaration of Independence in his own independence proclamation, the veteran nationalist leader was in effect offering the opening bid in what would prove to be a concerted, if ill-fated, campaign for U.S. backing. Later that day, a Vietnamese band joined the independence-day festivities in Hanoi with a rendition of the "Star-Spangled Banner." U.S. Army officers listened from the reviewing stand as a series of Vietnamese nationalists echoed Ho with their own glowing tributes to the United States' anticolonial heritage. The previous evening Ho had invited two members of the Office of Strategic Services (OSS) for dinner. After thanking them for the valuable material assistance rendered by the United States to his guerrilla movement during the war, he appealed for "fraternal collaboration" in the future.[9]

A shrewd tactician with the instincts of a born politician, the man previously known as Nguyen Ai Quoc was a communist, a revolutionary, but above all a Vietnamese nationalist. He sensed that the momentous events set in motion by the Japanese occupation of Indochina and the Nazi conquest of France had created a historic opportunity for the realization of his lifelong dream: independence from French rule. From the outset Ho calculated that the United States, if it remained true to its wartime statements, could become his most useful ally. That view was not born of naiveté. It grew, instead, from the mutually beneficial collaboration between U.S. military and intelligence officers and Vietminh guerrillas that had taken place in the jungles of northern Tonkin during the struggle against Japan. It was nourished by the Vietnamese leader's belief that the United States' global interests would compel it to oppose the reestablishment of French colonialism.[10]

Ho's assessment was not an unrealistic one. After all, Roosevelt had calculated that U.S. interests would best be served by the progressive evolution of colonial dependencies into self-governing states; the president's revulsion against French misrule in Indochina ran especially deep. Ho can hardly be faulted for failing to anticipate the shift in U.S. policy that occurred shortly before Roosevelt's death. Unaware that first Roosevelt and then Truman had reassured European allies that the United States would not block the reestablishment of the status quo antebellum, Ho appealed to Truman for recognition in a series of personal letters. "The carrying out of the Atlantic Charter and San Francisco Charter," he declared hopefully in one message, "implies the eradication of imperialism and all forms of colonial oppression."[11]

Truman never responded to Ho's appeals. Neither he nor any of his top advisers ever seriously contemplated direct support for or diplomatic recognition of the Democratic Republic of Vietnam. To do so would have represented a sharp break with the policy Truman had inherited from Roosevelt in an area that ranked relatively low on the overall scale of U.S. priorities. Such a course must have seemed inconceivable to a president still overwhelmed by the myriad responsibilities of his new office. On August 29, during a White House meeting with de Gaulle, Truman signaled that there would be no such break. He reassured France's provisional president that the United States recognized the right of French authorities to reestablish sovereignty in Indochina.[12] Ho's declaration of independence just three days later did not occasion a searching reexamination of that stance. Despite widespread respect for Ho's nationalist-credentials and leadership abilities among U.S. intelligence and military personnel serving in Indochina, top U.S. policymakers were far more concerned with the needs and viewpoints of France. To alienate France, a country whose active support in Europe was crucial, would have undermined the overall foreign policy goals of the Truman administration. To do so on behalf of a national independence movement in remote Southeast Asia would have represented the height of diplomatic folly.[13]

The United States instead pursued a policy of neutrality toward the colonial rebellion in Indochina, much as it did toward a contemporaneous colonial revolt in the Dutch East Indies. The Truman administration never questioned the legal right of the European sovereigns to reestablish control in Vietnam and Indonesia. At the same time, it realized that sheer pragmatism necessitated some concessions to indigenous nationalist movements. A harsh policy of political and military repression by the colonial powers would probably endanger not only the peace and order that the United States sought in Southeast Asia but the economic recovery and political stability that it sought in Western Europe.[14]

Throughout 1945 and 1946, U.S. diplomats consequently urged their

French counterparts to negotiate in good faith with Ho and his chief lieutenants in order to avert an outright conflict that would serve the interests of neither party. Washington applauded the conclusion of a preliminary Franco-Vietnamese accord on March 6, 1946, since it seemed to open the way for an amicable political compromise. Like Roosevelt administration planners before them, Truman administration analysts believed that only a more liberal approach to colonial issues, one pointing toward eventual self-government, could establish the essential preconditions for order, stability, and prosperity in the developing world.[15]

Those broad principles served as a general guidepost for U.S. policymakers during the four years following Vietnam's proclamation of independence. Although the principles were certainly sound, they produced little more than frustration for the Truman administration in a period punctuated by false hopes, failed negotiations, and savage fighting. The promise of the March 6 accord soon gave way to stalemated negotiations at Dalat and Paris. Although he was willing to accept less than immediate independence for all of Vietnam, Ho could not condone the retention of French supremacy in the southern province of Cochinchina. To this ardent patriot, Tonkin, Annam, and Cochinchina formed one unified country; he would rather fight than accept division. And fight he did. Following abortive talks at Fontainebleau in the summer of 1946, the imperatives of diplomacy yielded inevitably to preparations for war. In November, hostilities erupted with shattering suddenness. Following a vicious French naval bombardment of Haiphong that claimed more than 6,000 Vietnamese lives, Ho Chi Minh and his supporters fled Hanoi. The French moved quickly to establish their administrative control in the north, and the Vietminh mobilized for another guerrilla struggle. Conflict soon engulfed much of Vietnam. No one at the time could have imagined how many years would pass before peace returned to that embattled land.[16]

U.S. analysts privately expressed dismay with France's resort to the use of force. A colonial war of reconquest represented a regrettable return to the discredited methods of the past. Even worse, the French seemed to lack the military power necessary to accomplish their goals. John Carter Vincent, director of the State Department's Office of Far Eastern Affairs, offered a pessimistic appraisal of French prospects to Under Secretary of State Dean Acheson in a memorandum of December 23. "The French themselves admit that they lack the military strength to reconquer the country," he observed. Possessing "inadequate forces, with public opinion sharply at odds, [and] with a government rendered largely ineffective through internal division," the French were embarking on a most unpromising course. "Given the present elements in the situation," Vincent predicted, "guerilla warfare may continue indefinitely."[17]

For all of its misgivings about French policy in Indochina, the State Department carefully avoided open criticism of its European partner. On December 23, Acheson told French Ambassador Henri Bonnet of Washington's deep concern about "the unhappy situation in which the French find themselves." Calling existing conditions in Indochina "highly inflammatory," the under secretary stressed the importance of reaching a settlement as soon as possible. Only the most sensitive of diplomats could have read even an implied criticism into Acheson's mild remarks. Indeed, he made it clear that even though the United States had no wish to offer its services as a mediator, it did want the French government "to know that we are ready and willing to do anything which it might consider helpful in the circumstances."[18]

Nineteen forty-seven brought no respite to the fighting in Indochina—and no essential change in U.S. policy toward the conflict. The Truman administration continued to view French military exertions as a misguided effort to turn back the clock. In a February 3 cable to the U.S. Embassy in Paris, Secretary of State George C. Marshall expressed "increasing concern" with the stalemate in Indochina. He deplored both the "lack [of] French understanding [for] the other side" and their "dangerously outmoded colonial outlook and methods." At the same time, Washington displayed no inclination to intervene directly in yet another nettlesome regional conflict and even less interest in exerting unwanted pressure on an invaluable ally. "We have only [the] very friendliest feelings toward France," Marshall noted, "and we are anxious in every way we can to support France in her fight to regain her economic, political and military strength and to restore herself as in fact one of [the] major powers of [the] world."[19] The enunciation in mid-1947 of the containment strategy and the Marshall Plan just underscored France's indispensability to the broader foreign policy aims of the Truman administration. Both initiatives were conceived as part of the administration's overall strategy for containing Soviet influence and power by fostering the economic recovery and political stability of Western Europe. In the intensifying Cold War struggle between the United States and the Soviet Union, no area was more vital than Western Europe and no country more crucial than France.[20]

In view of its transcendent importance to the United States, France's persistence in a colonial conflict that most U.S. experts believed would leave it drained and weakened posed a fundamental dilemma to Truman and his senior advisers, one that they never adequately resolved. Precisely how could the United States help France recognize that its own self-interest required a nonmilitary solution in Indochina? And what specific course of action should the United States urge France to pursue? The dilemma was posed far more easily than it could be resolved. "Frankly we have no solution of [the] problem to suggest," Marshall conceded. "It is basically [a] matter for [the] two parties to work out [for] themselves."[21]

The communist character of the Vietnamese independence movement and the absence of viable noncommunist alternatives further clouded an already murky picture. U.S. officials were keenly aware that the movement's outstanding figure had a long record as a loyal communist. Not only had Ho Chi Minh received political training in Moscow, but he had served for decades as a dedicated Comintern agent outside Indochina. Most U.S. diplomatic and defense officials worried that if Ho prevailed over the French, it would lead to "an independent Vietnam State which would be run by orders from Moscow."[22] A handful of junior State Department officials dissented from that analysis, advancing the argument that Ho's ardent nationalism transcended any fraternal links to the Kremlin's rulers; they speculated that he might even emerge as an Asian Tito. Such unorthodox views never permeated the upper reaches of the Truman administration, however. Most senior policymakers calculated that, regardless of Ho's undeniably powerful credentials as a Vietnamese nationalist, the establishment of a Vietminh-dominated regime would benefit the Soviet Union. Moreover, other nations would almost certainly view the emergence of such a regime as a defeat for the West.[23]

Yet, as the State Department acknowledged in September 1948, "we are all too well aware of the unpleasant fact that Communist Ho Chi Minh is the strongest and perhaps the ablest figure in Indochina and that any suggested solution which excludes him is an expedient of uncertain outcome."[24] Much to Washington's consternation, the French search for an alternative figure with whom to negotiate produced only the weak and vacillating former emperor Bao Dai. Charles Reed, the U.S. consul in Saigon, reminded Washington that "the reputed playboy of Hong Kong" commanded little support. Bao Dai counted among his followers only "those whose pockets will be benefited if he should return."[25] Notwithstanding U.S. reservations and objections, the French promoted the pliant Bao Dai as their answer to Ho Chi Minh. Most U.S. analysts viewed France's "Bao Dai solution" as a transparent effort to retain colonial control; they saw it as confirmation of the bankruptcy of French policy. The restoration of Bao Dai as titular head of an "impotent puppet Gov[ernmen]t" prompted concern within the State Department that the democracies might be forced to "resort [to] monarchy as [a] weapon against Communism."[26]

In September 1948 the State Department offered an internal assessment of U.S. policy vis-à-vis the Indochina dispute, remarkable both for its candor and for its self-critical tone. "The objectives of US policy towards Indochina have not been realized," it admitted flatly. "Three years after the termination of war a friendly ally, France, is fighting a desperate and apparently losing struggle in Indochina. The economic drain of this warfare on French recovery, while difficult to estimate, is unquestionably large. The Communist control in the nationalist movement has been increased during this period. US influence in Indochina and Asia has suffered as a result." U.S. objectives could be attained only if France satisfied "the nationalist aspirations of the peoples of Indochina." Yet a series of fundamental impediments bedeviled all U.S. efforts to nudge the French in that direction: the communist coloration of the nationalist movement; the seeming dearth of popular noncommunist alternatives; the unwillingness of the Truman administration to offer unsolicited advice to an ally on such an emotional issue; Washington's "immediate interest in maintaining in power a friendly French government, to assist in the furtherance of our aims in Europe"; and, perhaps most basic of all, the administration's "inability to suggest any practicable solution of the Indochina problem."[27]

Over the next year and a half, the Truman administration engaged in a wide-ranging reexamination of U.S. policy toward Southeast Asia. A series of unsettling global developments, which deepened the administration's appreciation for Southeast Asia's strategic and economic salience, lent urgency to the internal debate. As a result of its reassessment, the Truman administration abandoned its quasi-neutral approach to the Indochina dispute in favor of a policy of open support for the French. On February 7, 1950, Secretary of State Acheson formally announced U.S. recognition of the Bao Dai regime, the nominally independent entity established by France the previous year, and its sister regimes in Cambodia and Laos. Emphasizing U.S. concern that neither security, democracy, nor independence could exist "in any area dominated by Soviet imperialism," he promised economic aid and military equipment for France and the Associated States of Vietnam, Cambodia, and Laos.[28]

The decision to lend U.S. money, equipment, and prestige to France's struggle against the Vietminh cannot be understood without reference to the wider forces shaping the foreign policy of the Truman administration in late 1949 and early 1950. Those forces led both to a searching reevaluation of the world situation and to a fundamental reassessment of U.S. tactics and strategy. In the six months preceding its commitment to the French, the Truman administration came face to face with probably the gravest global crisis of the entire postwar era. In the summer of 1949 the Soviet Union exploded its first atomic device, putting an end to the United States' brief atomic monopoly and posing a host of unprecedented challenges to U.S. national security. Truman and other leading officials feared that possession of the bomb might incline the Kremlin to take greater risks in an effort to extend its global reach and power. The collapse of the U.S.-backed Kuomintang regime in China and the establishment of a communist government in its stead provoked additional fears in U.S. policy circles. Events in China also gave rise to a round of nasty finger-pointing at home; a swelling chorus of Republican critics blamed the president personally for China's fate. Events outside the communist bloc appeared even more ominous to America's Cold Warriors. By the end of the year it was increasingly evident that the economic recoveries of Western Europe and Japan had stalled badly. U.S. decision makers feared that continued economic stagnation in those lands would generate social unrest and political instability, conditions that might prove a fertile breeding ground for communism.[29]

Taken together, those developments portended a potentially catastrophic threat to U.S. national security. As the communist world gained strength and self-confidence, the United States and its allies seemed poised to lose theirs. To Truman and his senior strategists, the stakes in this global struggle for power were extraordinarily high, involving nothing less than the physical safety and economic health of the United States. "The loss of Western Europe or of important parts of Asia or the Middle East," wrote Acheson, "would be a transfer of potential from West to East, which, depending on the area, might have the gravest consequences in the long run."[30] By early 1950, top U.S. diplomatic and defense officials concentrated much of their energy on defusing this hydra-headed crisis by resuscitating the economies of Western Europe and Japan and regaining the West's political and psychological momentum in the Cold War.

U.S. policymakers recognized that a multiplicity of links tied developments in Indochina to this daunting string of global crises. In Asia, the administration's overriding objective was to orient a politically stable and economically prosperous Japan toward the West. "Were Japan added to the Communist bloc," Acheson warned, "the Soviets would acquire skilled manpower and industrial potential capable of significantly altering the balance of world power."[31] The secretary of state and other leading officials were convinced that Japan needed the markets and raw materials of Southeast Asia in order to spark its industrial recovery. The revitalization of Asia's powerhouse economy would create the conditions necessary for stability and prosperity within both Japan and Southeast Asia. U.S. geopolitical and economic interests in this regard formed a seamless web. Truman administration planners envisioned a revitalized Japan emerging once again as the dynamic hub of commercial activity throughout Asia. Achievement of this objective would give a much-needed boost to the regional and global economic systems, thwart communism's military threat and ideological appeal, and ensure Tokyo's loyalty to the West. According to the logic subscribed to by nearly all top U.S. strategists, Japan's economic health demanded that peace and stability prevail throughout Southeast Asia. Consequently, the Vietminh insurgency in Indochina, which posed the most serious threat to regional peace and stability, had to be vanquished with the greatest possible dispatch.[32]

For a somewhat different set of reasons, U.S. strategic and economic interests in Europe pointed in the same direction. By the end of 1949, the optimism generated by the Marshall Plan on both sides of the Atlantic had long since dissolved. The unprecedented commitment of U.S. resources to the economic rehabilitation of Western Europe had not yet brought the dramatic transformation that the Truman administration so desperately sought. Instead, the United States' most important allies found themselves facing a frightening panoply of economic and political difficulties. The increasingly costly war in Indochina stretched France's resources to the breaking point, severely hampering its contribution to the European recovery program. Although West Germany's economic performance was not quite so dismal, U.S. officials continued to fret about the fragility of Bonn's commitment to the West. Certain that the ultimate success of the Marshall Plan required the reintegration of Germany into Europe, U.S. planners agonized about how to ease France's understandable fears about a resurgent Germany.[33]

The enormous trade and currency imbalance between the United States and its European economic partners posed an even more immediate threat to U.S. interests. This so-called dollar gap continued to grow, reaching over $3.5 billion by the middle of 1949, and posed a particularly painful problem for Great Britain.[34] "Unless firm action is taken," British Foreign Secretary Ernest Bevin implored Acheson in July 1949, "I fear much of our work on Western Union and the Atlantic pact will be undermined and our progress in the Cold War will be halted."[35] Experts in Washington shared Bevin's fears. Former Assistant Secretary of State William Clayton spoke for many when he conjured up the image of "the patient little man in the Kremlin [who] sits rubbing his hands and waiting for the free world to collapse in a sea of economic chaos."[36]

By early 1950, the Truman administration's senior planners were convinced that Western Europe's troubles, like Japan's, could be aided by the stabilization and pacification of Southeast Asia. France, Great Britain, and Holland had avoided a dollar gap problem during the prewar years through the establishment of triangular trading patterns in which their colonial dependencies in Southeast Asia earned dollars through the sale of raw materials to the United States. The health of the British sterling bloc had grown unusually dependent on American purchases of rubber and tin from Malaya. The disruption of traditional trading patterns as a result of raging colonial conflicts—an insurgency erupted in Malaya in 1948, joining those that already wracked Indochina and the East Indies—thus compounded the already desperate fiscal conditions plaguing Western Europe. The Truman administration's initial commitment to Southeast Asia, then, must also be placed within this context. U.S. officials believed that financial and material assistance to the French in Indochina would abet military pacification and political stabilization in Southeast Asia. At the same time, it would permit a more active French contribution to European recovery.[37]

Political pressures reinforced Truman's inclination to link Southeast Asian developments to larger issues. The ferocity of the partisan assaults on Truman in the wake of Chiang Kai-shek's (Jiang Jieshi's) collapse increased the political pressure on the president to show greater resolution vis-à-vis the communist challenge in Asia. Aid to the French in Indochina enabled the beleaguered Truman to answer his critics' charges by demonstrating a determination to hold the line against further communist advances *somewhere*. It is of no small significance that the initial U.S. dollar commitment of February 1950 was drawn from funds earmarked by the president's congressional critics for the containment of communism within "the general area of China."[38]

More diffuse psychological considerations also shaped the U.S. commitment to Southeast Asia. Administration analysts were convinced that the belief in many corners of the world was that historical momentum lay with communism and not with the West. U.S. strategists feared that such a perception, whether rooted in fact or fantasy, might take on a life of its own, producing a bandwagon effect that would have an extremely pernicious im-

pact on U.S. global interests. In the words of NSC-68, an April 1950 administration document providing a comprehensive reappraisal of U.S. national
security, the Soviet Union sought "to demonstrate that force and the will to
use it are on the side of the Kremlin [and] that those who lack it are decadent
and doomed."[39] Because the fighting in Indochina was widely viewed as a
contest between East and West, however erroneous that view might have
been, the challenge it posed to Washington was almost as much psychological as it was geostrategic. State Department and Pentagon officials agreed
that the U.S. commitment in Indochina helped meet that psychological
challenge by demonstrating to adversaries and allies alike Washington's
strength, resolution, and determination. The Truman administration's concern with such intangible matters as the United States' prestige, image, and
reputation—in a word, its credibility—thus also entered into the complex
policy calculus that made U.S. intervention in Southeast Asia seem as logical as it was unavoidable.[40]

With the outbreak of the Korean War in June 1950, the strategic, economic, political, and psychological fears undergirding that initial commitment intensified. Convinced that Moscow and Beijing had become even
more dangerously opportunistic foes, Truman and his senior advisers redou-
bled their efforts to contain the communist threat on every front. At the
same time, they pursued with even greater vigor initiatives designed to
strengthen the U.S. sphere of influence. Those vital global priorities demanded nothing less than an all-out effort to contain the communist threat
to Southeast Asia, a threat manifested most immediately and most seriously
by the Vietminh insurgency. Virtually all national security planners in the
Truman administration agreed that Indochina was the key to Southeast
Asia. If the Vietminh succeeded in routing the French, according to an analysis prepared by the Joint Strategic Survey Committee in November, "this
would bring about almost immediately a dangerous condition with respect
to the internal security of all of the other countries of Southeast Asia, as
well as the Philippines and Indonesia, and would contribute to their probable eventual fall to communism."[41] With uncommon unanimity, U.S. civilian and military policymakers agreed that a communist triumph in Indochina would represent a strategic nightmare for the United States. It would
probably destabilize the entire region, disrupt important trading ties to Japan and Western Europe, deny to the West and make available to the communist powers important raw materials, endanger vital transportation and
communication routes between the Pacific Ocean and the Middle East, and
render vulnerable the United States' chain of off-shore military bases in the

Pacific. "In addition, this loss would have widespread political and psychological repercussions upon other non-communist states throughout the world."[42]

If the intersection of geostrategic, economic, political, and psychological imperatives helped crystallize U.S. policy objectives in Indochina, they did little to clarify the means necessary for the attainment of those objectives. By the autumn of 1950, the Vietminh had achieved a string of stunning military successes; the French, increasingly demoralized and immobilized, appeared on the verge of defeat. U.S. intelligence experts feared that open intervention by Chinese communist units, which were already providing matériel along with technical and training assistance to the Vietminh, might precipitate a complete French collapse. State Department consultant John Foster Dulles called attention in November 1950 to "what might be a hopeless military situation."[43] A month later an interagency intelligence assessment, coordinated by the CIA, offered an equally grim prognosis. "If this [Chinese communist] aid continues and French strength and military resources are not substantially increased above those presently programmed," it forecast, "the Viet Minh probably can drive the French out of North Viet Nam (Tonkin) within six to nine months." The French position in the rest of Indochina would soon become untenable, leading eventually to "the transformation of Indochina into a Communist satellite."[44]

Determined to help prevent such a calamitous occurrence, the Truman administration steadily accelerated its military and economic aid commitments to the French. By the end of 1950, Washington had committed over $133 million in aid to Indochina. By fiscal year 1951, the total value of U.S. military supplies earmarked for the Indochina war had swelled to approximately $316.5 million. Indochina ranked second by then, behind only Korea, as a recipient of U.S. military aid. That aid helped reinvigorate a faltering French military effort. Together with the appointment of the flamboyant and self-assured General Jean de Lattre de Tassigny as the commander of French forces in Indochina, it led to a substantial—albeit short-lived—improvement in French military fortunes throughout 1951. U.S. observers exulted, hoping that the most acute phase of the crisis might be behind them.[45]

Still, realism tempered the Truman administration's appreciation of the de Lattre–inspired turnaround. Too much hinged on one man, an individual "not always concerned about how many eggs he breaks for his omelette."[46] Furthermore, no matter how vigorous a military campaign the French waged, and no matter how much aid the United States pumped into Indochina, U.S. analysts understood that those factors could not by themselves resolve the Indochina crisis and secure Southeast Asia for the West. Reflecting a view widely shared within the Truman administration, the Joint Chiefs of Staff noted that "without popular support of the Indochinese people, the French will never achieve a favorable long-range military settlement of the security problem of Indochina."[47]

U.S. officials in Washington, Saigon, and Paris were keenly aware that the political and military challenges of Indochina were inseparable. The more astute among them recognized as well that U.S. support for the French pacification effort might work at cross-purposes with U.S. encouragement of Vietnam's noncommunist elites. As early as May 1950, U.S. Ambassador to France David K. E. Bruce shrewdly put his finger on the core problem. The ultimate success of U.S. policy, he observed, "depends upon encouragement and support of both local nationalism and [the] French effort in Indochina. . . . Yet these two forces, brought together only by common danger of Communist imperialism, are inherently antagonistic and gains of one will be to some extent at expense of other."[48] Much to the dismay of U.S. officials, the military dynamism of de Lattre found no political counterpart. The French, who remained extremely unpopular among the Indochinese, simply refused to transfer any genuine power to Bao Dai and his associates. The independence of the Associated States remained a sham; the peoples of Indochina accordingly viewed with disdain the coterie of local leaders serving as little more than French puppets. Lamented U.S. minister in Saigon Donald R. Heath, the "fact is that Ho Chi Minh is [the] only Viet[namese] who enjoys any measure of national prestige."[49]

Notwithstanding its deep and well-founded misgivings about the direction of French policy, the United States carefully avoided open criticism of its European partner. Washington was footing a substantial portion of the bill for the Indochina war. Such a financial commitment would ordinarily bring a commensurate degree of leverage, but the Indochina conflict was anything but ordinary. The French military effort in Southeast Asia served U.S. interests at least as much as it served French interests, a point understood equally well in Paris and Washington. For all its dependence on the United States, France retained the ultimate leverage in the relationship. If U.S. advice became too meddlesome, or if the United States sought to tie strings to its aid, the French could simply withdraw from Indochina entirely. That threat, repeatedly made by French leaders, frightened U.S. decision makers, who worried that they might by default inherit direct responsibility for the Indochina morass.[50]

From the outset of U.S. involvement in Indochina, the Joint Chiefs of

Staff had insisted upon, and Truman had accepted, a critical limitation on available U.S. options: Namely, under no circumstances could U.S. troops be deployed in Southeast Asia. With U.S. resources already stretched to the breaking point by the nation's ever-expanding global commitments, the military establishment worried constantly about an increasingly dangerous over-extension of U.S. power.[51] Threats to U.S. interests may have been multiplying, but resources remained finite. John Ohly, deputy director of the Mutual Defense Assistance Program in the State Department, articulated the fundamental dilemma faced by U.S. planners. As he reminded Secretary of State Acheson: "We have reached a point where the United States, because of limitations in resources, can no longer simultaneously pursue all its objectives in all parts of the world and must realistically face the fact that certain objectives, even though they may be extremely valuable and important ones, may have to be abandoned if others of even greater value and importance are to be attained."[52] Ohly's argument applied with especial force to Indochina, an area where U.S. interests had escalated far more rapidly than had the resources available to military planners. State Department and White House officials were convinced, as were their counterparts in the Pentagon, that the United States must contain the communist threat in Southeast Asia without using U.S. ground forces. That consensus also pointed to an unresolved—and perhaps unresolvable—contradiction at the root of U.S. policy toward Indochina. If Southeast Asia was so vital that its loss to communism would deal a severe blow to U.S. national security, how could the United States accept *any* limits on its actions?

Throughout 1952, in the course of an extended reexamination of U.S. policy toward Southeast Asia, the Truman administration struggled in vain to resolve that contradiction. Its efforts were carried out against the backdrop of a deteriorating French military position (made more ominous by the death of de Lattre in January of that year), renewed fears about the possibility of direct Chinese communist intervention, and growing concern that domestic political pressures might lead to a French withdrawal from Indochina. The numerous reappraisals prepared by the State Department, the Defense Department, and the National Security Council emphasized once again the critical importance of Southeast Asia to the United States. During a meeting of the National Security Council in March 1952, Secretary of Defense Robert A. Lovett referred to "the grave danger to U.S. security interests" that would occur "should Southeast Asia pass into the Communist orbit."[53] Likewise, Acheson candidly informed British Foreign Secretary Anthony Eden several months later that "we are lost if we lose Southeast

Asia without a fight," and thus "we must do what we can to save Southeast Asia."[54]

According to NSC-124/2, a new statement of policy approved by Truman on June 25, 1952, "Communist domination, by whatever means, of all Southeast Asia would seriously endanger in the short term, and critically endanger in the longer term, United States security interests." The possibility of "overt or covert" aggression by Beijing posed the most immediate threat. If a single Southeast Asian nation succumbed as a result of Chinese intervention, it "would have critical psychological, political and economic consequences. In the absence of effective and timely counteraction, the loss of any single country would probably lead to relatively swift submission to or an alignment with communism by the remaining countries of the group." The long-term alignment of India and the nations of the Middle East with the communist bloc, the report noted, would almost certainly follow. "Such widespread alignment would endanger the stability of Europe." Further, a communist Southeast Asia would deprive the West of a range of strategic commodities, thus exerting even greater economic and political pressure on nations allied with the United States and probably impelling "Japan's eventual accommodation to communism."[55]

It was a nightmarish—if familiar—scenario. The president and his top civilian and military advisers were agreed that a set of interdependent global interests made the preservation of a noncommunist Southeast Asia vital to U.S. security. Developing a consensus within the administration on the steps essential to secure that critical objective, however, proved more elusive. Certain that French resistance would crumble rapidly if Communist Chinese divisions entered the fray, military and civilian analysts agonized over how the United States might respond to such a move. Some Pentagon officials believed that only military action against China itself, or the threat of such action, could deter Beijing, raising the frightening question of whether preserving a noncommunist Indochina might necessitate another Sino-American conflict. The pragmatic Lovett suggested that the United States should be prepared instead to spend more money—"perhaps at the rate of a billion or a billion and a half dollars a year"—to support the French; "this would be very much cheaper," he argued, "than an all-out war against Communist China, which would certainly cost us fifty billion dollars."[56]

Neither Truman, Acheson, Lovett, the service chiefs, nor any other senior administration official developed a satisfactory response to the multiple challenges posed by the Indochina conflict. In the end, the Truman administration had to content itself with an ever-deepening monetary commitment to the French. By the end of 1952, the United States was underwriting approximately 40 percent of the cost of the Indochina war. Obviously, as the formulators of U.S. policy themselves were quick to admit, it was an imperfect solution. "More and more dollars [are] being poured into an uninspired program of wait and see," acknowledged the service chiefs.[57] At best, the United States' swelling financial commitment simply postponed the inevitable reckoning. Even if the much-discussed Chinese intervention never materialized, the United States could expect little more than a continuation of the present stalemate; and in the absence of meaningful French political concessions to noncommunist Vietnamese leaders, such a stalemate would simply play into the hands of the Vietminh. The blunt Army Chief of Staff General J. Lawton Collins doubtless spoke for many when he predicted in March 1952 that "the French will be driven out—it is just a question of time."[58]

The Truman administration, which had done so much to elevate Southeast Asia to a diplomatic prize of the greatest importance, failed to develop the means necessary to secure that prize. It never reconciled strategy with tactics. Nor did the administration ever decide on an appropriate U.S. response should the French position suddenly collapse. Truman simply passed those daunting issues, along with an increasingly perilous U.S. commitment to Southeast Asia, on to his successor. It was a legacy fully as problematic and as wracked with contradictory currents as the one he had inherited from Roosevelt.

Notes

1. See, for example, Robert Shaplen, *The Lost Revolution* (New York: Harper & Row, 1965); Arthur Schlesinger, *The Bitter Heritage: Vietnam and American Democracy* (Boston: Houghton Mifflin, 1967). For a useful summary of the early literature, see Leslie H. Gelb and Richard K. Betts, *The Irony of Vietnam: The System Worked* (Washington, D.C.: Brookings Institution, 1979), 9–26.

2. Among the most important scholarly works on Truman's Indochina policies are Gary R. Hess, "The First American Commitment in Indochina: The Acceptance of the 'Bao Dai' Solution, 1950," *Diplomatic History* 2 (Fall 1978): 331–50; Robert M. Blum, *Drawing the Line: The Origin of the American Containment Policy in East Asia* (New York: Norton, 1982); Michael Schaller, "Securing the Great Crescent: Occupied Japan and the Origins of Containment in Southeast Asia," *Journal of American History* 69 (September 1982): 392–414; William Borden, *The Pacific Alliance: United States Foreign Economic Policy and Japanese Trade Recovery, 1947–1955* (Madison: University of Wisconsin Press, 1984); Michael Schaller, *The American Occupation of Japan: The Origins of the Cold War in Asia* (New York: Oxford University Press, 1985); Gabriel Kolko, *Anatomy of a War: Vietnam, the*

United States, and the Modern Historical Experience (New York: Pantheon, 1985); Andrew J. Rotter, *The Path to Vietnam: Origins of the American Commitment to Southeast Asia* (Ithaca, N.Y.: Cornell University Press, 1987); Gary R. Hess, *The United States' Emergence as a Southeast Asian Power, 1940-1950* (New York: Columbia University Press, 1987); Lloyd C. Gardner, *Approaching Vietnam: From World War II through Dienbienphu* (New York: Norton, 1988); Richard H. Immerman, "Prologue: Perceptions by the United States of Its Interests in Indochina," in Lawrence S. Kaplan, Denise Artaud, and Mark R. Rubin, eds., *Dien Bien Phu and the Crisis of Franco-American Relations, 1945-1955* (Wilmington, Del.: Scholarly Resources, 1990), 1-26; and Melvyn P. Leffler, *A Preponderance of Power: National Security, the Truman Administration, and the Cold War* (Stanford, Calif.: Stanford University Press, 1992).

3. Alonzo L. Hamby, "Harry S. Truman: Insecurity and Responsibility," in Fred I. Greenstein, ed., *Leadership in the Modern Presidency* (Cambridge, Mass.: Harvard University Press, 1988), 60-67; Leffler, *Preponderance of Power*, 25-30.

4. For Roosevelt's colonial policy, see especially W. Roger Louis, *Imperialism at Bay: The United States and the Decolonization of the British Empire, 1941-1945* (New York: Oxford University Press, 1978).

5. Quoted in ibid., 227, 356.

6. Cordell Hull, *Memoirs*, 2 vols. (New York: Macmillan, 1948), 2:1597. For Roosevelt's policy toward French Indochina, see Gary R. Hess, "Franklin D. Roosevelt and Indochina," *Journal of American History* 59 (September 1972): 353-68; Walter LaFeber, "Roosevelt, Churchill, and Indochina, 1942-1945," *American Historical Review* 80 (December 1975): 1277-95; and Christopher Thorne, "Indochina and Anglo-American Relations, 1942-1945," *Pacific Historical Review* 45 (February 1976): 73-96.

7. Robert J. McMahon, *Colonialism and Cold War: The United States and the Struggle for Indonesian Independence, 1945-49* (Ithaca, N.Y.: Cornell University Press, 1981), 54-73.

8. Ibid.

9. Bernard B. Fall, ed., *Ho Chi Minh: On Revolution* (New York: Praeger, 1967), 143; George C. Herring, *America's Longest War: The United States and Vietnam, 1950-1975*, 2d ed. (New York: Knopf, 1986), 3; Gardner, *Approaching Vietnam*, 64-65.

10. On Ho, see especially Jean Lacouture, *Ho Chi Minh: A Political Biography* (New York: Vintage, 1968).

11. Quoted in Gardner, *Approaching Vietnam*, 66.

12. George C. Herring, "The Truman Administration and the Restoration of French Sovereignty in Indochina," *Diplomatic History* 1 (Spring 1977): 110-11.

13. Acting Secretary of State Dean Acheson to the Embassy in China, October 5, 1945, *Foreign Relations of the United States, 1945*, vol. 6, *The British Commonwealth: The Far East* (Washington, D.C.: GPO, 1969), 313 (hereafter cited as *FRUS*, with year and volume). The most complete account of U.S. intelligence and military contacts with the Vietminh can be found in Archimedes L. A. Patti, *Why Vietnam? Prelude to America's Albatross* (Berkeley: University of California Press, 1980).

14. For the U.S. response to developments in the Netherlands East Indies, see McMahon, *Colonialism and Cold War*.

15. *FRUS, 1946*, 8:32–43.

16. Hess, *The United States' Emergence*, 197–204.

17. Vincent to Acheson, December 23, 1946, *FRUS, 1946*, 8:75–76.

18. Secretary of State James F. Byrnes to the Embassy in France, December 24, 1946, ibid., 77–78.

19. Marshall to the Embassy in France, February 3, 1947, *FRUS, 1947*, 6:67–68.

20. See, for example, ibid., 3: 204–53.

21. Marshall to the Embassy in France, February 3, 1947, ibid., 6:67–68.

22. Charles S. Reed II (consul in Saigon) to the Department of State, July 11, 1947, ibid., 114.

23. On the Asian Tito option, see especially House Committee on Armed Services, *United States-Vietnam Relations, 1945-1967: Study Prepared by the Department of Defense (Washington, D.C.: GPO, 1971)*, 1:c1–c7; Blum, *Drawing the Line*, 118–23.

24. Department of State Policy Statement on Indochina, September 27, 1948, *FRUS, 1948*, 6:48.

25. Reed to the Department of State, July 11, 1947, *FRUS, 1947*, 6:114.

26. Marshall to the Embassy in France, May 13, 1947, ibid., 97; Hess, "The First American Commitment in Indochina."

27. Department of State Policy Statement on Indochina, September 27, 1948, *FRUS, 1948*, 6:43–49. Similar analyses of the U.S. policy dilemma can be found in CIA Report ORE 25-48, "The Break-up of the Colonial Empires and Its Implications for U.S. Security," September 3, 1948, President's Secretary's File, Harry S. Truman Papers, Harry S. Truman Library, Independence, Mo.; Policy Planning Staff (PPS) Paper 51, "United States Policy toward Southeast Asia," March 29, 1949, in *The State Department Policy Planning Staff Papers*, vol. 3, 1949, introduction by Anna Kasten Nelson (New York: Garland, 1983), 32–53.

28. U.S. Department of State, *Bulletin* 24 (February 20, 1950): 291–92. See also Bruce to Acheson, December 11, 1949, and NSC-48/2, December 30, 1949, *FRUS, 1949*, 7:105–10, 1215–20; and Acheson to Truman, February 2, 1950, *FRUS, 1950*, 6:716–17.

29. For the broader context of these challenges to U.S. foreign policy, see especially Leffler, *Preponderance of Power*, ch. 8; Thomas J. McCormick, *America's Half-Century: United States Foreign Policy in the Cold War* (Baltimore: Johns Hopkins University Press, 1989), 88–98.

30. Memorandum by Acheson, December 20, 1949, *FRUS, 1949*, 1:612–17.

31. Acheson to British Ambassador Oliver Franks, December 24, 1949, ibid., 7:927.

32. The crucial link between Japan and Southeast Asia is emphasized in a number of important secondary works, including Borden, *The Pacific Alliance*; Schaller, *The American Occupation of Japan*; Rotter, *The Path to Vietnam*; and Leffler, *Preponderance of Power*.

33. Michael J. Hogan, *The Marshall Plan: America, Britain, and the Reconstruction of Western Europe, 1947-1952* (New York: Cambridge University Press,

1987), ch. 6; Melvyn P. Leffler, "The United States and the Strategic Dimensions of the Marshall Plan," *Diplomatic History* 12 (Summer 1988): 277–306.

34. PPS/61, "Policy Relating to the Financial Crisis of the United Kingdom and the Sterling Area," August 31, 1949, in *The State Department Policy Planning Staff Papers*, 3:150–56; Leffler, "Strategic Dimensions," 298.

35. Quoted in Rotter, *The Path to Vietnam*, 54.

36. Quoted in ibid., 141.

37. Ibid., chapters 3, 7, 8.

38. This argument is developed most fully and most effectively in Blum, *Drawing the Line*.

39. Quoted in John Lewis Gaddis, *Strategies of Containment: A Critical Appraisal of Postwar American National Security Policy* (New York: Oxford University Press, 1982), 92. For the full text of NSC-68, see *FRUS, 1950*, 1:237–92.

40. On this point, see Robert J. McMahon, "Credibility and World Power: Exploring the Psychological Dimension in Postwar American Diplomacy," *Diplomatic History* 15 (Fall 1991): 455–71; and Gaddis, *Strategies of Containment*, 91–92.

41. Analysis prepared for the Joint Chiefs of Staff by the Joint Strategic Survey Committee, November 17, 1950, *FRUS, 1950*, 6:949–50.

42. Ibid. See also Joint Chiefs of Staff to Secretary of Defense George C. Marshall, November 28, 1950, ibid., 945–48.

43. Dulles to Acheson, November 30, 1950, ibid., 163.

44. NIE-5, "Indochina: Current Situation and Probable Developments," December 29, 1950, ibid., 958–63.

45. Progress Report on NSC-64, March 15, 1951, Under Secretary of State James E. Webb to Truman, September 13, 1951, *FRUS, 1951*, 6:397–400, 496–97.

46. Edmund Gullion (chargé in Saigon) to the Department of State, August 18, 1951; Heath to the Department of State, July 20, 1951; NIE-35, "Probable Developments in Indochina during the Remainder of 1951," August 7, 1951; J. Lawton Collins (army chief of staff) memorandum, November 13, 1951, ibid., 480–84, 457–59, 469–75, 544–45.

47. Joint Chiefs of Staff to Marshall, November 28, 1950, *FRUS, 1950*, 6:946.

48. Bruce to the Department of State, May 31, 1950, ibid., 819–20.

49. Heath to the Department of State, February 24, 1951, *FRUS, 1951*, 6:385. On U.S.-French policy differences, see George C. Herring, "Franco-American Conflict in Indochina, 1950–1954," in Kaplan, Artaud, and Rubin, *Dien Bien Phu*, 29–48.

50. See, for example, memorandum of discussion at State-JCS meeting, December 21, 1951, *FRUS, 1951*, 6:569–70.

51. Secretary of Defense Louis Johnson to Acheson, April 14, 1950, memorandum prepared in the Policy Planning Staff, August 16, 1950, *FRUS, 1950*, 6:780–85, 857–58; Joint Chiefs of Staff to Marshall, January 10, 1951, *FRUS, 1951*, 6:347–48. See also Robert Buzzanco, "Prologue to Tragedy: U.S. Military Opposition to Intervention in Vietnam, 1950–1954," *Diplomatic History* (forthcoming); Walter S. Poole, *The Joint Chiefs of Staff and National Policy*, vol. 4, *1950–1952* (Wilmington, Del.: Michael Glazier, 1980), 419–22.

52. Ohly to Acheson, November 20, 1950, *FRUS, 1950*, 6:929.

53. Memorandum of discussion at NSC meeting, March 5, 1952, *FRUS, 1952–54*, vol. 12, pt. 1, 70–74.

54. Memorandum of discussion among Acheson, Eden, and others, May 26, 1952, ibid., 96–97.

55. NSC-124/2, June 25, 1952, ibid., 127–32. See also NIE-43, "The Strategic Importance of the Far East to the USSR," November 13, 1951, *FRUS, 1951*, 6: 107–15.

56. Memorandum of discussion at NSC meeting, March 5, 1952, *FRUS, 1952–54*, vol. 12, pt. 1, 71–72. On the U.S. policy reassessment of 1952, see also Leffler, *Preponderance of Power*, chapter 11.

57. Secretaries of the Army, Navy, and Air Force to Lovett, April 8, 1952, CD 092 (Indochina) 1952, Records of the Office of the Administrative Secretary, Office of the Secretary of Defense, Record Group 330, National Archives, Washington, D.C.

58. Memorandum of discussion at a State-JCS meeting, March 5, 1952, *FRUS, 1952–54*, vol. 12, pt. 1, 63.

3
Dwight D. Eisenhower and Wholehearted Support of Ngo Dinh Diem

David L. Anderson

"The loss of South Vietnam would set in motion a crumbling process that could, as it progressed, have grave consequences for us and for freedom," President Dwight D. Eisenhower declared in an April 1959 speech.[1] This statement reaffirmed the famous "falling domino" analogy that he had used five years earlier to explain the strategic importance of Indochina. If the states of Southeast Asia fell under "the Communist dictatorship," he asserted in April 1954, the result would be a "disintegration" with the "most profound influence" for "millions and millions and millions of people."[2] Throughout his eight years as president, Eisenhower never wavered in his conviction that the survival of an independent, noncommunist government in southern Vietnam was a vital strategic imperative for the United States. This objective, which Eisenhower's successors in the White House would also support, was the cornerstone of his policies in Southeast Asia, but it left open the question of the means of achieving that goal.

Eisenhower and his foreign policy advisers went through two stages in attempting to devise a successful method of securing U.S. interests in Vietnam. The first approach, which lasted through 1954 and into 1955, was to continue the Truman tactic of working with and through the French and other Western allies to contain communism in Southeast Asia. During this early phase, Eisenhower showed remarkable restraint considering the administration's Cold War rhetoric about the global danger of communist expansionism. He managed to avoid involving the United States militarily in Indochina as France suffered a humiliating defeat at Dienbienphu at the hands of the communist-led Vietminh army. After the French surrender at Dienbienphu, an international conference at Geneva, Switzerland, arranged a

Eisenhower and Secretary of State John Foster Dulles greet President Ngo Dinh Diem at the White House in May 1957. (National Park Service, courtesy Dwight D. Eisenhower Library)

Franco-Vietminh cease-fire in July 1954. In the following months, the Eisenhower administration tried to maintain an allied strategy in Indochina. It established the Southeast Asia Treaty Organization (SEATO) and sent a special mission to Vietnam headed by General J. Lawton Collins to attempt, among other things, to continue a joint U.S.-French program in the region.

By the spring of 1955, however, the administration had begun a second, essentially unilateral approach in which the United States sought to protect its strategic interests in Southeast Asia by building a new Vietnamese nation around a reclusive autocrat named Ngo Dinh Diem. For the remainder of the Eisenhower presidency, the United States pegged its Vietnam policy on the questionable ability of Diem. In contrast to the cautious good judgment of the first phase that limited U.S. risks in Southeast Asia, the second phase exhibited a tragic irresponsibility by enmeshing the United States in the tangled web of Vietnamese politics and exposing Americans and American interests to considerable danger.

Eisenhower brought with him to the White House the conviction that the areas of the world "in which freedom flourishes" were under assault from a "Communist-regimented unity."[3] In his first State of the Union address in February 1953, he described France's struggle against the Vietminh as holding "the line of freedom" against "Communist aggression throughout the world."[4] As he prepared to leave office eight years later, his bipolar perception of the world divided between freedom and tyranny—with Southeast Asia at the center of that conflict—had not altered. Eisenhower's farewell address to the nation is remembered primarily for its warning against the dangerous influence of the military-industrial complex in America, but the speech opened with the stern reminder that the nation had faced and would continue to confront "a hostile ideology—global in scope, atheistic in character, ruthless in purpose, and insidious in method."[5] The next day, on January 19, 1961, he warned president-elect John Kennedy that the civil war then raging in Laos threatened to spread communism throughout the entire region.

Besides his commitment to no compromise with world communism, the other hallmark of Eisenhower's policies in Indochina and elsewhere was cost reduction. In a strategy labeled the New Look, his administration sought the most economical ways to protect U.S. security. Commonly associated with the threat to use nuclear force for "massive retaliation," the New Look also called for a greater reliance on military alliances and covert operations.[6]

The New Look was apparent during the initial phase of the administration's Indochina policies in the effort to work with France to defeat the Vietnamese communists. Although they shared the Truman administration's displeasure at the French intent to recolonize Indochina, the Republicans decided that the Cold War required them to stand with their North Atlantic Treaty Organization (NATO) ally. Secretary of State John Foster Dulles candidly admitted to the Senate Foreign Relations Committee that U.S. choices in this situation were distasteful, but in "the divided spirit" of the world today, the United States would have to tolerate the colonialists a bit longer to help block Soviet and Chinese infiltration of Southeast Asia.[7] Dulles also felt compelled to cooperate with France in Indochina because he wanted French officials to accept a rearmed West Germany (a frightening prospect for many in France) as part of a U.S.-backed plan for NATO called the European Defense Community. To bolster French resolve in both Indochina and Europe, the Eisenhower administration increased U.S. aid to the point that it accounted for almost 80 percent of France's military expenditures in Southeast Asia by January 1954.[8]

As the Eisenhower administration observed its first anniversary in office, however, Paris's perseverance was waning. The French public and politicians were tiring of the seven-year burden of the Indochina war. The resilient Vietminh, under the charismatic leadership of Ho Chi Minh, continued to exact a heavy price in blood and treasure from their would-be masters. To the regret of Washington, French leaders accepted a Soviet proposal for a multinational conference at Geneva, set to begin in April, that would attempt to structure a diplomatic settlement in Indochina. Then, in March, the Vietminh assaulted an entrenched French garrison at Dienbienphu with such overwhelming force that a French military disaster appeared possible on the eve of the truce talks. The French might decide at Geneva to capitulate to their communist foes.

The prospect of a socialist ally of the Soviet Union and the People's Republic of China (PRC) emerging triumphant over a member of NATO that had been openly aided by the United States deeply troubled U.S. leaders, who began serious consideration of the New Look's trump card—massive retaliation. Although this option implied the possibility of using nuclear weapons, few U.S. planners believed that the atomic bomb was necessary to balance the military scales at Dienbienphu. In this case, the proposal involved a staggering conventional bombardment of the attacking force using as many as 350 planes from U.S. aircraft carriers and from bases in Okinawa and the Philippines.[9]

Throughout March and April, Eisenhower, Dulles, and other top administration officials weighed the air strike idea but never used it. In early May, the French garrison surrendered after sustaining heavy losses, and this outcome set the stage for the signing of a cease-fire agreement between France and the Vietminh at Geneva. This turn of events has long fascinated observers of Eisenhower's foreign policies. The president and his secretary of state encouraged the image that their hands were tied by congressional and allied reluctance to countenance a risky and perhaps unwarranted rescue of France's failed ambitions. Although this characterization made the White House appear passive, it paid excellent political dividends. It helped shield Eisenhower from personal attacks that he had "lost" something in Vietnam, as Truman had been excoriated for allegedly losing China.

While in office, Eisenhower was beloved by many Americans who admired his leadership of the Allied forces that defeated Nazi tyranny during World War II and who appreciated his humble demeanor and engaging grin. At the same time, however, he seemed to be a rather lackadaisical chief executive who presided over but did not propel his administration. The later declassification of confidential White House files reversed this picture dramatically. The record revealed Eisenhower to be directly and often decisively involved in key decisions such as those on Indochina in 1954. His management of the Dienbienphu crisis has become something of a centerpiece of the rehabilitation of his presidential image in recent years. He utilized the skills of talented subordinates such as Dulles and let them absorb some of the public pressure produced by controversial actions, but the president kept a firm, if hidden, hand on the administration's helm.[10]

The origin of Eisenhower's leadership ability is clear. His rise to the pinnacle of the nation's military structure as a five-star general provided him with a wealth of experience that prepared him to be president. The military had been his leadership laboratory, and his advancement up the ranks in competition with other extremely able officers revealed that he was an adept student of management theory. His method of handling subordinates, for example, was carefully considered. During World War II, he delegated extensive responsibility to such forceful commanders as George Patton and Omar Bradley, but he retained the authority to call them to account when necessary. Similarly, his approach to public relations, contingency planning, and other areas of executive responsibility demonstrated active leadership and effective management style.[11]

The details of the Dienbienphu decision have especially enhanced Eisenhower's reputation. Confronted with a military-diplomatic problem that corresponded to his personal experience, he confidently shaped the policy deliberations. Neither Dulles nor Vice-President Richard M. Nixon, both of whom often spoke out publicly and stridently on foreign policy, fashioned the administration's actions. The president made the decisions that kept U.S. ground and air forces out of combat. "It would be a great mistake for the United States to enter the fray in partnership only with France," Eisenhower believed; "united action by the free world was necessary, and in such action the U.S. role would not require use of its ground troops."[12] The prudence of his course appears statesmanlike in contrast to the steps of later presidents who plunged U.S. forces into hostile action in Southeast Asia.[13]

Yet praise for the decision can easily be overdrawn. Eisenhower's restraint had more to do with the immediate predicament of the French and the perception that Paris had lost the will to fight than with any careful reassessment of U.S. purposes in Vietnam. He was willing to accept a tactical setback in the Cold War at Dienbienphu but was not prepared to question the proclaimed importance of Indochina in the global balance of power. Also, it is a mistake to conclude that Eisenhower was an energetic leader just because the career soldier chose to involve himself personally in a national security issue. A few days after the French garrison surrendered, for example, the U.S. Supreme Court issued its momentous school desegregation decision, *Brown v. the Board of Education of Topeka.* On the matter of racial injustice, which burdened millions of American citizens every day, the president chose to stay uninvolved, declaring that he would express neither "approbation nor disapproval" of the Court's action.[14]

When the Court ruled on the *Brown* case, U.S. delegates were sitting at the Geneva Conference deliberating the fate of Vietnam. The Vietminh victory at Dienbienphu made it likely that the French would accept a compromise with the communists. The Eisenhower administration took a largely passive role in the proceedings to avoid any responsibility for the outcome, but the United States maintained a presence there because the president and his advisers were not willing to embark on a separate, solitary course in the region. With Britain, the USSR, and the PRC mediating, the French and Vietminh reached a cease-fire agreement that temporarily partitioned the country at the 17th parallel. The communist-led Democratic Republic of Vietnam (DRV) would control the North, and France would regroup its military forces in the South. An all-Vietnam election was to be held in two years to determine the future political structure of the nation. The U.S. delegation publicly acknowledged these terms but did not sign or verbally endorse any of them.[15]

Determined to salvage the southern part of Vietnam from communist domination and to do so by collective defense if possible, the Eisenhower administration championed the creation of SEATO in September 1954. Comprising the United States, France, Britain, Australia, New Zealand, the Philippines, Thailand, and Pakistan, this alliance was not a binding security pact like NATO, but it did provide a mechanism for possible joint action in future crises like Dienbienphu and especially in the event of overt aggression by the DRV or PRC. Under the terms of the Geneva Accords, Vietnam and neighboring Laos and Cambodia could not enter into military agreements, but the SEATO pact extended a vague commitment to their security in an attached protocol. Despite the treaty's weaknesses, Dulles hailed it as a "no trespassing" sign to warn away potential communist aggressors, and Eisenhower and his successors in the White House cited SEATO as the authority for U.S. intervention in the region's affairs.[16]

Eisenhower's handling of Dienbienphu, Geneva, and SEATO, taken together, highlighted the strengths and weaknesses of his leadership style. He was managing the Vietnam issue politically but not solving it substantively. Using Dulles as his primary spokesman, Eisenhower had urged "united action" during the siege of Dienbienphu to counter the communist threat in Southeast Asia. With the formation of SEATO, such allied unity seemed possible. Opinion polls indicated that the American public favored this kind of multilateral approach over unilateral action. Similarly, Eisenhower's decision to maintain a discreet distance from the negotiations and final settlement at Geneva avoided a charge that he had accepted a compromise with communists—an allegation that critics had made against Franklin Roosevelt after the Yalta Conference of 1945. The American people wanted toughness in U.S. policy without the risk of war, and the administration's coolness toward the Geneva Accords and its creation of SEATO suited this public mood. In terms of policy, however, toughness alone was not a solution. The true alternatives were either to use force to break DRV power or to accept DRV success. The administration would do neither and hence only deepened the U.S. commitment in Southeast Asia with no realistic prospect for resolving the dilemma of how to protect U.S. interests without war.[17]

Although France entered SEATO, U.S.-French cooperation in Southeast Asia after the Geneva Conference was strained almost to the breaking point. Eisenhower and many of his aides believed that Paris had essentially forfeited its influence on Western policies in Indochina with its weak performance against the Vietminh. The president complained that he was "weary" of the French and their "seemingly hysterical desire to be thought such a 'great power.' "[18] Still, many of the French had strong economic and personal ties with Indochina and were loath to surrender what remained of their position.

In an effort to reestablish a working relationship with French officials in South Vietnam, Eisenhower sent General J. Lawton Collins, a trusted World War II colleague and former army chief of staff, to Saigon in November 1954 as his personal representative. "Lightning Joe" Collins was also to formulate "a crash program to sustain the Diem government and establish security in Free Vietnam." The president thought that French officials in Saigon would cooperate, but, if not, "we ought to lay down the law to the French," he told the National Security Council. "It is true that we have to cajole the French with regard to the European area," Eisenhower added, "but we certainly didn't have to in Indochina."[19]

Collins had some success with military training programs and bureaucratic changes, but eventually his mission and U.S. policy in general reached an impasse with the French over the internal political structure of the South. At issue was the leadership of Ngo Dinh Diem. While the Geneva Conference was under way, Emperor Bao Dai had made Diem prime minister of the

State of Vietnam, the vacuous regime that French officials had created as a Vietnamese nationalist alternative to the Vietminh and their alien Marxist ideology. It was this government, currently under the protection of the French in their regroupment zone south of the 17th parallel, that would face the DRV and its president Ho Chi Minh in the Geneva-mandated elections. Not all Vietnamese approved of the Vietminh, who had often ruthlessly silenced their political rivals, but the leaders of the DRV enjoyed the advantage of having forced the capitulation of the colonialists. Diem's regime would have to prove its ability and its patriotism if it was going to shake the appearance of dependence on the Westerners. Some Americans thought Diem might be able to meet this challenge, but only if the French allowed him the true independence to do so.

Diem himself was a complex individual. He was personally honest and courageous and had a well-established record of resistance to French domination of his homeland. These qualities were assets for a Vietnamese politician. He had genuine liabilities, though, that the French were quick to emphasize. He had no political base except his own large family, which had a well-earned reputation for clannish self-interest. His Catholic religion may have pleased the French but only served to isolate him from his predominantly Buddhist countrymen. His personality was aloof, even monkish—the opposite of the modern politician. In addition, he had lived briefly in the United States and knew some influential American politicians and church leaders, such as Senator Mike Mansfield (D-Mont.) and Francis Cardinal Spellman. In fact, it may have been Diem's ties to the United States that prompted Bao Dai to name him prime minister, in a move to court official U.S. support as French power waned in Vietnam.[20]

How Bao Dai came to appoint Diem, a man whom he disliked immensely, is not known with certainty. Some accounts have speculated that the CIA or some other secret U.S. influence was behind the selection. There is no particular evidence available for this scenario, however, and Bao Dai may well have had his own reasons. Clandestine American contact with Diem after he became prime minister has become well known. Covert initiatives were an explicit element of the New Look, and CIA Director Allen W. Dulles (the secretary of state's brother) sent a special agent to Saigon at the same time that Diem assumed office. Allen Dulles's choice was Air Force Colonel Edward G. Lansdale, an unconventional warfare officer who had aided the Philippine government's successful resistance of a communist rebellion. Lansdale quickly became Diem's confidant and an ardent advocate for firm U.S. support of the prime minister.[21]

Despite endorsement of Diem from Lansdale and others, Eisenhower had given explicit instructions to Collins to evaluate Diem's leadership qualities.[22] After five months of close observation, Collins reported that he judged Diem incapable of providing South Vietnam with the dynamic leadership it needed. Diem and his brothers were running a "practically one-man government," the general informed Washington, and they were stubbornly resistant to helpful advice. Collins recommended other Vietnamese officials whom he thought could better organize a broad-based coalition to compete with the communists. Collins's report shocked Secretary of State Dulles. Although initially dubious of Diem's prospects, the secretary had come to accept the argument of Diem's American friends that the prime minister was the best hope for a nationalist alternative to Ho and that all Diem needed was the confidence that he had the *"wholehearted* backing" of the United States.[23]

Unlike the Dienbienphu discussions of the previous year, debate on the Diem issue in the spring of 1955 did not directly engage the president. Eisenhower chose to stand aside and let Secretary Dulles and General Collins reach a conclusion. The president was preoccupied with the Taiwan Straits crisis and the approach of his first summit conference with Soviet leaders. Meeting with Dulles and other State Department officials in Washington on April 25, Collins maintained his position that Diem was not indispensable, and the secretary reluctantly agreed. Literally at the moment these decisions were being made, street fighting erupted in Saigon. Probably instigated by Diem himself in a desperate demonstration to Washington, the violence enabled the prime minister to obtain enough backing from the fledgling South Vietnamese armed forces to quell the unrest. As Collins rushed back to Saigon to oversee U.S. interests in the unstable situation, Dulles's Asian advisers convinced him to reverse himself and to make wholehearted support of Diem the basis of U.S. policy. The aides argued that the violent outbreak proved that it was an inopportune time to tamper with Saigon's internal politics.[24]

Once the Eisenhower administration had determined that it would stick with Diem, the task remained to convince the French to accept this course. In early May, exactly a year after the surrender of Dienbienphu, Dulles met several times with French premier Edgar Faure. The sessions were stormy, but Faure finally acquiesced to Dulles's insistence on Diem.[25] It was clear that Paris no longer wished to contest Washington over the direction of Western policy in Vietnam. Through the rest of 1955, the French rapidly withdrew the remainder of their forces in South Vietnam and left the fate of the would-be nation to the Americans and their client Diem.

In the long-term history of U.S. involvement in Southeast Asia, Washington had turned an important corner. SEATO had provided a semblance of collective sanction to the U.S. intent to bolster South Vietnam, but the departure of the French demonstrated that the effort actually would be a unilateral U.S. program. The feasibility of the plan hinged on the questionable judgment that Diem could make it work. The administration entered a new and perilous policy phase.

With the basic decision having been made to build a nation around Diem, the implementation now fell to the foreign policy bureaucracy with little additional input from the president or Dulles. After Eisenhower suffered a heart attack in September 1955, many issues that his staff deemed routine, such as Vietnam, were kept from his schedule. The following year, Dulles developed abdominal cancer, and although he remained in office almost until his death in 1959, his personal agenda too became more restricted.[26] Yet the course that Eisenhower and Dulles had set in Vietnam remained the administration's policy until the end of Eisenhower's presidency, and occasionally the two men would publicly reaffirm the concept of wholehearted support for Diem.

The task of nation building loomed large before the administration. The legitimacy of Diem's regime rested only on his appointment by the heir of Vietnam's last royal dynasty, and Sa Majesté Bao Dai had taken up permanent residence on the French Riviera. The State of Vietnam had a small army of 150,000 led by an inexperienced officer corps that, under the French, had never been allowed to have any command or staff authority. The civil bureaucracy consisted only of *fonctionnaires* trained to take orders, not to solve problems. Industry was virtually nonexistent in South Vietnam, and the agricultural base of rice and rubber, although potentially valuable, had been wrecked by exploitative landlords who had impoverished much of the peasantry. Diem himself had no political following that could compete with the regimented and motivated cadre in the DRV.[27]

Diem's political weakness seemed especially important because of the national reunification elections that were supposed to occur in 1956. Although many observers of all ideological perspectives believed that Ho Chi Minh would win any truly free countrywide election, the chances of a referendum occurring were slim from the beginning. The Geneva conferees had drafted a vague proposal for elections because they could not fashion any workable political formula themselves. How the Vietnamese were to vote and on what was never specified. No official in North or South Vietnam had ever organized or conducted a free election, and there was no reason to expect that the Vietnamese would do so now under these strained circumstances. In the months following the Geneva Conference, it was clear that Diem and his American patrons had no enthusiasm for an election, but there was also no pressure for a vote from China, the Soviet Union, Britain, or France. None of these governments was inclined to assume any risk to itself to champion elections in Vietnam for the benefit of the DRV. The Eisenhower administration can be given little credit or blame for the failure of the election provisions of the Geneva agreements.[28]

Even without the serious possibility of a reunification vote, Diem's specious political legitimacy posed grave difficulties for U.S. objectives. Kenneth T. Young, the State Department officer in charge of Southeast Asian affairs, saw the problem as a paradox. He believed that if South Vietnam did not become a republic the anachronistic State of Vietnam would be easy prey for the revolutionary line of the DRV. At the same time, though, he feared that voting for a representative assembly in the South might open the door to political anarchy.[29] While Young and other Americans worried, Diem acted. He staged a lopsided referendum in October 1955 to depose Bao Dai and to make himself president of a newly created Republic of Vietnam (RVN). In March 1956, Diem organized an election of a constituent assembly, heavily stacked in his favor, to draft a constitution. The voting was not an exercise in democracy, but it was impressive evidence of the ability of the Ngo family, especially Diem's brothers Ngo Dinh Nhu and Ngo Dinh Can, to manipulate ballots. The RVN provided a facade of popular government for an ambitious family aspiring to centralized authority.[30]

Evidence of the emerging Ngo family dictatorship mounted. Nhu and Can operated a secret organization, the Can Lao, that used bribery and intimidation to garner personal support for Diem from key members of the military and bureaucracy. Vietminh "suspects," that is, persons thought disloyal to the regime, were arrested and sent to "reeducation camps." An RVN ordinance abolished elected village councils and substituted government appointees to run local affairs. Some U.S. officials, including Secretary Dulles, excused this authoritarianism as typical of Asia and even saw it as prudent because it provided a measure of stability in a nation still developing its institutional structure. Among his criticisms of Diem, Collins had warned that the Ngos' penchant for self-protection would only isolate Diem from the people and weaken the regime. That caution had been rejected, however, in favor of wholehearted support for Diem. As Collins had predicted, the Ngos increasingly behaved as if they could take U.S. aid for granted regardless of how they acted.[31]

The level of U.S. assistance to South Vietnam was high, almost $250 million annually through the end of the Eisenhower years. Some of these funds were designated for economic development. Very little aid went to the agricultural sector, but after U.S. urging, the Diem government announced some rent controls and land transfer plans, which went largely unimplemented. In the urban areas, a U.S.-designed Commercial Import Program made U.S. dollars available to subsidize imports. Rather than stimulate economic activity, however, the plan produced an influx of consumer goods, such as refrigerators and motorbikes, that created an appearance of prosperity but masked the lack of real economic growth.[32]

The bulk of U.S. aid, about 80 percent of it, went directly to the South Vietnamese armed forces. During the Eisenhower presidency, the number of U.S. military personnel in the RVN never exceeded 700, but the large percentage of U.S. aid that went for military purposes revealed the high priority placed on the military security of the new nation. Eighty-five percent of the funds for paying, equipping, and training the RVN's 150,000-man force came from the U.S. Treasury.[33]

Eisenhower and his advisers chose to declare Diem's leadership of South Vietnam a grand success, despite the repressive nature of the Saigon regime and its heavy dependency on aid. On May 8, 1957, the president himself stood on the hot parking apron at Washington National Airport to greet Diem as the RVN leader arrived for a highly publicized state visit. During the next four days, among lavish receptions and private meetings, Diem conferred with Eisenhower, Dulles, and other officials and addressed a joint session of Congress. This pageantry was part of a series of such events hosted by the administration for a number of Asian and African dignitaries. The purpose was to improve U.S. relations with the Third World, which, as Washington had learned during the Suez Canal crisis of 1956, could be vitally important. Diem was a beneficiary of this administration initiative in personal diplomacy.[34]

Eisenhower and other American speakers hailed Diem as a "tough miracle man" and the "savior" of South Vietnam.[35] The administration congratulated Diem and itself on his survival since 1954 and characterized the RVN as a stalwart ally in the struggle against world communism. Behind closed doors the rhetoric was friendly but somewhat more restrained. When Diem asked for an increase in U.S. aid, for example, Eisenhower rebuffed him with the explanation that U.S. global aid commitments prevented greater assistance. The Eisenhower-Diem summit reconfirmed the administration's earlier decisions to treat South Vietnam as strategically important and to give wholehearted endorsement to Diem's regime. It also showed that, even in a region of vital interest, the New Look principle of fiscal restraint still applied.[36]

In the late 1950s, Congress too was determined both to contain foreign aid budgets and to continue assistance to the Diem regime. Only once during the decade did congressional committees hold hearings specifically on Indochina, and that occasion was an investigation of alleged corruption in the management of the aid program in Saigon. Although both Democratic and Republican members questioned the amounts and uses of some funds, the probe uncovered no serious misconduct. At no time during the Eisenhower presidency did Congress as a body challenge the goals of the administration's policies in Vietnam. During the Dienbienphu crisis, some congressional leaders, including Senator Lyndon B. Johnson (D-Tex.), urged the White House to avoid a unilateral U.S. intervention in the French war, but that position was already preferred by the president. Later, as the U.S. commitment to Diem grew, a bipartisan alignment of lawmakers—many of them in an interest group called the American Friends of Vietnam that included Senator John F. Kennedy (D-Mass.)—staunchly defended U.S. involvement in the region.[37]

During Eisenhower's second term, two pressures largely shaped the conduct of U.S. policy in Southeast Asia: (1) the proclaimed value of South Vietnam to U.S. security and (2) the need to manage economically the United States' global obligations. These twin concerns often exasperated the diplomats and military officers charged with devising and implementing appropriate actions. The problem was how to do more with less. With his attention on Sputnik, Cuba, and elsewhere, the president provided no additional direction to U.S. policymakers as conditions within Vietnam worsened.

By 1957 and 1958, terrorism and armed insurrection were on the rise in South Vietnam. This violence often represented retaliation and resistance to Diem's increasingly repressive regime. Most of these incidents occurred without the instigation of Hanoi. The DRV had not given up its objective of reuniting Vietnam under its rule, but its leaders had ordered their southern cadres to be patient. Hanoi preferred to try propaganda and other destabilizing techniques first rather than to plunge into an armed conflict that could prompt a U.S. military attack on the North. Southern resistance leaders, who faced being jailed and even executed, refused to wait, however, and began acting on their own with assassinations, firebombings, and small attacks on RVN military units and outposts.[38]

Both Vietnamese and American officials in Saigon shared a mounting feeling of crisis, but the instructions from Washington remained clear that the nation-building program would have to make do with what it was already receiving, or likely even less, as the total foreign aid budget shrank.[39] The result was a bitter and debilitating battle between American diplomats and the Ngo family and among the Americans themselves over how to utilize the available resources. The issue was whether to increase the already high percentage of U.S. funds that went to military use or to place more emphasis on economic development and political reform.

U.S. Ambassador in Saigon Elbridge Durbrow took the lead in arguing that the RVN government would remain under attack from within as a neocolonialist dependent as long as it failed to take genuine steps toward improving the economic and social welfare of its citizens. He even went so far as to suggest to Washington that helicopters and other military items that Diem desired be withheld until the RVN president demonstrated progress on land reform, civil rights, and other abuses—urgent problems that were fueling the hostility toward his regime. Meanwhile, Diem and Nhu vehemently demanded more military aid of all types with which to increase the size and armament of their forces.[40]

Lieutenant General Samuel T. Williams, the chief of the U.S. Military Assistance Advisory Group in Vietnam, took sharp exception to Durbrow's views and sided with the Ngos. He argued that economic and political reforms remained impossible until the partisan violence had been crushed militarily. He also considered it deplorable that Durbrow would propose threatening to deny matériel to Diem at a time when the RVN government was under attack by armed and ruthless opponents. The general complained privately that the ambassador was better suited to be a salesman in a ladies' shoe store than a diplomat in Asia. Williams got support from Lansdale, now a brigadier general in the Pentagon, who advised his Defense Department superiors that Durbrow was "insulting, misinformed, and unfriendly" toward Diem.[41]

Lansdale's and Williams's personal attacks on the ambassador demonstrated that there was more to the policy debate than just the merits of military versus economic aid. In question was the long-standing Eisenhower administration commitment to wholehearted support of Diem. The generals contended that rather than criticism and pressure, Diem needed Washington's acceptance and reassurance. With the backing of the State Department's Southeast Asia specialists, Durbrow maintained that no one, including Diem, was indispensable. In a pointed comment to his diplomatic colleagues, the ambassador recalled his Pentagon critic's past association with Diem: "We have to recognize that we are dealing with a somewhat more complicated situation in the case of the GVN [Government of Vietnam]," Durbrow declared, "and that we have left the 'Lansdale days' behind."[42] The intensity with which both sides argued revealed how important these officials considered Vietnam to be to the United States. The debate also gave no indication that any of these policymakers thought of doing nothing and simply leaving the outcome in Vietnam up to the Vietnamese.

In January 1961, a few days before John Kennedy took the oath of office as Eisenhower's successor, Lansdale returned from an inspection visit to South Vietnam with a dire report. The RVN was in "critical condition," he declared, and the Vietcong (Washington's new term for Vietnamese communists) "have started to steal the country and expect to be done in 1961."[43] His urgent tone may have derived in part from his ongoing debate over tactics with State Department officers, but it also revealed that the time had come for either reaffirmation or reassessment of the United States' wholehearted support of Diem and the RVN.

As Lansdale delivered his evaluation to the Pentagon, Eisenhower was briefing the president-elect on current world conditions. With a civil war under way in Laos in which the United States and the Soviet Union were supplying weapons to the contending sides, their discussion turned to Southeast Asia. The retiring chief executive claimed that the SEATO treaty obligated the United States to defend the region from communist encroachment. The United States should protect the area's security in cooperation with the SEATO allies if possible, but if not, Eisenhower advised, "then we must go it alone."[44] The next day, January 20, Eisenhower's constitutional authority over the direction of U.S. foreign policy expired, but the course that he had charted in Vietnam would continue.

A review of the long-term significance of the two phases of Eisenhower's Vietnam policies reveals that the second or post-1955 stage with its unilateral and assertive commitment to South Vietnam prevailed over the original multilateral and cautious approach. The goal during both periods was the same: to deny Vietnam or as much of it as possible to the Vietnamese communists. Phase one was a setback to this objective because it ended with de facto acceptance of communist control of the northern half of the country. Eisenhower's negative decision—to avoid taking overt action to resist this outcome—appears as a wise, statesmanlike acceptance of the reality of the

Vietminh's success in resisting French colonialism. It was a caution dictated by the immediate circumstances, however. The second phase was also based upon a negative decision—to avoid acceptance of an internal Vietnamese resolution of political authority in the country.[45] This decision was far from statesmanlike. It failed to acknowledge Diem's neocolonial dependence on U.S. support. It placed U.S. actions in conflict with the manifest Vietnamese desire for national independence. Yet Washington's wholehearted support of Diem continued. By the time Eisenhower left office in 1961, the goal of a noncommunist South Vietnam and the means of obtaining that objective—nation building premised on the survival of the Diem regime—were so deeply embedded in U.S. global strategy as to be virtually unassailable.

Eisenhower's personal strengths served him well during the first phase. His knowledge of military affairs and the politics of war enabled him to perceive clearly the military and political costs inherent in U.S. intervention in the French war. His talent for utilizing a good staff organization also enhanced his analysis of policy options and enabled him to present the outcome as a bureaucratic decision. This maneuvering mitigated potential criticism about being pusillanimous in Vietnam.[46] During the second phase, these same strengths failed him. Once the Geneva cease-fire took effect, the issue in Vietnam was not one of military strategy but of the internal political and economic development of a new nation. Although his experience on General Douglas MacArthur's staff in the Philippines in the 1930s made Eisenhower sensitive to the aspirations of Asian nationalists and familiar with the frustrations of dealing with them, he had no personal acquaintance with any Vietnamese leaders and little grasp of the complex sociopolitical realities of the Asian communism that Diem faced.[47] His one meeting with Diem was largely ceremonial. Similarly, his system of having his staff sift through options did not help alleviate this problem of comprehending complexity. Indeed, the key staff member upon whom he relied for foreign policy advice, Secretary Dulles, generally accepted the single-minded fixation on Diem. It could be argued that Eisenhower's 1955 heart attack made him excessively dependent on his staff, but even after his recovery and return to a rather heavy work load, he gave little personal attention to the details of Vietnam, which his staff presented to him as an issue that was being managed well.[48] He accepted their optimistic assessments and, during Diem's 1957 visit, lent his voice to the chorus of praise for the RVN's achievements. Beneath the miracle facade, however, were serious problems: Diem's narrow political base, his regime's weak military structure, South Vietnam's weak economy, and the growing insurgency. When Eisenhower yielded the White

House to Kennedy, the policy of wholehearted support of Diem remained in place not because it was achieving U.S. objectives but because to waver even slightly could risk collapse of the administration's eight-year effort to keep the dominoes from falling. Eisenhower's accomplishments in Vietnam were negative: no war, but no peace. It was a record of nonsolution and ever-narrowing options.

Notes

1. *Public Papers of the Presidents of the United States: Dwight D. Eisenhower, 1959* (Washington, D.C.: GPO, 1960), 311–13.
2. *Public Papers: Eisenhower, 1954* (Washington, D.C.: GPO, 1958), 382–84.
3. Dwight D. Eisenhower, *Crusade in Europe* (Garden City, N.Y.: Doubleday, 1948), 476.
4. *Public Papers: Eisenhower, 1953* (Washington, D.C.: GPO, 1958), 16.
5. *Public Papers: Eisenhower, 1960* (Washington, D.C.: GPO, 1961), 1035–40. See also Clark Clifford memorandum to Lyndon Johnson, September 29, 1967, U.S. Department of Defense, *The Pentagon Papers: The Defense Department History of United States Decision Making on Vietnam*, Senator Gravel edition, 4 vols. (Boston: Beacon Press, 1971), 2:635–37.
6. John L. Gaddis, *Strategies of Containment: A Critical Appraisal of Postwar American National Security Policy* (New York: Oxford University Press, 1982), 145–61.
7. U.S. Senate, *Executive Sessions of the Senate Foreign Relations Committee (Historical Series)*, vol. 5, 83d Cong., 1st sess., 1953 (Washington, D.C.: GPO, 1977), 385–88.
8. George McT. Kahin, *Intervention: How America Became Involved in Vietnam* (New York: Knopf, 1986), 42; George C. Herring, *America's Longest War: The United States and Vietnam, 1950–1975*, 2d ed. (New York: Knopf, 1986), 25–29.
9. Arthur W. Radford, *From Pearl Harbor to Vietnam: The Memoirs of Admiral Arthur W. Radford*, ed. Stephen Jurika, Jr. (Stanford, Calif.: Hoover Institution Press, 1980), 391–95; Ronald H. Spector, *The United States Army and Vietnam: Advice and Support: The Early Years, 1941–1960* (Washington, D.C.: GPO, 1983), 199–202; John Prados, *The Sky Would Fall: Operation Vulture: The Secret U.S. Bombing Mission to Vietnam, 1954* (New York: Dial Press, 1983), 152–56.
10. For examples of this Eisenhower revisionism, see Fred I. Greenstein, *The Hidden-Hand Presidency: Eisenhower as Leader* (New York: Basic Books, 1982); John P. Burke and Fred I. Greenstein, *How Presidents Test Reality: Decisions on Vietnam, 1954 and 1965* (New York: Russell Sage Foundation, 1989); Stephen E. Ambrose, *Eisenhower*, 2 vols. (New York: Simon & Schuster, 1983–84); and Robert A. Divine, *Eisenhower and the Cold War* (New York: Oxford University Press, 1981). For an appraisal of this revisionism, see Chester J. Pach, Jr., and Elmo Richardson,

The Presidency of Dwight D. Eisenhower, rev. ed. (Lawrence: University Press of Kansas, 1991), 237–39.

11. Fred I. Greenstein, "Dwight D. Eisenhower: Leadership Theorist in the White House," in Fred I. Greenstein, ed., *Leadership in the Modern Presidency* (Cambridge, Mass.: Harvard University Press, 1988), 76–107.

12. Arthur Minnich memorandum of conversation, no date, U.S. Department of State, *Foreign Relations of the United States, 1952–1954*, vol. 13, *Indochina* (Washington, D.C.: GPO, 1982), 1413 (hereafter cited as *FRUS*).

13. Melanie Billings-Yun, *Decision against War: Eisenhower and Dien Bien Phu, 1954* (New York: Columbia University Press, 1988); Richard E. Neustadt, *Presidential Power and the Modern Presidents: The Politics of Leadership from Roosevelt to Reagan* (New York: Free Press, 1990), 295–302; Richard H. Immerman, "Between the Unattainable and the Unacceptable: Eisenhower and Dienbienphu," in Richard A. Melanson and David Myers, eds., *Reevaluating Eisenhower: American Foreign Policy in the Fifties* (Urbana: University of Illinois Press, 1987), 120–21, 142–44.

14. Quoted in Harvard Sitkoff, *The Struggle for Black Equality, 1954–1980* (New York: Hill & Wang, 1981), 25. See also Robert Burk, *The Eisenhower Administration and Black Civil Rights* (Knoxville: University of Tennessee Press, 1984); George C. Herring and Richard H. Immerman, "Eisenhower, Dulles, and Dienbienphu: 'The Day We Didn't Go to War' Revisited," *Journal of American History* 71 (September 1984): 343–63; and Robert J. McMahon, "Eisenhower and Third World Nationalism: A Critique of the Revisionists," *Political Science Quarterly* 101 (Fall 1986): 453–73.

15. Herring, *America's Longest War*, 37–40; Lloyd C. Gardner, *Approaching Vietnam: From World War II through Dienbienphu, 1941–1954* (New York: Norton, 1988), 248–56, 281–84.

16. Memorandum of conversation, June 29, 1954, *FRUS, 1952–54*, vol. 12, *East Asia and the Pacific* (Washington, D.C.: GPO, 1984), 588. See also U.S. Department of State, *Bulletin* (September 20, 1954): 394–96; and Immerman, "Between the Unattainable and the Unacceptable," 145–46.

17. Burke and Greenstein, *How Presidents Test Reality*, 269–70; David L. Anderson, "China Policy and Presidential Politics, 1952," *Presidential Studies Quarterly* 10 (Winter 1980): 79–90.

18. Eisenhower to Alfred M. Gruenther, June 8, 1954, *FRUS, 1952–54*, 13: 1667–69.

19. Discussion at the 218th NSC meeting, October 22, 1954, ibid., 2157.

20. For various interpretations of Diem's appointment, see Herring, *America's Longest War*, 49; Kahin, *Intervention*, 78; Chester L. Cooper, *The Lost Crusade: America in Vietnam* (New York: Dodd, Mead, 1970), 20–21; Bui Diem and David Chanoff, *In the Jaws of History* (Boston: Houghton Mifflin, 1987), 71–72, 86; William C. Gibbons, *The U.S. Government and the Vietnam War: Executive and Legislative Roles and Relationships*, part 1, *1945–1960* (Princeton, N.J.: Princeton University Press, 1986), 266–67; and Robert Scheer, *How the United States Got Involved in Vietnam* (Santa Barbara, Calif.: Center for the Study of Democratic Institutions, 1965), 13–15.

21. Edward G. Lansdale, *In the Midst of Wars: An American's Mission to Southeast Asia* (New York: Harper & Row, 1972).

22. Eisenhower to Collins, November 3, 1954, *FRUS, 1952–54*, 13:2207; Andrew J. Goodpaster memorandum of conference with the president, November 3, 1954, box 3, Diary series, Ann Whitman File, Dwight D. Eisenhower Papers, Dwight D. Eisenhower Library, Abilene, Kans.

23. Dulles to Collins, April 20, 1955, *FRUS, 1955–57*, vol. 1, *Vietnam* (Washington, D.C.: GPO, 1985), 270–72 (Dulles's italics). See also Collins to Dulles, March 31, 1955, and April 7, 1955, ibid., 168–71, 218–21.

24. J. Lawton Collins, *Lightning Joe: An Autobiography* (Baton Rouge: Louisiana State University Press, 1979), 405–7.

25. John Foster Dulles, "An Historic Week—Report to the President," May 17, 1955, pp. 4–5, box 91, John Foster Dulles Papers, Princeton University Library.

26. Pach and Richardson, *Eisenhower*, 113–14, 203–4.

27. For a good description of Diem's Vietnam, see Robert Scigliano, *South Vietnam: Nation under Stress* (Boston: Houghton Mifflin, 1963).

28. William J. Sebald memorandum to Dulles, May 10, 1956, *FRUS, 1955–57*, 1:680–82; Kahin, *Intervention*, 88–92; Gibbons, *U.S. Government and the Vietnam War*, 1:299–300.

29. Kenneth T. Young memorandum to Walter S. Robertson, October 5, 1955, Young to G. Frederick Reinhardt, October 5, 1955, *FRUS, 1955–57*, 1:550–54.

30. Reinhardt to Dept. of State, November 29, 1955, ibid., 589–92; Reinhardt to Dulles, March 3, 1956, file 751G.00/3-356, and Reinhardt to Dulles, March 8, 1956, file 751G.00/3-856, U.S. Department of State General Records, Record Group 59, National Archives, Washington, D.C. (hereafter cited as RG 59).

31. Reinhardt to Dulles, December 6, 1955, file 751G.00/12-655, RG 59; G. Frederick Reinhardt interview by Philip A. Crowl, October 30, 1965, John Foster Dulles Oral History Project, Princeton University Library; Bernard B. Fall, *The Two Viet-Nams: A Political and Military Analysis*, rev. ed. (New York: Praeger, 1964), 246–68.

32. Arthur Z. Gardiner to Dept. of State, August 2, 1956, file 751G.5-MSP/8-256, and C. E. Lilien memorandum of conversation, December 10, 1957, file 751G.131/12-1057, RG 59; Kahin, *Intervention*, 84–88.

33. Scigliano, *South Vietnam*, 193; Fall, *Two Viet-Nams*, 289–306.

34. Program for Ngo Dinh Diem Visit, May 3, 1957, box 73, Subject series, White House Central Files (Confidential File), Eisenhower Library; Burton I. Kaufman, *Trade and Aid: Eisenhower's Foreign Economic Policy* (Baltimore: Johns Hopkins University Press, 1982), 99–110.

35. United States Department of State, *Bulletin* (May 27, 1957): 851; *Public Papers: Eisenhower, 1957* (Washington, D.C.: GPO, 1958), 417.

36. Elbridge Durbrow memorandum of conversation, May 9, 1957, *FRUS, 1955–57*, 1:794–99; Ambrose, *Eisenhower*, 2:376–81.

37. Gibbons, *U.S. Government and the Vietnam War*, 1:301–5, 320–27; John D. Montgomery, *The Politics of Foreign Aid: American Experience in Southeast Asia* (New York: Praeger, 1967), 221–35; Eisenhower, *Crusade in Europe*, 347; Dulles memorandum for the file, April 5, 1954, *FRUS, 1952–54*, 13:1224–25.

38. Kahin, *Intervention*, 109–15; Jeffrey Race, *War Comes to Long An: Revolutionary Conflict in a Vietnamese Province* (Berkeley: University of California Press, 1972), 105–22; William J. Duiker, *The Communist Road to Power in Vietnam* (Boulder, Colo.: Westview, 1981), 187–99.

39. Dulles to Durbrow, November 19, 1957, *FRUS, 1955–57*, 1:863–64.

40. Durbrow to Christian Herter, May 3, 1960, Durbrow to Daniel V. Anderson, July 18, 1960, *FRUS, 1958–60*, vol. 1, *Vietnam* (Washington, D.C.: GPO, 1986), 433–37, 514–15.

41. Lansdale to Edward J. O'Donnell, September 20, 1960, ibid., 580. See also memorandum prepared in Dept. of Defense, May 4, 1960, ibid., 439–41; and Samuel T. Williams to R. E. Lawless, May 15, 1962, box 8, Samuel T. Williams Papers, Hoover Institution Archives, Stanford, Calif.

42. Durbrow to Richard E. Usher, April 18, 1960, *FRUS, 1958–60*, 1:394.

43. Lansdale to Williams, January 17, 1961, box 8, Williams Papers. See also Lansdale to secretary of defense and deputy secretary of defense, January 17, 1961, box 49, Edward G. Lansdale Papers, Hoover Institution Archives.

44. Clifford to Johnson, September 29, 1967, *Pentagon Papers*, 2:635–37.

45. See James David Barber, *The Presidential Character: Predicting Performance in the White House*, 3d ed. (Englewood Cliffs, N.J.: Prentice-Hall, 1985), 134, 148, for a description of Eisenhower as a "passive-negative" president. For a favorable view of Eisenhower's negative achievements, see Divine, *Eisenhower*, 154–55.

46. Billings-Yun, *Decision against War*; Burke and Greenstein, *How Presidents Test Reality*, 268; Ambrose, *Eisenhower*, 2:185.

47. Burke and Greenstein, *How Presidents Test Reality*, 263–64; Ambrose, *Eisenhower*, 1:104–18.

48. Neustadt, *Presidential Power*, 133–34, 301.

4
Commitment in the Age of Counterinsurgency: Kennedy's Vietnam Options and Decisions, 1961–1963

Gary R. Hess

In November 1960, John F. Kennedy narrowly won election to the presidency. Throughout his campaign, Kennedy's promise of a more vigorous foreign policy addressed the concerns of Americans who sensed that their nation was losing ground in its global Cold War struggle. Anti-Americanism had been evident in hostility toward Vice-President Richard Nixon during his 1958 tour of Latin America, in the 1959 Panamanian riots protesting U.S. control of the canal, in the violent demonstrations in Japan that forced cancellation of President Eisenhower's visit to that country, and in other episodes. Above all, the Cuban revolution that brought Fidel Castro to power in 1959 underlined the depth of antagonism toward American hegemony. Castro's turn toward the Soviet Union had brought a communist state to the Caribbean, just ninety miles from the United States. Leftist movements exploited anti-Western sentiments in the newly independent countries of Asia and Africa. It was in the Third World that the specter of communism, linked to the Soviet Union and the People's Republic of China (at the time, commonly called Communist China), was seen as making its greatest gains. The sense that time was running against the United States was enhanced by the fear—derived from the evidence that China's growth was surpassing that of democratic India—that the communist model of economic development would be irresistible to Third World peoples.

Adding to the insecurity was the sense that the country's diplomacy had been unimaginative and inept in responding to these challenges. Soviet Premier Nikita Khrushchev had exploited the embarrassing U-2 incident to cancel the Paris summit conference and to repudiate "the spirit of Camp David" that had characterized his meetings with Eisenhower during his Sep-

*Kennedy receives a briefing from Brigadier General William P. Yarborough of the
U.S. Army Special Forces (Green Berets) during a training demonstration in 1961.
(U.S. Army, courtesy National Archives)*

tember 1959 visit to the United States. A year later Khrushchev was back in
the United States, this time to attend the United Nations meetings, where his
boorish behavior and rude outbursts were calculated to appeal to anti-
American sentiments.

November 1960 was also an important month in Vietnam—one of the many trouble spots confronting the American president-elect. On November 11, three battalions of the South Vietnamese army surrounded the presidential palace in Saigon in an attempt to overthrow the government of Ngo Dinh Diem. Dissident officers demanded political reforms and new leadership that would facilitate the battle against the communist insurgency. Exploiting the inept implementation of the coup and promising reforms, Diem outmaneuvered the rebels and survived the challenge.

The abortive coup, however, had ominous overtones. It surprised both American personnel in South Vietnam and the inner circle of the South Vietnamese government, centering on Diem and his brother Ngo Dinh Nhu. Indeed, reports of U.S. military and diplomatic officers had minimized the likelihood of any revolt and had portrayed Diem as enjoying wide support. The coup attempt underscored the dissatisfaction with Diem's leadership among those very elements of South Vietnamese society that had to be the basis of an effective government, for the rebels represented the concerns of a large portion of the urban professional and business classes. Both victors and losers learned important lessons: Diem, feeling betrayed by supposedly loyal officers, became ever more determined to control the army. His opponents, feeling betrayed as Diem reneged on his promised reforms, concluded that working with Diem was impossible and that next time there would be no bargaining.[1]

As Kennedy fashioned his administration, no one foresaw the extent to which the problems in South Vietnam evident in the attempted coup would absorb the attention and resources of the United States over the next decade. Yet no one in the Kennedy White House doubted the United States' ability to meet the challenges it faced. Called to guide America's destiny, the talented and resourceful men of the New Frontier relished confronting a world in crisis. In his book *The Best and the Brightest*, journalist David Halberstam described the mood of the Kennedy era: "A remarkable hubris permeated the entire time. Nine years earlier Denis Brogan had written 'probably the only people who have the historical sense of inevitable victory are the Americans.' Never had that statement seemed more true."[2] Arthur M. Schlesinger, Jr., the distinguished historian who served as an adviser to Kennedy, later reflected: "Euphoria reigned; we thought for a moment that the world was plastic and the future unlimited."[3]

The self-styled grand theorist of the Kennedy foreign policy team was the renowned economist Walt W. Rostow, who served as deputy special assistant for national security affairs and saw that "the first charge of the Kennedy Administration in 1961—somewhat like the challenge faced by the Truman administration in 1947—was to turn back the Communist offensive."[4] Secretary of Defense Robert McNamara, National Security Adviser McGeorge Bundy, special military adviser General Maxwell Taylor, Rostow, Schlesinger, and other "action intellectuals" embodied the "can-do" style that Kennedy inspired. Taylor, the former army chief of staff, had written a critique of the Eisenhower administration's overreliance on nuclear weapons, *The Uncertain Trumpet*, in which he called for "flexible response" in meeting the challenges posed by the communist powers. In terms of Southeast Asian policy, a key Kennedy official was Roger Hilsman, who served as assistant secretary of state for Far Eastern affairs and whose memoir and history of Kennedy's foreign policy, published shortly after the president's death, is revealingly titled *To Move a Nation*. The self-effacing and deliberative Dean Rusk served as secretary of state. He was something of an anomaly in the Kennedy inner circle, but he shared the worldview of his more outspoken colleagues. Moreover, he embodied Kennedy's determination to have a low-profile secretary of state and was unswerving in his loyalty to the president.[5]

Scholarship on the Kennedy presidency offers a variety of insights into his style and accomplishments. The early and wholly adulatory accounts by Kennedy insiders—Schlesinger's *A Thousand Days* and Theodore Sorensen's *Kennedy*—helped mold an enduring popular image of a decisive, imaginative, and idealistic leader. To Schlesinger, Kennedy's murder in 1963 deprived America of "the life-affirming zest, the brilliance, the wit, the cool commitment, the steady purpose" that the young president provided. Kennedy "gave his country back to its best self," Schlesinger continued, because he "re-established the republic as the first generation of our leaders saw it . . . transformed the American spirit . . . [and] gave the world for an imperishable moment the vision of a leader who greatly understood the terror and the hope, the diversity and the possibility, of life on this planet and who made people look beyond nation and race to the future of humanity."[6] To Sorensen, Kennedy could not be measured "by any ordinary historical yardstick. For he was an extraordinary man, an extraordinary politician and an extraordinary President. . . . Without demeaning any of the great men who have held the Presidency in this century, I do not see how John Kennedy could be ranked below any one of them."[7]

With the passage of time and the opportunity to judge the long-term impact of Kennedy's policies, perhaps above all in Vietnam, some historians have judged Kennedy quite harshly. In particular, Thomas Paterson sees Kennedy as relentlessly, but unnecessarily, pursuing victory in the Cold War to the point that he eroded U.S. power. Ignoring the realities of divisions within the communist bloc, exaggerating communist influence in the Third World, and assuming that all international problems were susceptible to American solution, Kennedy formulated policies that accelerated the arms race, overcommitted the United States in the Third World, alienated the United States' allies and neutrals, and weakened the U.S. economy. To those who see Kennedy as the "young, fallen hero who never had a chance," Paterson responds: "actually, he had his chance and he failed."[8] A different but still flawed Kennedy—one that is less arrogant and more cautious, less belligerent and more conciliatory—emerges in Michael R. Beschloss's *The Crisis Years: Kennedy and Khrushchev 1960–1963*. From the beginning of his presidency, Kennedy sought a reduction in tensions with the Soviet Union, although he mismanaged that relationship in ways that precluded any movement in that direction until the resolution of the Cuban Missile Crisis. Yet Beschloss, like Paterson, criticizes Kennedy's judgment and tactics, finding that he "rarely showed the magnanimity that should have been expected of a great power," exaggerated the communist threat, and needlessly provoked the Soviet Union.[9] Despite differences in the tones of their studies, both Paterson and Beschloss question whether Kennedy understood the nature of the threat facing the United States.

Kennedy still has his defenders, though. In his account of the Kennedy presidency, Herbert S. Parmet essentially reaffirms the Schlesinger-Sorensen perspective. Although acknowledging Kennedy's shortcomings, Parmet sees Kennedy as reacting imaginatively to international changes and modifying his Cold War policy in the interest of promoting international peace. Moreover, through the Peace Corps and Alliance for Progress, Kennedy embodied "the idealism much of the world preferred to associate with America." By the time of his death, Kennedy had become identified "with the universal aspirations that are elusive to so many" and had brought to the presidency "a new style and tone . . . that evoked national pride and hope."[10]

Vietnam is vital to any assessment of Kennedy because, during the thousand days of his administration, the United States' commitment to the Saigon government deepened. Faced with evidence that the U.S. effort to buttress the South Vietnamese government was failing, the Kennedy administration increased economic and military assistance. Most visibly, the number of military advisers grew from approximately 700 to 16,000. This enhanced investment meant that the United States had far greater political and military influence. First, it enabled Washington to pressure Saigon to undertake new initiatives, notably the Strategic Hamlet Program, to rally the support of the peasantry. Second, it brought some military advisers into combat roles (the United States began officially tabulating its casualties in Vietnam in 1961) and into the position of supporting South Vietnamese covert raids against North Vietnam. Finally, it increased the American presence in ways that permitted manipulation of South Vietnamese politics, ultimately resulting in the overthrow of the government of Ngo Dinh Diem. By November 1963, Vietnam constituted a far greater commitment of U.S. resources and prestige than had been the case in January 1961.

That deepening U.S. involvement, with its ominous overtones, reflected several related developments: Kennedy's approach to the world in general and Vietnam in particular, the ideas of the "best and the brightest" who worked with Kennedy, the ways that U.S. interests in Vietnam were defined, and, above all, the political and military changes in Vietnam itself. Although the direction of U.S. policy was clear, it was not without considerable debate within the administration. Through it all, Kennedy remained somewhat above the fray, opting for what seemed to be the minimum level of involvement to sustain the American-South Vietnamese enterprise but also avoiding any detailed analysis of the situation.

Perhaps that lack of inquiry resulted from Kennedy's confidence that he understood the Vietnam problem. On several occasions during the previous decade, he had addressed U.S. policy in Indochina. His interest in the region, however, had not led Kennedy to any special insights; indeed, his thinking was representative of the nation's foreign policy elite in that he had defined U.S. interests in Southeast Asia within a Cold War context, had criticized French colonial and military policy during their struggle against the Vietminh, and had identified U.S. interests with the emergence of an anticommunist Vietnamese nationalism.

As a thirty-four-year-old congressman, Kennedy had visited the Middle East and Southeast Asia in 1951 and had embraced the thinking of American officials of that time who saw the problem in Indochina in terms of an outdated French colonialism. In Saigon, Kennedy renewed his acquaintance with Edmund Gullion, a foreign service officer who was the American counselor in Saigon. They had met four years earlier when Secretary of State Dean Acheson, responding to Kennedy's request for advice on Asian policy, had recommended Gullion. Gullion influenced Kennedy's thinking on the nature of the situation in Indochina. Upon his return to Washington, Kennedy criticized French reliance on a military solution. Like Gullion and other American observers, Kennedy was convinced that a noncommunist nationalist movement would emerge if the French would grant genuine independence.

As a senator in 1953, Kennedy had urged the Eisenhower administration to force French concessions to the Vietnamese that would result in a "reliable and crusading native army." In a Senate speech during the Dienbienphu crisis, Kennedy had warned against providing military support for the French because their policies were undermining the U.S. objective of fostering nationalism. After the French withdrawal, Kennedy had seen Diem's government as the embodiment of the genuine aspirations of the Vietnamese. In 1956 he had spoken of Vietnam as representing "the cornerstone of the Free World in Southeast Asia, the keystone in the arch, the finger in the dike, and should the red tide of Communism pour into it . . . much of Asia would be threatened."[11]

As president, Kennedy faced a series of difficult policy choices resulting from the mounting problems of the South Vietnamese government, and these decisions eventually forced him to confront Diem's shortcomings. Kennedy never altered his fundamental thinking, however, about the problems facing the United States in Vietnam. That consistency was reinforced by the way in which problems were presented to him. Assuming that U.S. interests necessitated support of the South Vietnamese government, policymakers submitted choices in terms of determining the appropriate levels of increased U.S. support. Only rarely did officials question the basic U.S.-South Vietnamese connection, and, when they did, they had to move cautiously to avoid losing influence. Bureaucracies tend to force conformity, which at first glance seems incongruent in an administration that prided itself on its use of expertise and its intellectual atmosphere. Yet an arrogance born of the certainty that they understood U.S. interests and capabilities characterized the intellectuals in command of the White House.

Four words—commitment, credibility, consequences, and counterinsurgency—are central to the assumptions about Vietnam that run throughout the documents of the Kennedy administration. Together, they justified the conclusion that U.S. national security was tied to South Vietnam's survival. The Kennedy administration inherited a commitment to South Vietnam that had to be upheld partly because it was already in place. Schlesinger observed that "whether we were right in 1954 to undertake this commitment will long be a matter of interest to historians, but it had ceased by 1961 to be of interest to policy-makers."[12] Chester Cooper, a diplomat with wide experience in Southeast Asia, wrote that "Kennedy's inheritance [was] an American commitment in Vietnam which, while less specific in form and smaller in substance than it later became, was nonetheless concrete and substantial enough that American prestige in Asia—and beyond—was intimately tied to the declining fortunes of Ngo Dinh Diem."[13]

As Cooper's observation implies, commitment begot credibility; a failure to stand by Saigon would risk American stature everywhere. Following his 1961 visit to Southeast Asia, Vice-President Lyndon Johnson told Kennedy that the only alternative to standing by our allies was to "throw in the towel . . . and pull our defenses back to San Francisco." If that occurred, "we would say to the world . . . that we don't live up to treaties and don't stand by our friends."[14] Historian John Gaddis, in his analysis of Kennedy's national security strategy, has maintained that credibility was the overriding consideration: "What the Kennedy and Johnson administrations came to fear most, one gathers, was not communism, which was too fragmented, or the Soviet Union, which was too committed to détente, or even China, which was too impotent, but rather the threat of embarrassment, of humiliation, of appearing to be weak. . . . [C]ommitments, once made, could not be abandoned without appearing to call into question more vital obligations elsewhere."[15]

Like its predecessor, the Kennedy administration deemed Vietnam to be the key to the future of Southeast Asia. The consequences of defeat or withdrawal were monumental: communist ascendancy throughout the region. This prospect was linked to the concern about credibility, for the feared "loss" of the region was generally perceived as resulting from the global erosion of confidence in U.S. resolve and the attendant sense that communism was the wave of the future.

This concern with consequences took on added significance as 1961 brought a new factor to policy calculations: Vietnam as a vital test of the United States' capacity to resist communist-led wars of national liberation. A speech by Khrushchev on January 6, 1961, seemingly challenged the new administration. Khrushchev's call for all communists to support "liberation wars and popular uprisings" alarmed the Kennedy foreign policy team. Describing conflicts such as those in Algeria and Vietnam as "just and inevitable," Khrushchev contended that communist solidarity would intimidate the "imperialists." To Kennedy and his advisers, whom he had instructed to read the speech, this meant that the United States had to be prepared to confront communist insurgency throughout the Third World. In Vietnam, the struggle had been under way for several years, and the step-up of Vietcong activity in 1960 seemed to confirm Khrushchev's threat of communist initiatives.[16]

In an April 1961 speech, Kennedy warned that "we are opposed around the world by a monolithic and ruthless conspiracy that relies primarily on covert means for expanding its sphere of influence." Communist strategy had shifted to insurrection and subversion, and, if successful in places like Vietnam, "the gates will be opened wide."[17] A National Intelligence Estimate (NIE) of August 1961 addressed specifically how the "gates" would be opened. Thailand, Cambodia, Burma, Indonesia, and the Philippines saw Indochina as a "gauge of U.S. willingness to help an anti-Communist Asian government stand against a Communist 'national liberation' campaign." According to the NIE authors, these nations "will almost certainly look upon the struggle for Vietnam as a critical test of such U.S. willingness and ability. All of them, including the neutrals, would probably suffer demoralization and loss of confidence in their prospects for maintaining their independence if the Communists were to gain control of South Vietnam. This loss of confidence might even extend to India."[18] This commitment to counterinsurgency quickly became an important part of national security thinking. Numerous popular and scholarly works stressed the necessity of learning how to fight guerrilla wars, and books such as Lieutenant Colonel T. N. Greene's *The Guerrilla and How to Fight Him* conveyed the urgency of the moment. On the Senate floor, the prominent liberal Hubert Humphrey (D-Minn.) spoke for many when he stated that the United States had to act quickly if it was to counter wars of national liberation.[19]

Throughout Kennedy's first months in office, American officials pressed the need to dramatize the U.S. commitment to Diem. Early advice came from Brigadier General Edward Lansdale, an almost legendary figure. Lansdale, already known for his role in helping the Philippine government resist communist insurgency, had gone to Vietnam in 1954 where, as head of a special CIA mission, he had worked tirelessly to assure the survival of Diem's government. Lansdale was characteristically blunt: "We have to show him by deeds, not words alone, that we are his friend. This will make our influence effective again."[20] A task group headed by Deputy Secretary of Defense Roswell Gilpatrick similarly maintained that "South Vietnam is nearing the decisive phase in its battle for survival." Describing the situation as "critical but not hopeless," the task force recommended that the United States demonstrate "to our friends, the Vietnamese and our foes, the Viet Cong, that come what may, the United States intends to win this battle."[21] In May, Vice-President Johnson undertook a fact-finding mission to Southeast Asia that included the folksy, homespun Texan beguiling people on the streets of Saigon. He quickly identified with the Diem government, describing its president as the "Churchill of Asia." He wrote to Kennedy: "The country can be saved—if we move quickly and wisely. We must decide to support Diem—or let Vietnam fall. . . . The most important thing is imaginative, creative American management of our military aid team."[22]

The deteriorating situation in Vietnam by the fall of 1961 confirmed the alarmist tone of these early reports. American analysts calculated that increased infiltration from North Vietnam meant that the number of armed, full-time Vietcong had grown from 4,000 to 16,000 within the previous year. As the insurgency intensified, American and South Vietnamese officials feared major Vietcong efforts to "liberate" wide areas. A beleaguered Saigon government pressed Washington for additional economic assistance, and the Joint Chiefs of Staff considered the deployment of U.S. forces.[23]

Kennedy had been preoccupied with more urgent issues—recovering from the disastrous Bay of Pigs operation against Cuba and his ill-fated meeting in Vienna with an obtuse Khrushchev, and then responding to Khrushchev's subsequent igniting of a Berlin crisis reprise. Forced to deal with the deteriorating situation in Vietnam, Kennedy dispatched two of his most trusted advisers—Taylor and Rostow—on a special mission. Finding a "deep and pervasive crisis of confidence and a serious loss in national morale," they urged a "limited partnership" to bolster the Diem government and to enable the Army of the Republic of Vietnam (ARVN) to take the military initiative. Taylor and Rostow recommended a significant increase in the level of U.S. support. They urged dispatching advisers who would engage in a wide range of training and consultative activities and providing the ARVN with equipment, including helicopters, that would enhance its mobility and effectiveness.

Taylor and Rostow also proposed sending a small U.S. combat unit: an 8,000–man "logistic task force" for the stated purpose of repairing massive damage caused by flooding in the Mekong Delta. Its real purpose, however, was to demonstrate U.S. resolve and to facilitate a direct military role should that be necessary. Taylor assured Kennedy that the risks of war with North Vietnam were "present but . . . not impressive." Indeed, he argued that the risks to Hanoi were so great that they should be exploited by the United States: "North Vietnam is extremely vulnerable to conventional bombing, a weakness which should be exploited diplomatically in convincing Hanoi to lay off South Viet Nam."[24]

The Taylor-Rostow recommendations forced the first high-level debate over Vietnam policy in the Kennedy White House. Rusk and McNamara followed with a ringing message to Kennedy, warning that defeat in Vietnam meant that the rest of Southeast Asia "*would move to a complete accommodation with Communism, if not formal incorporation, within the Communist bloc.*" They urged that "the United States should commit itself to the clear objective of preventing the fall of South Viet-Nam to Communism."[25] They questioned only the timing, but not the strategy, of sending U.S. forces. That step could disrupt current negotiations to end the civil war in Laos, but once that issue was settled, the presence of an American unit could help stabilize the situation in both Laos and Vietnam.[26]

On the other side, Under Secretary of State Chester Bowles and the highly respected diplomat W. Averell Harriman, whom Kennedy had designated to head the U.S. negotiating team on Laos, warned about the consequences of commitment to a narrowly based and dictatorial South Vietnamese government. Bowles saw the United States "headed full blast up a dead end street." Rather than increasing the level of U.S. support, he thought that Kennedy should seek a negotiated settlement. Assuming that a settlement could be reached in Laos, it could serve as the basis for an expanded conference to address the Vietnamese situation. Even one member of the Taylor-Rostow mission, Sterling Cottrell, who chaired the State Department's Vietnam task force, raised questions about the increased level of U.S. support. In an appendix to the report, he wrote that "since it is an open question whether [South Vietnam] can succeed even with U.S. assistance, it would be a mistake for the United States to commit itself irrevocably to the defeat of the communists in South Vietnam."[27] George Ball, under secretary of state for economic affairs, made that point directly to Kennedy, warning that an unequivocal commitment to Diem, as urged by McNamara and Rusk, would inevitably lead to more U.S. troops in Vietnam. An annoyed Kennedy dismissed such projections as "crazy." Ball, who had frequent conversations with Kennedy but not a close relationship with him, henceforth kept his reservations about the escalating U.S. involvement to himself.[28]

Kennedy opted for a middle course. He rejected the Taylor-Rostow call for a task force and the Harriman-Bowles recommendation for a negotiated settlement. Curiously, the situation in Laos influenced the repudiation of both extreme alternatives. Kennedy, like McNamara and Rusk, feared that the introduction of a task force in Vietnam would undermine the delicate negotiations in Laos. He also believed, however, that the very pursuit of a negotiated settlement in Laos rendered a similar approach in Vietnam impolitic, since any compromise with communists risked criticism at home and the appearance of weakness. Kennedy was obsessed with demonstrating U.S. resolve to his adversary in the Kremlin. Rejecting the forebodings of

Harriman and Bowles, Kennedy accepted Rostow's view that "the gut issue" was not the character of Diem's government but whether the United States would help resist North Vietnam's "aggression." Credibility was at stake, and the response of the United States would be "examined on both sides of the Iron Curtain . . . as a measure of the administration's intentions and determination."[29] Kennedy's rejection of the task force also reflected his skepticism about whether it would have a significant effect on South Vietnamese morale and his foreboding that it would lead to demands for more regular forces.

Describing Kennedy's decision as a middle course risks obscuring the fact that by embracing the greater part of the Taylor-Rostow recommendations, he significantly increased the U.S. presence and influence. The United States ignored the Geneva Accords limitation on foreign advisers to which it had adhered since 1955. As Americans went to Vietnam by the hundreds and undertook far-reaching military obligations and as equipment and supplies flowed to Saigon, a vitally important step toward "Americanization" of the conflict was taken.

The victory of those seeking a greater U.S. role discouraged debate within the Kennedy administration. Those who questioned the Taylor-Rostow recommendations either fell in line or were subsequently ignored. Ball, who became a persistent critic of Vietnam policy during the Johnson administration, never detailed his criticisms of Kennedy's course for the president's benefit. His reservations appended to the Taylor-Rostow report notwithstanding, Cottrell still endorsed its recommendations. Bowles's questioning of the administration's strident anticommunism led to his removal as under secretary of state for political affairs (and Ball's elevation to that post) and appointment as ambassador-at-large. Exiled from the inner circle, the loquacious Bowles continued his warnings about becoming ensnarled in Vietnam and advocated negotiations toward the neutralization of Southeast Asia. Similar advice came from the ambassador to India, John Kenneth Galbraith, the eminent economist and Kennedy confidant. The White House and State Department ignored their entreaties. Harriman, as he diligently pursued positions of influence in the Kennedy administration, muted his concerns about the Vietnam commitment.[30]

The outcome of the policy debate of late 1961 also signaled a shift toward treating Vietnam as a military problem. The hawkish elements of the Kennedy administration—Taylor, Rostow, Bundy, and McNamara—came closer to their objectives than the naysayers—Ball, Harriman, Bowles, and Cottrell. Significantly, the latter were all part of the State Department, whose head tended to defer to the aggressive McNamara, who confidently saw Vietnam as a manageable problem. This trend was reflected in the field; under terms of an understanding reached by Rusk and McNamara, the commander of U.S. military operations dealt directly with the Diem government on military matters and operated independently of the U.S. ambassador. Sharp divisions eventually surfaced between the State Department and Defense Department, but by that time the militarization of U.S. policy made it very difficult for the State Department to regain influence. "Perhaps the single most important detail in understanding what happened in the Kennedy administration's approach to Vietnam," Anthony Short wrote in *The Origins of the Vietnam War*, "is that its Secretary of State never went to Vietnam. . . . Rusk's notable absence from Vietnam underlines why so many people felt that the State Department generally and he personally had abdicated responsibility and had turned it over to McNamara, to the Department of Defense and to the military in general."[31]

In the short run, the increased U.S. role appeared to be working. The Strategic Hamlet Program, modeled on a successful effort to resist communist insurgency in Malaya, was intended to isolate the rural population from the Vietcong and to introduce social and economic reforms that would win the "hearts and minds" of the peasantry. The South Vietnamese army's capabilities and performance improved as a result of the vastly increased number of U.S. military advisers (a total of over 9,000 by the end of 1962) and the influx of U.S. aircraft, armored personnel carriers, and other equipment. Americans not only supplied and trained the ARVN, but they also directly supported and participated in military operations against the Vietcong. In many ways, the South Vietnamese government seemed to gain strength: The Vietcong reduced its insurgency, and other opponents of Diem were muted. At a press conference in March 1962, Kennedy cautiously described the situation as "very much up and down . . . [making] it impossible to draw any long-range conclusions." By the end of 1962, he was more optimistic: "So we don't see the end of the tunnel, but I must say I don't think it is darker than it was a year ago and in some ways lighter."[32]

Yet as so often happened during the years of U.S. involvement in Vietnam, evidence of progress was superficial. It had been assumed that the introduction of more Americans would result in effective reporting, but in fact the opposite occurred. The South Vietnamese, anxious to please their benefactor and aware of the American penchant for statistics, produced data that conformed to Washington's objectives. For example, the Diem government drastically inflated the number of operational strategic hamlets. Moreover, the program, intended to gain the support of the peasantry, had the opposite effect. It alienated the peasantry in various ways. Likewise, Saigon's reports of the ARVN's military initiatives ignored the fact that about one-third of those offensives were into areas where the Vietcong were not active. Like the Saigon government, the U.S. military command had a vested interest in documenting progress. Advisers who questioned the effectiveness of operations found their reports discarded or ignored by their superiors.[33]

By late 1962, the shortcomings of the past year's investment and initiatives were becoming evident. After months of relative inactivity, the Vietcong renewed widespread guerrilla operations; there was no indication that the Strategic Hamlet Program had altered the alienation of the peasantry from the Diem government. Moreover, the repression carried out under the authoritarian Diem and Nhu became widely known in the United States, principally through the reporting of American correspondents in Saigon. David Halberstam of the *New York Times*, Neil Sheehan of United Press International, and Malcolm Browne of Associated Press criticized the corruption and repressiveness of the Diem government and the ineffectiveness of the entire counterinsurgency effort.[34]

Characteristically, Kennedy sought the advice of special emissaries. In December, the respected Senator Mike Mansfield (D-Mont.), whose advice and friendship Kennedy valued, visited Vietnam at the president's request. The blunt Mansfield publicly stated that he found little evidence of progress, and, in a private message to Kennedy, the senator warned that the United States was being drawn into a large and futile war. This assessment prompted Kennedy to send Hilsman and Michael Forrestal, a National Security Council staff member, on a fact-finding mission. Differing substantially from Mansfield's assessment, their report, although "not rosily optimistic," still found that the United States was "probably winning." A basically sound strategy confronted a number of operational problems that were remediable. Yet the realization of U.S. objectives, Hilsman and Forrestal foresaw, would take "longer . . . [and] cost more in terms of both lives and money than we had anticipated."[35]

Kennedy's response to the worsening situation in late 1962 and early 1963 is revealing, for although he sought the recommendations of special emissaries, he resisted unwelcome advice. Rather than confronting the implications of Mansfield's stark warning, Kennedy sought more information from two officials who had vested interests in the existing policy. Hilsman was one of the principal architects of the counterinsurgency strategy, and Forrestal was a strong proponent of it. Their advice essentially and predictably called for continuing the existing policy.

Yet that approach came under strong criticism as the weaknesses of the Diem government became glaringly evident. Opposition surfaced in the cities, where Diem had his strongest political base, and the leadership came not from communists but from the large Buddhist community, which resented the dominance by the Catholic minority within Diem's inner circle. The arrogance of the Ngo family and, in particular, Ngo Dinh Nhu's insensitivity to the practices and beliefs of the Buddhist majority especially inflamed the situation. The growing American presence and influence added to the Buddhists' alienation from the Saigon government. Historically, Buddhist monks had used their moral power to effect political changes in times of crisis. By 1963, Buddhist leaders had concluded that the nation's well-being demanded the overthrow of Diem, an end to U.S. influence, and a neutral South Vietnam, leading eventually to reunification with the North under a coalition government.

The "Buddhist crisis" began in Hue on May 8—the celebration of the birth of the Buddha—when provincial police enforced a hitherto ignored law prohibiting the display of religious flags. In the face of protests, the police fired into the crowd, killing nine people. A subsequent protest demonstration demanded an end to religious persecution. Then on June 11, the protest took on another traditional form when at a busy intersection in Saigon, Thich Quang Duc, an elderly monk, sat down and crossed his legs in the middle of a circle of monks and nuns. One of them poured gasoline over his body, and another ignited him. The victim left a plea to the Diem government to show "charity and compassion" to all religions. The self-immolation received wide attention in the international media, and the photograph of the monk in flames brought increased attention to the problems confronting the United States in a country that had previously been of remote concern to most Americans.

As more of the Vietnamese urban middle class, including large numbers of students, rallied to support the Buddhist cause, the Diem government forced a showdown. In the face of mounting protests and more acts of self-immolation, the Diem government sent its U.S.-trained and -equipped special forces to attack Buddhist pagodas in Saigon, Hue, and other cities. They ransacked the pagodas and arrested some 1,400 monks. Unpopular as ever in the countryside and more and more alienated from the urban population, the Saigon government was unraveling.[36]

After the raid on the pagodas, a group of South Vietnamese generals established secret contacts with Americans. They warned that a desperate Diem government would not relent in its suppression and was making contacts with North Vietnam. U.S. officials were alarmed by the prospects of a deal between Saigon and Hanoi and saw the generals' overture as an opportunity for alternative leadership. In Washington, three key State Department officials—Hilsman, Forrestal, and Harriman—took the initiative. On August 24, they cabled instructions to Ambassador Henry Cabot Lodge to warn Diem that, unless he removed Nhu, the United States would find it difficult to sustain Diem's position. Lodge was also given authority to inform the dissident generals that the United States would not support Diem unless he modified his policies; if there was a breakdown of authority, the United States would provide backing for the generals. The essence of the instructions to Lodge was clear: The United States was prepared to abandon Diem and to support a government established by the group of South Vietnamese generals. Quickly implementing the cable, Lodge carried the warning to Diem. A CIA agent secretly conveyed assurances to the generals that the United States would not become involved in a coup but would support the generals if they succeeded in overthrowing Diem.

Kennedy's role in this key step was muted, but clear. Vacationing at the time the State Department prepared the cable, he was contacted and approved its contents. Two days later, a White House meeting revealed deep disagreement within the administration, as McNamara and Taylor questioned the new political commitments undertaken in the cable to Lodge. Although the criticism unnerved Kennedy, he kept the administration on the course set in the August 24 message. In fact, he gave Lodge considerable latitude in its implementation, including authorization to announce a reduction in U.S. aid to Diem, the signal that the generals had requested as an indication of U.S. support for their cause. Lodge aptly described U.S. policy as being "launched on a course from which there is no respectable turning back." Kennedy, however, reserved the prerogative to change course. "I know from experience," he told Lodge, "that failure is more destructive than an appearance of indecision. . . . If our national interest should require a change of mind, we must not be afraid of it."[37]

To Kennedy's chagrin, the course set in late August did not bring immediate change. Diem remained steadfast; he retained Nhu and made no conciliatory gestures toward the Buddhists. The generals, however, did not act and backed away from a coup. The situation seemed to defy comprehension. In September, the White House dispatched another special mission, and its members reached completely opposite conclusions. The Defense Department member minimized the opposition to Diem and urged unswerving support of his government, but the State Department representative reported political chaos and the likelihood of religious warfare and Vietcong victory unless, at a minimum, Diem removed Nhu. After listening to these disparate projections, an incredulous Kennedy asked: "You two did visit the same country, didn't you?"[38]

Kennedy's course reflected the consensus of congressional and media thinking on Vietnam. The reporting of Halberstam, Sheehan, Browne, and others blamed the United States' problems principally on Diem. In their reports, the war against the Vietcong was going badly because of Diem's repression of his opponents, his lack of popular support, and the ineffectiveness of his army. As newspaper and television coverage of South Vietnam's turmoil increased, it focused on the dramatic events—most notably the self-immolations of Thich Quang Duc and other monks and the raids on the pagodas—which worsened the already negative image of Diem.[39] This reporting completely reversed the exaggerated praise for Diem of a few years earlier. "A handful of Americans had created a myth about the 'miracle' Diem had wrought in South Vietnam," Ellen Hammer wrote. "They had sold and oversold him to the American government and press, giving rise to inflated and unreal expectations in the United States for which Diem (and Vietnam) was now going to pay dearly."[40] In the midst of the debate on Vietnam, only a few voices questioned the basic U.S. commitment there. In the Senate, George McGovern (D-S.Dak.) stated in late September: "The U.S. position has deteriorated so drastically that it is in our national interest to withdraw from that country our forces and our aid."[41] Yet such views were a distinct minority, for the preponderance of opinion in the press and Congress never questioned whether U.S. interests necessitated involvement in Vietnam.

By the time of McGovern's speech, Kennedy was sending still another special mission to Saigon, this one headed by Taylor and McNamara. Given the Defense Department's well-established inclination to view Vietnam as a military problem, their recommendations for working with Diem were predictable. Finding little evidence of a prospective coup and recognizing Diem's loyalty to his brother, they essentially saw no choice but to continue to tolerate Diem. Through "selective pressures," however, the United States could push Diem to be more conciliatory toward his opponents. Noting the relative inactivity of the Vietcong in the fall of 1963 (which was actually a ploy to encourage negotiations between the North and South), the report defended the effectiveness of the counterinsurgency program. "Tactics and techniques employed by the Vietnamese under U.S. monitoring are sound," it claimed, "and give promise of ultimate victory."[42] Seeking to exploit the evident success of that effort, McNamara and Taylor recommended the reduction of the U.S. advisory group by 1,000 and the withholding of certain levels of assistance "to impress upon Diem our disapproval of his political program . . . [and] to see what steps [he] is taking to reduce repressive practices and to improve the effectiveness of the military effort."[43]

Kennedy endorsed the McNamara-Taylor recommendations. A subsequent White House statement attracted attention with its projection that the principal U.S. military effort would be completed within two years, but little notice was given to the more pessimistic next paragraph: "The political situation . . . remains deeply serious. The United States has made clear its continuing opposition to any repressive actions in South Viet-Nam. While such actions have not yet significantly affected the military effort, they could do so in the future."[44]

Implementation of the McNamara-Taylor recommendations failed to provide coherence to U.S. policy, and the effect was the opposite of what had been intended. Rather than stabilizing Diem's position through reform, the pressures contributed to his demise. Reductions in support for the ARVN and the suspension of selected shipments under the commodity import program, which subsidized the Diem regime's budget, were seen by dissident generals as evidence of U.S. backing for a coup. The announcement of these measures shortly after the generals renewed their contact with U.S. officials only added to the U.S. role in the intrigue. As he had in August, Lodge again received instructions that had "been discussed with President." The ambassador was to indicate that although the United States would not openly support a coup, it would "not thwart a change of government or deny economic and military assistance to a new regime if it appeared capable of increasing effectiveness of military effort, ensuring popular support to win [the] war and improving working relations with U.S."[45]

Kennedy's hand quietly guided the tactics that would lead to a showdown between Diem and the generals. His administration remained divided, with the Defense Department and CIA warning that the State Department's determination to remove Diem would lead to an unpredictable and uncontrollable situation in South Vietnam. Kennedy's actions from August 25 onward indicated that he was resigned to the necessity of Diem's removal. In a sense, it was decision by indecision. He allowed the cuts in aid, knowing that such actions would encourage the plotters, and he gave wide latitude to Lodge, whose animosity toward Diem was well known.

Yet Kennedy doubted the wisdom of the course about to be undertaken. In meetings with key advisers in late October, he was searching for information on the relative strength of the pro-Diem and anti-Diem military forces and on the effects of a coup on the South Vietnamese political structure and on the anti-Vietcong campaign. Events, however, had overtaken Kennedy. The complicity of the Saigon embassy and CIA operatives in planning for the coup meant that failure to support it would alienate the dissident generals, and a failed coup would cause Diem to turn against the United States. Kennedy wanted Lodge to return to Washington for consultations, but the timing of the coup could not be controlled by the White House. The generals seized power on November 2.[46]

November 1963 was as momentous as that same month had been three years earlier. The course of events ran to its predictable outcome, with the coup ending in the assassination of Diem and Nhu. Although U.S. officials abhorred the murders, they anticipated that the new government would bring stability. Kennedy never lived to see the consequences of Diem's downfall: the continuing downward spiral of the Saigon regime characterized by frequent political changes and a virtual "revolving door" of military and civilian leaders.

Kennedy's thinking about Vietnam never went notably beyond fulfilling a commitment while avoiding military intervention. He seemed determined to draw a distinction between the U.S. supportive role and the military mission of the South Vietnamese. He never had to face the difficult choice between accepting the loss of Vietnam and increasing U.S. military intervention. In a television interview with Walter Cronkite in September 1963, Kennedy stated that "in the final analysis, it is the people and the Government itself who have to win or lose this struggle. All we can do is help, and we are making it very clear." Yet Kennedy went on to rule out withdrawal as a "great mistake . . . [for] this is a very important struggle even though it is very far away."[47] A week later in another television interview, Kennedy emphatically endorsed the domino theory: "I believe it. I believe it. . . . China is so large . . . [Vietnam's fall] would also give the impression that the wave of the future in Southeast Asia was China and the Communists. So I believe it." Kennedy again went on to reject any suggestion of withdrawal because that "only makes it easy for the Communists. I think we should stay. We should use our influence in as effective a way as we can, but we should not withdraw."[48] What Kennedy never resolved—because his administration was not forced to do so—was the U.S. response in the eventuality that the South Vietnamese could not win militarily on their own.

Reflecting on Kennedy's handling of the evolving Vietnam situation, one finds little of the skillful diplomacy that brings praise from such writers as Sorensen, Schlesinger, and Parmet. Indeed, there is much to support Paterson's image of the determined Cold Warrior leading the country toward disaster. And there is also evidence that reinforces Beschloss's portrait of a leader at once determined, but also cautious and, in some ways, lacking a firm sense of direction. Yet the Kennedy apologists are probably correct in their emphasis on his reluctance to send U.S. forces to Vietnam. Throughout the debates on Vietnam policy, Kennedy remained skeptical; he accurately foresaw that escalation would beget escalation, that bombing once begun would likewise expand, and that military victory would prove elusive.

Much has been written about how Kennedy would have dealt with Vietnam had he lived beyond November 1963. After the Americanization of the war, some of Kennedy's staffers and others contended that he had planned to get out of Vietnam after the 1964 election and that he would never have led the country to war. The military historian Bernard Brodie has argued that Kennedy's temperament, intelligence, and wariness of expert advice all distinguished him from his successor and would have led to a different approach to the crises of 1964–1965. In *Kennedy in Vietnam*, William J. Rust argues that Kennedy would have opted for the role of the "good doctor" who would have provided all feasible help before withdrawing from an impossible situation. Far more controversial is John M. Newman's *JFK and Vietnam: Deception, Intrigue and the Struggle for Power*, which is a scholarly companion to Oliver Stone's motion picture *JFK*. Newman charges that the Joint Chiefs of Staff and senior military officers sought intervention in Vietnam and sabotaged Kennedy's plans for withdrawal. The assassination enabled them to fulfill their plans because Lyndon Johnson, upon succeeding to the presidency, immediately opted for a more belligerent course, although military intervention had to be delayed until after the 1964 election. Other scholars, notably Lawrence J. Bassett and Stephen E. Pelz, see the firmness of Kennedy's commitment and the extent to which he sank the United States more deeply into the Indochina quagmire as evidence that Kennedy was as determined as his successor to hold South Vietnam.[49]

There was a certain logic in what Kennedy pursued. Given the inherited commitment, the concern with credibility, the consequences of defeat, and the heightened sense of the urgency of combating wars of national liberation, it may have been expecting too much for Kennedy to call for a more careful analysis of the assumptions underlying U.S. policy. It seems that as the intractability of the problems of Vietnam became more evident, Kennedy was thinking on two levels: the commitment to South Vietnam was still integral to U.S. national security, but the price of upholding it seemed less controllable. That he said contradictory things about Vietnam in 1963 should not be surprising. Yet the historical and political reasons for the Diem government's weakness and the Hanoi government's and the southern insurgency's resilience ought to have been examined, rather than accepted as developments that the United States had to remedy. Perhaps Kennedy's greatest fault was the tendency—not unique to his administration by any means—to approach Vietnam as a series of problems, without fully considering the reasons for the commitment to South Vietnam or the ramifications of the steps being taken. American officials, Kennedy included, accepted the proposition that there was a noncommunist nationalist movement of sufficient strength to sustain an independent South Vietnam. For nearly a decade, Diem had seemed to represent that alternative, but when Diem failed, Americans accepted, without careful analysis, that alternative leadership would somehow succeed in building a viable noncommunist government with broad popular support and the capacity to take the initiative from the Vietcong. To Kennedy and his fellow New Frontiersmen, it was a doctrine of faith that the problems of Vietnam lent themselves to an American solution.

Notes

I would like to acknowledge the research assistance of Bruce Olav Solheim.

1. Ronald H. Spector, *Advice and Support: The Early Years of the U.S. Army in Vietnam, 1941–1960* (New York: Free Press, 1985), 369–71; George McT. Kahin, *Intervention: How America Became Involved in Vietnam* (New York: Knopf, 1986), 122–26.

2. David Halberstam, *The Best and the Brightest* (New York: Random House, 1972), 153.

3. Arthur M. Schlesinger, Jr., *A Thousand Days: John F. Kennedy in the White House* (Boston: Houghton Mifflin, 1965), 217.

4. Walt W. Rostow, "The Third Round," *Foreign Affairs* 42 (October 1963): 5–6.

5. Maxwell D. Taylor, *The Uncertain Trumpet* (New York: Harper, 1960); Roger Hilsman, *To Move a Nation: The Politics of Foreign Policy in the Administration of John F. Kennedy* (Garden City, N.Y.: Doubleday, 1967); Warren I. Cohen, *Dean Rusk*, vol. 19 in Samuel Flagg Bemis and Robert Ferrell, eds., *The American Secretaries of State and Their Diplomacy*, n.s. (Totowa, N.J.: Cooper Square, 1980).

6. Schlesinger, *A Thousand Days*, 1030–31.

7. Theodore Sorensen, *Kennedy* (New York: Harper & Row, 1965), 758.

8. Thomas G. Paterson, "Kennedy's Quest for Victory and the Global Crisis," in Thomas G. Paterson, ed., *Kennedy's Quest for Victory: American Foreign Policy, 1961–1963* (New York: Oxford University Press, 1989), 3–23; see also Thomas G. Paterson, *Meeting the Communist Threat from Truman to Reagan* (New York: Oxford University Press, 1988), 191–210.

9. Michael R. Beschloss, *The Crisis Years: Kennedy and Khrushchev, 1960–1963* (New York: HarperCollins, 1991), 702.

10. Herbert S. Parmet, *JFK: The Presidency of John F. Kennedy* (New York: Dial, 1983), 357–58.

11. John F. Kennedy, "America's Stake in Vietnam," *Vital Speeches* 22 (August 1956): 617–19. See also Lawrence J. Bassett and Stephen E. Pelz, "The Failed Search for Victory: Vietnam and the Politics of War," in Paterson, *Kennedy's Quest for Victory*, 112–29; George C. Herring, *America's Longest War: The United States and Vietnam*, 2d ed. (New York: Knopf, 1986), 36–37; and Schlesinger, *A Thousand Days*, 320–23.

12. Schlesinger, *A Thousand Days*, 537–38.

13. Chester L. Cooper, *The Lost Crusade: America in Vietnam* (Greenwich, Conn.: Fawcett, 1970), 208.

14. Johnson to Kennedy, May 23, 1961, United States Department of Defense, *The Pentagon Papers: The Defense Department History of United States Decision Making on Vietnam*, Senator Gravel edition (Boston: Beacon Press, 1971), 2:58–59.

15. John L. Gaddis, *Strategies of Containment: A Critical Appraisal of Postwar American National Security Policy* (New York: Oxford University Press, 1982), 212.

16. Anthony Short, *The Origins of the Vietnam War* (London: Longman, 1989), 234–35.

17. Speech to American Newspapers Publishers Association, April 27, 1961, *Public Papers of the Presidents of the United States: John F. Kennedy, 1961* (Washington, D.C.: GPO, 1962), 336.

18. Excerpts from NIE, August 15, 1961, *Pentagon Papers*, 2:72.

19. Leslie Gelb with Richard K. Betts, *The Irony of Vietnam: The System Worked* (Washington, D.C.: Brookings Institution, 1979), 211.

20. Excerpts from Lansdale Report, January 1961, cited in *Pentagon Papers*, 2:26.

21. Report of Task Force, April 27, 1961, in House Committee on Armed Services, *United States-Vietnam Relations, 1945–1967: Study Prepared by the Department of Defense* (Washington, D.C.: GPO, 1971), 2:25, 27.

22. Johnson to Kennedy, May 23, 1961, *Pentagon Papers*, 2:59.

23. Short, *Origins of the Vietnam War*, 244–46.

24. Excerpts from Taylor to Kennedy, November 3, 1961, *Pentagon Papers*, 2:92–93.

25. Rusk and McNamara to Kennedy, November 11, 1961, ibid., 111 (emphasis in original).

26. Ibid., 110–16; Short, *Origins of the Vietnam War*, 248–49.

27. Chester Bowles, *Promises to Keep: My Years in Public Life* (New York:

Harper, 1971), 409; excerpts from Cottrell Appendix to Taylor Report, *Pentagon Papers*, 2:96; Bowles memorandum to secretary of state, October 5, 1961, *Foreign Relations of the United States, 1961–1963*, vol. 1, *Vietnam* (Washington, D.C.: GPO, 1988), 322–25 (hereafter cited as *FRUS*).

28. David L. Di Leo, *George Ball, Vietnam, and the Rethinking of Containment* (Chapel Hill: University of North Carolina Press, 1991), 56–59.

29. Rostow memorandum to Kennedy, November 14, 1961, *FRUS, 1961–63*, 1:601–3. See also Herring, *America's Longest War*, 82–84. As the Laotian settlement progressed, Kennedy indeed had to reassure Diem that it did not indicate a lack of resolve in Vietnam. Kennedy to Diem, July 9, 1962, *FRUS, 1961–63*, vol. 2, *Vietnam 1962* (Washington, D.C.: GPO, 1990), 511–13.

30. Beschloss, *The Crisis Years*, 590–92; Bowles, *Promises to Keep*, 336–37, 408–11, 424–25, 450–53; Galbraith memorandum to Kennedy, April 4, 1962, Bowles memorandum to Kennedy, April 4, 1962, *FRUS, 1961–63*, 2:297–303; Bowles memorandum to Kennedy, March 27, 1963, *FRUS, 1961–63*, vol. 3, *Vietnam January–August 1963* (Washington, D.C.: GPO, 1991), 136–40. David Di Leo notes a few instances of Ball's indirect and informal efforts to alter Kennedy's approach to Vietnam. See Di Leo, *Ball, Vietnam, and the Rethinking of Containment*, 56–63.

31. Short, *Origins of the Vietnam War*, 261–63.

32. Kennedy's press conferences, March 7 and December 12, 1962, *Public Papers: Kennedy, 1962* (Washington, D.C.: GPO, 1963), 199, 807. See also Forrestal memorandum to Kennedy, September 18, 1962, *FRUS, 1961–63*, 2:649–50.

33. Herring, *America's Longest War*, 86–93; Gaddis, *Strategies of Containment*, 255–64; Kahin, *Intervention*, 136–45.

34. Ellen J. Hammer, *A Death in November: America in Vietnam, 1963* (New York: Oxford University Press, 1988), 42–45, 65, 84–85, 144–45, 156–57, 172–73; David Halberstam, *The Making of a Quagmire: America and Vietnam during the Vietnam Era*, rev. ed. (New York: Knopf, 1988), 1–98.

35. Hilsman and Forrestal report to Kennedy, January 25, 1963, *FRUS, 1961–63*, 3:49–62. See also Mike Mansfield oral history interview, John F. Kennedy Library, Boston, Mass.; and Mansfield report to Kennedy, December 18, 1962, and memorandum by Heavner, December 27, 1962, *FRUS, 1961–63*, 2:779–87, 797–98.

36. Kahin, *Intervention*, 146–56; Halberstam, *Making of a Quagmire*, 99–155; Hammer, *A Death in November*, 103–33.

37. Forrestal memorandum to Kennedy, August 24, 1963, Forrestal telegram to Kennedy, August 24, 1963, State Dept. telegram to Lodge, August 24, 1963, memorandum by V. H. Krulak, August 24, 1963, memorandum of White House meeting, August 26, 1963, Forrestal memorandum to Kennedy, August 27, 1963, memorandum of conference with Kennedy, August 27, 1963, *FRUS, 1961–63*, 3:625, 627–31, 638–41, 658–65; memorandum of conference with Kennedy, August 28, 1963, memorandum of conversation at White House, August 28, 1963, Lodge telegram to State Dept., August 29, 1963, memorandum of conversation with Kennedy, August 29, 1963, State Dept. telegram to Lodge, August 29, 1963, *FRUS, 1961–63*, vol. 4, *Vietnam August–December 1963* (Washington, D.C.: GPO, 1991), 1–6, 12–14, 20–22, 26–33, 35–36; Kahin, *Intervention*, 156–68; Hammer, *A Death in November*, 169–

219; Short, *Origins of the Vietnam War*, 266–72; Hilsman, *To Move a Nation*, 483–94.

38. Hilsman, *To Move a Nation*, 502.

39. Halberstam, *The Making of a Quagmire*, 133–55.

40. Hammer, *A Death in November*, 45.

41. *Congressional Record*, 88th Cong, 1st sess., 1963, vol. 109, pt. 13:18205.

42. McNamara-Taylor Report, October 2, 1963, *Pentagon Papers*, 2:751–66, quote on p. 754.

43. Ibid., 752–53. See also Herring, *America's Longest War*, 102–3.

44. White House Statement, October 2, 1963, *Public Papers: Kennedy, 1963* (Washington, D.C.: GPO, 1964), 759–60. See also summary record of National Security Council meeting, October 2, 1963, *FRUS, 1961–63*, 4:350–52.

45. CIA to Lodge, October 9, 1963, *FRUS, 1961–63*, 4:393.

46. Kahin, *Intervention*, 168–81; memoranda of conferences with Kennedy, October 29, 1963, Bundy telegram to Lodge, October 29, 1963, Lodge telegrams to State Dept., October 30, 1963, Bundy telegram to Lodge, October 30, 1963, *FRUS, 1961–63*, 4:468–75, 484–88, 493–95, 500–502.

47. Transcript of broadcast, September 2, 1963, *Public Papers: Kennedy, 1963*, 652.

48. Transcript of broadcast, September 10, 1963, ibid., 659–60.

49. Bernard Brodie, *War and Politics* (New York: Macmillan, 1973), 187–98; William J. Rust, *Kennedy in Vietnam* (New York: Scribners, 1985), 179–82; John M. Newman, *JFK and Vietnam: Deception, Intrigue and the Struggle for Power* (New York: Warner Books, 1992); Bassett and Pelz, "The Failed Search for Victory," 112–29.

5
The Reluctant Warrior: Lyndon Johnson as Commander in Chief

George C. Herring

Drawing parallels with his illustrious predecessors Woodrow Wilson and Franklin Roosevelt, Lyndon B. Johnson, on the eve of his momentous decision for war in July 1965, lamented that "every time we have gotten near the culmination of our dreams, the war bells have rung. . . . If we have to fight," he added, "I'll do that. But I don't want . . . to be known as a War President."[1]

Whatever his wish, Johnson *is* remembered as a war president, and as a U.S. commander in chief, he generally rates among the least effective. He is, of course, popularly viewed as the only U.S. president to lose his war, something he greatly feared and on more than one occasion vowed he would not let happen. He is scored, on the one side, as the stereotypical shoot-from-the-hip Texan, the warmonger who destroyed Vietnam to save his own ego. He is attacked from the other side as a timid, all-too-political war leader who refused to do what was necessary to win an eminently winnable war.

Such criticisms tell a great deal about the way Johnson fought the war, but they do not get at the fundamental problems of his leadership. To be fair, limited war is extraordinarily difficult to fight, especially within the U.S. system, and Vietnam was a war that probably could not have been won in any meaningful sense. Still, the deficiencies of Johnson's leadership contributed to the peculiar frustrations of the Vietnam War and its outcome, and these deficiencies derived to a large extent from his personality and leadership style. Looking at such crucial issues as his handling of public opinion and his management of strategy, this essay will examine the ways in which Johnson exercised the duties of commander in chief in America's longest war.

Johnson studies the details of the siege of Khe Sanh in January 1968 as his national security adviser, Walter W. Rostow, points to a model of the battle area. (Y. R. Oka-moto, courtesy Lyndon Baines Johnson Library)

The president's role in limited war is admittedly a difficult one. In total war, he can wrap himself in the flag, rally the nation, employ the trappings of his office to boost his own image and leadership position, even suppress the criticism that in peacetime normally goes with the office. A fundamental principle of limited war, however, is that it should be waged without too much intrusion into the life of the nation. The commander in chief must set the tone and cannot appear preoccupied with the war to the exclusion of other things. But with men and women dying in the field, he cannot appear indifferent either. He must walk a very high and thin tightrope. Johnson was in many ways miscast in the role. To some degree he shared the yearning for military glory common to his generation. He took great pride in the Silver Star he had won in World War II. Draping the Congressional Medal of

Honor around the neck of a chaplain who had distinguished himself in battle, he was overheard to exclaim: "Son, I'd rather have one of these babies than be President."[2] Yet he had little of the boyish fascination with war of his mentor and idol Franklin Roosevelt. He had no lust for combat, and his one day under fire in World War II was deliberately contrived as a military means to a political end.[3] He was innately suspicious of military men. More important, much of his political career had been devoted to the cause of domestic reform, and he resented the Vietnam War as an intrusion on his ambition to go down in history as the greatest American reform president. He later complained that he had been forced to shun "the woman I really loved"—the Great Society—for that "bitch of a war on the other side of the world."[4]

In terms of personality, Johnson was particularly ill suited to be commander in chief in a limited war, especially the confusing and intractable war in Vietnam. He was a flamboyant and impulsive man in a situation that demanded restraint, an emotional man given to wild mood swings in circumstances that required calmness and steadiness. He was a man with a passion for success and a yearning for greatness, whose whole life had been a single-minded quest for measurable achievement in the form of bills passed, wells dug, and schools built, fighting a war in which it was difficult to establish criteria for progress, much less measure it. He was a restless and impatient man waging war against an enemy who thought in terms of years, not days, centuries, not decades. He was a man for whom defeat was intolerable, even unthinkable, entrapped in a conflict that probably could not be won.

From the outset, Johnson dutifully grappled with the challenge. His credo from his youth had been that if you work hard enough you will win. He brought to his war the same enormous energy and compulsive attention to detail that characterized his approach to politics, the presidency, and life in general.[5] He demanded the final word on the tonnage, timing, and targets of air strikes against North Vietnam. He insisted on being informed of every troop movement. "He sleeps fitfully at night when he knows that U.S. pilots are on their way against the enemy," a journalist observed. "He often arises in the small hours of the morning to check the White House situation room for cables about rescue operations and troop casualty lists from Saigon."[6]

Whatever public image Johnson sought to convey, during most working days he could not escape the burdens of war leadership. His mornings usually began with a National Security Council (NSC) staffer's edited summaries of cables reporting the latest developments in Vietnam.[7] It was not unusual, however, for him to call the White House situation room at midnight,

4:30 A.M., and 6:30 A.M. and ask in a concerned voice: "What's going on?"[8] During rare minutes of free time in his daily schedule, he might scan summaries of damage done by the bombing of North Vietnam, examine a report from General William C. Westmoreland in Saigon, or fret over rising domestic opposition to the war.[9]

The same standards applied at the end of his tenure in office. In the early days of the Tet Offensive, *Time* wrote, he was on constant alert, "pouncing on more than 25 reports rushed to him through the evening and night." He was up at 5:00 A.M. for a situation room briefing and talked to Secretary of Defense Robert McNamara twice before a breakfast meeting with congressional leaders. "He's working like a dog," Press Secretary George Christian observed, "keeping tabs on everything." "Not a sparrow falls," a former aide noted, "that he doesn't know about it."[10]

His passion for information was legendary. In the morning, he would devour several major newspapers and the *Congressional Record* while watching three television networks simultaneously. NSC staffers were amazed to see him tear pieces out of his "earlybird" morning briefings and send them back to the situation room with the instruction to fill in a reporter about them. During the siege of Khe Sanh in 1968 he called directly to the beleaguered fortress to talk to the commander on the scene.[11]

Despite conscious efforts to do so, he was not able to balance Vietnam with other concerns, and his absorption in it became near total. He insisted through much of his presidency that the war was not diverting him from other foreign policy issues and domestic concerns, that his critics were the ones preoccupied with the war. He had accomplished great things at home, but the press could only whine "Veetnam, Veetnam, Veetnam, Veetnam." To emphasize the point, he would savagely mimic a baby crying.[12] Yet those close to him knew better. As early as August 1965, *Time* noted, Vietnam was "devouring the great majority of Johnson's hours" and disrupting his regular routine.[13] Admiral Thomas Moorer later recalled that when you were with Johnson, "you always discussed Vietnam, no matter where you were."[14]

From early on, it is equally clear that Vietnam was a source of great frustration for him. "He stalks the White House corridor," a journalist observed, "longingly paraphrasing to aides the World War II order that Franklin Roosevelt gave to General Eisenhower: 'Seek out the German army and destroy it.'"[15] If only Vietnam were that simple. When Senate dove George McGovern (D-S.Dak.) presented him a memorandum explaining why the United States had erred in intervening in Vietnam, he exploded: "Don't give me another goddamn history lesson. . . . I don't need a lecture on where we went wrong. I've got to deal with where we are now."[16] As the war dragged on, opposition mounted, and that elusive light failed to appear at the end of the tunnel, his frustration grew. "I can't get out," he complained. "I can't finish with what I've got. So what the hell do I do?"[17]

For the emotional Johnson, the war became a source of great personal grief. "No man felt more deeply and more heavily the burdens and responsibilities of the decisions he was called on to make," a sympathetic Secretary of the Treasury Henry Fowler later remarked. "And if the American public could have seen the Lyndon Johnson that I saw in those private sessions with this deep and overpowering concern for the lives of . . . the men, women, and children in the war zone . . . people would be ashamed of the things they've said."[18] Johnson in fact believed that his position required him to keep to himself the grief that he felt, lest it show weakness to his own people and his foes in Hanoi. But it is poignantly captured in a photo, not released until twenty years later, of a president, bent over in distress, head in his hands, after listening to a tape sent to his daughter from Vietnam by her husband, Charles Robb.[19] Fowler compared Johnson to Lincoln, a comparison the president himself used as a source of comfort, adding that "if the mothers of the men who went to Viet Nam could have seen him on occasion as I saw him reading their letters with the deepest emotion they would have felt as sorry for him as I did, for the grief he had to suppress publicly, but gave way to privately, of carrying on this dreadful conflict."[20]

Grief sometimes gave way to melancholy and self-pity. He told a group of labor leaders in August 1967 that the first thing he reviewed each morning was a list of the men who had died in Vietnam the day before, and he added: "Remember that every time you criticize me it is just another rock of cement that I must carry."[21] His mentor and confidant, Senator Richard Russell (D-Ga.), stopped going to the White House alone because, he explained, Johnson would start crying uncontrollably, and he could not stand to be subjected to that kind of emotionalism.[22] Another close friend, journalist William S. White, confirmed that more than once he saw Johnson "weep surreptitiously" when reports of the day's casualties were placed before him.[23]

Although he took on the job of commander in chief with the greatest reluctance, Johnson gave it his full attention, applying himself with characteristic single-mindedness. He carried out the ceremonial aspects of the position with restraint and quiet dignity. He worked hard at managing the war, seeking to oversee each detail, agonizing over it, eventually suffering from it. His failure was not from want of trying. Rather, he can be more readily faulted for getting too involved in the day-to-day details of the war, for letting the trees obscure his view of the forest.

One of the most important tasks of the commander in chief in the U.S. system is to generate and maintain public support, and in a limited war this is especially difficult to do. Unlike his counterpart engaged in total war, the president cannot rally the nation to the war and himself, yet he must sustain public support. How to balance these conflicting demands especially vexed Johnson, and as the war grew more unpopular, anything he did or did not do subjected him to ridicule, abuse, indignation, or outrage. If he attempted to raise morale, as with his notorious injunction to the troops to "nail those coonskins to the wall," he was pilloried by those who opposed the war. If he did nothing, he was charged with failing to lead. Johnson never resolved this dilemma. At the outset, he and his advisers went by the book, playing it low-key, hoping to hold public support without exciting popular passions. This did not happen, of course, and by 1967 they were fighting a desperate rearguard action to prevent the collapse of the home front.

At least moderately concerned about the matter of public support, some administration officials in the summer of 1965 proposed a variety of activities to prepare the nation for war. McNamara advocated creation of a blue-ribbon task force to explain the war to the American people. Presidential aides suggested the creation of a citizens' committee like the Committee for the Marshall Plan to mobilize support at the grass-roots level. White House staffer Horace Busby even pressed Johnson to go out and rally the people in the mode of Franklin Roosevelt or Winston Churchill.[24]

Johnson rejected all such proposals. Complacency may have been one reason. After World War II, within the larger confines of the Cold War consensus, the executive branch had developed the knack of analyzing and manipulating public opinion into a fine art. Postwar administrations were never free from criticism, but in no case was a major foreign policy initiative frustrated by lack of public support. Perhaps because of this record of success, the administration assumed that the American people would tolerate large-scale involvement in Vietnam. Drawing a sharp distinction between the political liabilities that had bedeviled France in the First Indochina War and the political advantages of the United States in 1965, McGeorge Bundy advised Johnson that "while there is widespread questioning and uneasiness about the way in which we may be playing that role, the public as a whole seems to realize that the role must be played."[25]

The administration also dismissed the warning raised by Under Secretary of State George Ball on July 21, 1965, that, based on the Korean analogy, if the war dragged on and casualties mounted, public support would erode. Johnson and his advisers acted, aide Bill Moyers later conceded, in the expectation that "reason and mutual concessions" would prevail, that North Vietnam could be enticed or intimidated into negotiating and a drawn-out war would be avoided.[26] Thus a fatal miscalculation about Hanoi's response to U.S. escalation may have been behind an equally fatal miscalculation about the longevity of public support.

The administration totally missed the significance of the budding peace movement. Rusk compared the campus protest of the spring of 1965 to the 1938 Oxford Union debate, observing that most of those who "took the pledge" later served in World War II.[27] Bundy later admitted that "we simply hadn't estimated the kinds of new forces that were loose in the land."[28]

More important, perhaps, was the war's impact on the president's beloved domestic programs. He was deeply committed to the Great Society, and he knew that if the United States were driven out of Vietnam his dreams of domestic reform would be crushed. He also feared that a public debate on Vietnam would jeopardize the Great Society legislation then pending in Congress, and he knew that if he was candid with the American people and revealed the prospective costs of the war, his goals would be jeopardized.[29]

Other, more important reasons for the administration's approach derived from prevailing theories about the way limited wars should be fought. Johnson and his top advisers feared that mobilizing the nation for war would lead to pressures for escalation and victory, which might provoke the larger war with the Soviet Union and China that the commitment in Vietnam was designed to deter in the first place. As Rusk later put it, "in a nuclear world it is just too dangerous for an entire people to get too angry and we deliberately tried to do in cold blood what perhaps can only be done in hot blood."[30] "I don't want to be dramatic and cause tension," the president told the National Security Council on July 27, 1965.[31]

For Secretary of Defense McNamara, the person who gave practical application to limited war theory, Vietnam was the prototype for the way wars must be fought in the nuclear age. "The greatest contribution Vietnam is making," he observed on one occasion, "is developing an ability in the United States to fight a limited war . . . without arousing the public ire." This was almost a necessity, he added, "since this is the kind of war we'll likely be facing for the next fifty years."[32]

Johnson and his advisers thus gambled that without taking exceptional measures they could hold public support long enough to achieve their goals in Vietnam. As a result, the United States went to war in July 1965 in a way that was uniquely quiet and underplayed. The president ordered his July decisions implemented in a low-key manner. He announced the major troop increase at a noon press conference instead of during prime time. It was even lumped in with a number of other items in a way that downplayed its importance.[33]

With the exception of several hastily arranged, typically Johnsonian public-relations blitzes, the administration persisted in this low-key approach until the summer of 1967. It created no special machinery to monitor or manipulate public opinion. It took only modest steps to promote public support. Administration officials did conduct briefings for state governors and put together packets of materials to be used by friends to generate public support. They closely monitored press and congressional debates, watching for and answering criticisms. Inasmuch as they attempted to sell the war, however, they did so from behind the scenes, leaving it to ostensibly private groups such as the Junior Chamber of Commerce, the Young Democrats, and the American Friends of Vietnam to take the lead.[34]

Johnson himself faithfully and at times even eloquently executed his public, ceremonial role as commander in chief. He regularly visited wounded war veterans, expressing to them the country's pride in their service and gratitude for their sacrifice. These visits were moving experiences for the highly emotional president and became much more difficult as the war went on.[35] He presented Medals of Honor to war heroes, on one occasion quoting an eve-of-battle prayer attributed to George Washington: "Good God, what brave men must I lose today?"[36]

In late October 1966 he made the famous visit to Camranh Bay, a trip that became the subject of ridicule at home but that had a significant impact on Johnson himself. It was the first visit by a president to a war zone since Franklin Roosevelt's journey to Casablanca in 1943. Clark Clifford called it one of the "emotional high points" of Johnson's presidency. Clifford further surmised that because he had seen the war firsthand with his troops, the commander in chief's personal and emotional commitment to it increased "exponentially." "I have never been more moved by any group I have ever talked to," Johnson observed upon his return, "never in my life."[37]

Throughout much of 1966 and into 1967, however, almost to the point of being conspicuous about it, Johnson followed the low-key approach he had imposed on his administration, remaining, in the words of *Time* magazine, "strangely silent" on the war. He made few public appearances and fewer speeches. He spent three months at his ranch in Texas in 1966 and two months in 1967. In 1966 he held forty press conferences, the following year only twenty-one. At first, his silence was justified in terms of strategic necessity. Aides confided that he feared that statements of optimism might sway hawks to press for all-out escalation and victory, and doves to redouble their clamor for a negotiated peace. Journalists later speculated that he was lying low as a way of dealing with his own sagging popularity. Increasingly, he was criticized for being the most aloof chief executive since Calvin Coolidge and for being unable to communicate to the nation a sense of what it was doing in Vietnam and why the war was necessary. *Time* reported in August 1967 that he was holed up in a small study away from the Oval Office, "strangely insulated from his countrymen's doubts and fears."[38]

Increasingly on the defensive, administration officials responded to criticism in a way that was typically Johnsonian and generally counterproductive. If Ronald Reagan was the Teflon president, to whom nothing stuck, Johnson—to a large degree by choice—was the flypaper president, to whom everything clung. A compulsive reader, viewer, and listener who took every criticism personally and to heart, he was at first intent on and then obsessed with answering every accusation, responding to every charge. When General Matthew Ridgway came out against the war, the president ordered Army Chief of Staff General Harold Johnson to get statements of support from two leading World War II generals.[39] Reams of paper were devoted to proving critical columnist Walter Lippmann wrong, and thousands of man-hours were wasted by harried White House staffers compiling dossiers on critics such as Senator J. William Fulbright (D-Ark.) and especially the despised Kennedy brothers.[40]

By mid-1967, the administration belatedly recognized that its greatest crisis was at home. As the war dragged on with no end in view and domestic unrest grew, the president's job-approval rating steadily declined. More ominous was the sharp increase in the number of people who thought that sending troops to Vietnam was a mistake, raising disturbing parallels with Korea. Still more unnerving was the mood of the nation—anxious, frustrated, and increasingly divided. This "pinpoint on the globe [Vietnam]," old New Dealer and presidential adviser David Lilienthal lamented, was "like an infection, a 'culture' of some horrible disease, a cancer where the wildly growing cells multiply and multiply until the whole body is poisoned."[41]

Signs of waning support left the administration deeply troubled. Johnson complained about his inability to get his message across. He and his advisers were particularly worried about the public perception, fed by the press, that the war had become a stalemate. The president groped for some magic formula to reverse the spread of disillusionment, on one occasion even longing for "some colorful general like McArthur [*sic*] with his shirt neck open" who could dismiss as "pure Communist propaganda" the talk of a stalemate and go to Saigon and do battle with the press.[42] Anticipating the dramatic decision he would make on March 31, 1968, a despondent president wondered aloud at a top-level meeting in early October 1967 how the country would be affected if he decided not to run again.[43]

Vietnam was not fundamentally a public-relations problem, and a more vigorous and effective public-relations campaign would not have changed the outcome. Still, what stands out quite starkly is the strangely limited and notably cautious effort made by the Johnson administration between 1965 and 1967 to promote public support for the war. The president and his advisers thought that they were following the limited war doctrine and hoped that they could achieve their objectives without arousing popular passions. They failed, and by late 1967 their problem was magnified. "The temperament of our people seems to be, 'you must get excited, get passionate, fight it and get it over with, or we must pull out,' " Lady Bird Johnson confided to her diary. "It is unbearably hard to fight a limited war."[44]

Limited war, in particular, requires the most sophisticated strategy, precisely formulated in terms of ends and means, with special attention to keeping costs at acceptable levels. The most important tasks of the commander in chief are to oversee the conception and implementation of that strategy, shape war aims, and devise appropriate means to achieve them. In Vietnam, perhaps the most complex war ever fought by the United States, there was never any systematic discussion at the highest levels of government of the fundamental issue of how the war should be fought. The crucial discussions of June and July 1965 focused on the numbers of troops that would be provided rather than how and for what ends they would be used. There was no other discussion of strategy until the communist Tet Offensive forced the issue in 1968.

Simple overconfidence may be the most obvious explanation for this curious lack of strategy. Americans could not conceive that the United States would be unable to impose its will on what Lyndon Johnson once referred to as that "raggedy ass little fourth rate country." But the explanation goes much deeper than that. Although Johnson worked hard at the job of commander in chief, he never took control of his war, as had Polk, Lincoln, or Franklin Roosevelt. In contrast to these presidents or even to Truman, Johnson had no illusions of military expertise. He was fond of quoting his political mentor, Sam Rayburn, to the effect that "if we start making the military decisions, I wonder why we paid to send them to West Point." Perhaps he was rationalizing his own ignorance and lack of security in an alien field.[45]

Secretary of Defense McNamara might have filled the strategic void, but he was no more willing to take control than Johnson. When asked on one occasion why he did not tell the military what to do, as Churchill had done, McNamara responded that he was no Churchill.[46] Thus, as Stephen Peter Rosen has observed, Johnson and McNamara refused to do what the civilian leadership must do: "They did not define a clear . . . mission for the military and did not establish a clear limit to the resources to be allocated for that mission."[47] They saw their primary task as maintaining tight operational control over the military.

For Johnson, a compulsive determination to micromanage everything was an essential part of his makeup. Even as a young congressman, he had insisted on overseeing the most minute detail, never sure "things would go right," an aide later recalled, "unless he was in control of everything."[48] The tendency to micromanage also derived from other factors. Johnson brought to the White House the southern populists' suspicion of the military. Suspecting that generals and admirals needed war to boost their reputations, he was determined to keep close check on them. It also reflected the deep-seated and pervasive civil-military tension of the 1960s. Operating in an age of profound international stress with weaponry of enormous destructive potential, civilians were determined to keep the military in check. During the Cuban Missile Crisis, McNamara had haunted the Navy command center, and even then he had had difficulty preventing provocative actions; this experience reinforced his determination to keep control tightly in his own hands. The result in Vietnam was a day-to-day intrusion into the tactical conduct of the war on an unprecedented scale. The larger result, Rosen concludes, was an unhappy combination of "high level indecision and micromanagement."[49]

Even more crippling was Johnson's decision to finesse rather than resolve the deep divisions among his advisers on how the war should be conducted. No one in the administration really liked the way the war was being fought or the results that were being obtained. What is even more striking, however, is that despite the rampant dissatisfaction, there was no change of strategy or even systematic discussion of a change in strategy. Indeed, in many different ways the system seems to have been rigged to prevent discussion, debate, and adaptation.

From July 1965, there were sharp differences over strategy within the administration. The running battle over the bombing of North Vietnam, especially between McNamara and the Joint Chiefs of Staff (JCS), is well known.[50] But there was also widespread and steadily growing dissatisfaction with General Westmoreland's ground strategy. From the outset, the marines strongly objected to Westmoreland's determination to fight guerrillas by staging decisive battles "along the Tannenberg design."[51] More significant was the growing concern about Westmoreland's conduct of the war within the army itself. Army Chief of Staff Harold Johnson increasingly questioned the wastefulness of search-and-destroy operations, as did Vice Chief of Staff Creighton Abrams and some of Westmoreland's top field officers.[52]

Divisions within the military paled in comparison to the growing conflict between the military and civilians. The military bristled at Johnson's refusal to mobilize the reserves and protested the micromanagement of the war.[53] The civilians worried about relentless military pressure for escalation of the war. They increasingly pressed to cut back or even stop the bombing, put a ceiling on the number of ground troops, and shift to a less costly and less wasteful ground strategy.[54]

Despite these divisions, there was no change of strategy or even systematic and sustained discussion of a change of strategy. The military tradition of the field commander's autonomy inhibited debate on and possible alteration of the ground strategy. More important was the leadership style of the commander in chief. Lyndon Johnson's entirely political manner of running the war, his consensus-oriented modus operandi, effectively stifled debate. On such issues as bombing targets, bombing pauses, troop levels, and troop use, he managed to keep dissent and controversy under control by making concessions to each side without giving any side what it wanted. From the beginning of the war to the end, as Johnson's second secretary of defense Clark Clifford has noted, Johnson acted more like a legislative leader maintaining consensus among his divided colleagues than the commander in chief of a nation at war.[55]

The president and his top advisers also insisted on rigid standards of loyalty in an increasingly divided administration. Unlike his hero Franklin Roosevelt, Johnson had no tolerance for internecine conflict, and he imposed on his government the "Macy's window" variety of loyalty made legendary by David Halberstam.[56] Unfortunately, the two men who might have influenced him in another direction, McNamara and Secretary of State Dean Rusk, shared Johnson's perverted notions of team play. In-house devil's advocate George Ball later recalled that McNamara treated his dissenting memos like "poisonous snakes." He was "absolutely horrified by them" and considered them "next to treason."[57] Rusk agreed with McNamara.

"When the president has decided what the policy shall be," he later wrote, "an officer should either support that policy or resign."[58]

Finally, and perhaps most important, is what might be called the MacArthur syndrome: the pervasive fear among civilians and military alike of a repetition of the illustrious general's challenge to civilian authority. Johnson lived in mortal terror of a military revolt and did everything in his power to squelch the slightest tendency in that direction. In a February 1966 meeting in Honolulu, Westmoreland later recalled, the president carefully sized him up, eventually satisfying himself that *his* general was "sufficiently understanding" of the constraints imposed on him and was a "reliable" and "straightforward soldier who would not get involved in the politics of the war."[59]

An encounter in July 1967 is even more revealing of the delicate game played between the commander in chief and his top general. An increasingly frustrated and restive Westmoreland reminded Johnson that he had made every effort to ease the president's burden by his conduct, but added an only slightly veiled warning that he must think of his own requirements first. Johnson flattered Westmoreland by expressing great admiration for the way he had handled himself. He cleverly sought to appease the general by hinting that he did not always favor his civilian advisers over his military.[60]

Having learned from Korea, the military carefully refrained from anything approaching a direct challenge to civilian authority. General Earle Wheeler, chairman of the Joint Chiefs of Staff, emphasized short-term acquiescence and silence. Hoping to break down the restrictions imposed by the White House, he encouraged Westmoreland to continue to push escalation and accept half a loaf to "get his foot in the door." He even instructed Westmoreland to keep his subordinates quiet. If escalation were to occur following reports of military dissatisfaction, it might be concluded that the military was "riding roughshod" over civilians. Officers must understand the "absolute necessity for every military man to keep his mouth shut and get on with the war."[61]

For a variety of reasons, then, the president kept a tight lid on dissent. Even in the spring and summer of 1967, with McNamara pressing for an end to the bombing and a negotiated settlement and with civilians and military deeply divided, Johnson characteristically avoided a confrontation. There was no debate on the issues at the highest levels. He delayed a decision for months, and when he finally acted he did so on a piecemeal basis, carefully avoiding the larger strategic questions. When the air war became an open subject of dispute between the JCS and McNamara during hearings before

Senator John Stennis's (D-Miss.) Preparedness Subcommittee in August, the president dealt with the problem by denying its existence. There were "no quarrels, no antagonisms" within his official family, he insisted. "I have never known a period when I thought there was more harmony, more general agreement, and a more cooperative attitude."[62]

Writing to Johnson in late 1967, Under Secretary of State Nicholas Katzenbach posed the question: "Can the tortoise of progress in Vietnam stay ahead of the hare of dissent at home?"[63] Katzenbach's Aesopian analogy made clear the dilemma faced by the commander in chief at this crucial point in his war. To stave off collapse of the home front, progress had to be demonstrated in Vietnam. Yet real progress in the war was perhaps not possible without clear-cut indications of public support at home.

By late 1967, Katzenbach and other civilian advisers pressed Johnson to do what he had thus far staunchly refused to do: address head-on the issue of how the war was being fought. A now blatantly dissident McNamara, civilians in the State Department and Pentagon, and establishment figures outside the government urged the president to check dissent at home by changing strategy in Vietnam. They pressed for cutbacks in or an end to the bombing. More important, they urged scrapping Westmoreland's costly search-and-destroy strategy and shifting to a "clear and hold strategy" that might stabilize the war at a politically acceptable level and perhaps save South Vietnam without risking a wider war. They also pushed for an incipient form of what would later be called Vietnamization, the shifting of greater military responsibility to the South Vietnamese.[64]

Speech writer Harry McPherson and presidential adviser McGeorge Bundy pointed out the flaws in Johnson's exercise of presidential powers in wartime. McPherson gently chided his boss for expanding the bombing to silence military criticism. "You are the Commander in Chief," he affirmed. "If you think a policy is wrong, you should not follow it just to quiet the generals and admirals."[65] Bundy pressed Johnson to take control of the war and arrange a "solid internal understanding" between Rusk, McNamara, and the Joint Chiefs on the bombing—a "basic command decision" to settle the issue once and for all. He urged Johnson to initiate a full review of the ground strategy at the "highest military and civilian levels." Conceding that it was a "highly sensitive matter" to question the field commander, Bundy went on to say that if the strategy was not wise or effective, the work of the field commander "must be questioned." Now that the principal battleground was at home, he added, the "Commander in Chief has both the right and duty . . . to visibly take command of a contest that is more political in character than any in our history except the Civil War (where Lincoln interfered *much* more than you have)." It was essential to end the conflict in the government and stabilize the home front.[66]

Johnson was not moved by the appeals of his closest advisers. He was unsympathetic to repeated JCS appeals for expansion of the ground and air wars. He also doubted that McNamara's proposals for a bombing halt would work. "How do we get this conclusion?" he scrawled on a memo in which the secretary had predicted that stopping the bombing would lead to peace talks.[67] As before, he refused to make the hard decisions, and he refused to take control of the war. He "resolved" the strategic questions politically without addressing the strategic issues. He kicked McNamara downstairs to the World Bank and tossed the military a bone in the form of a few new bombing targets. In regard to ground operations, he would go no further than privately committing himself to review Westmoreland's search-and-destroy strategy at some undetermined point in the future.[68]

To resolve the dilemma posed by Katzenbach, Johnson attempted to slow down the runaway hare of dissent at home rather than speed up or shift the direction of the tortoise of progress in Vietnam. In the late summer and early fall of 1967, he mounted a large-scale, many-faceted public-relations campaign to rally support for the war. A group was established in the White House to work full time monitoring public reactions and addressing public-relations problems as they surfaced. From behind the scenes, administration officials helped organize the Committee for Peace with Freedom in Vietnam, an ostensibly private organization modeled on the Committee for the Marshall Plan and designed to mobilize the "silent center."[69]

Believing that his major problem was a widespread public perception that the war was a stalemate, the president designed much of the campaign to persuade a skeptical public that the United States was in fact winning. He ordered the embassy and military command to find evidence of progress. U.S. officials dutifully responded, producing reams of statistics to show a steady rise in enemy body counts and pacified villages. The White House arranged for influential citizens to go to Vietnam and observe the progress firsthand. As part of the offensive at home, Westmoreland was brought home in November, ostensibly for top-level consultations, but in reality to reassure a troubled nation.[70]

The president himself assumed the lead in the public-relations campaign, for the first time taking the offensive against his critics. Emerging from months of isolation and seclusion, he launched a 5,100-mile tour of eight military bases in November 1967. In a fighting Veterans' Day speech, he made clear that "Viet Nam is no academic question. It is not a topic for cocktail parties, office arguments or debate from some distant sidelines." The lives of men were "tied by flesh and blood to Viet Nam. Talk does not come cheap for them."[71]

At a press conference on November 17, he abandoned the stiff, formal style that had been his trademark and defended his policies in a conversational manner with great vigor and emotion. In war, as in football, he said, Americans wanted quick decisions and clear-cut results, but this was not the kind of conflict that was being fought in Vietnam. He reiterated the administration's claims of progress. He reserved special comment for dissent. Reminding his listeners that there had been protest in every American war, he defended "responsible dissent," adding, with rare self-deprecation, that if he had done anything as president it was to "insure that there are plenty of dissenters." But he condemned the tactics of some of his critics, chided the press for not defending the First Amendment on which it relied, and warned that "storm trooper bullying," "rowdyism," and the suppression of free speech were "extremely dangerous" and undermined America's fighting men in Vietnam.[72] *Time* noted that the "real Johnson" had reemerged— "combative, spontaneous, self-assured." The time of "defensive silence" had passed, and he was "once more taking the stance of leadership."[73]

Johnson's public-relations campaign was a qualified short-term success but an unmitigated long-term disaster. Polls taken late in 1967 indicated a slight upswing in support for the war and even in the president's job-approval rating, and it is possible that under different circumstances the campaign might have bought him some time.[74] In fact, it merely deepened his problems. On January 31, 1968, the North Vietnamese launched a series of massive, coordinated military attacks throughout the cities and towns of South Vietnam. As perhaps nothing else could have, the so-called Tet Offensive put the lie to the administration's year-end claims of progress, eroding public support even more and forcing the internal reassessment of strategy that Johnson had dreaded and deferred for so long.

The Tet Offensive is generally regarded as a major turning point of the Vietnam War, and in many ways it was. But in terms of Johnson's management of the conflict, there was no real change. The president still refused to take control of the war. He continued to evade rather than confront the fundamental strategic issues. His dramatic March 31, 1968, speech, in which he announced a limit on the bombing, a readiness to negotiate, and his withdrawal as a candidate for reelection, is often cited as a major change of policy. It was designed, however, as much to quiet the home front as anything else. Like most of his earlier decisions, it was driven by a search for consensus, the result of picking and choosing from conflicting approaches rather than developing a coherent strategy to achieve a clearly defined objective. In the aftermath of that speech, the ambiguity persisted. The president's advisers were more divided than ever, and the lame duck Johnson was less certain of whose counsel to heed.

Tet did force the first full-scale consideration of strategy undertaken by the administration. Once the initial enemy attacks had been repulsed, Westmoreland and Wheeler sought to capitalize on the new mood of urgency in Washington, pressing for 206,000 additional troops and mobilization of the reserves. Westmoreland also revived his 1967 proposals to intensify the bombing of North Vietnam, conduct ground operations against North Vietnamese sanctuaries in Laos and Cambodia, and launch an "amphibious hook" across the 17th parallel. Not inclined to make a hasty decision on a matter fraught with such grave implications, Johnson turned the matter over to newly appointed Secretary of Defense Clark Clifford with the grim instruction: "Give me the lesser of evils."[75]

Clifford immediately began raising questions that had been skirted for years. He instructed his civilian advisers to study all the implications of the request and review the alternatives. He demanded of Wheeler and Westmoreland precise information on how the additional troops might be deployed and what results could be expected. He was "appalled" to discover that the JCS had no apparent plan to win the war. "Nothing had prepared me for the weakness of the military's case," he later recalled.[76]

The conflict that had simmered throughout 1967 was joined with renewed vigor in the frenzied aftermath of Tet. Clifford's civilian advisers insisted that even with the additional troops, the prevailing strategy promised no end to the conflict, and the costs would be heavy. Further Americanization of the war would reinforce the South Vietnamese tendency to do nothing. Additional escalation would bring increased U.S. casualties and require new taxes, risking a "domestic crisis of unprecedented proportions."[77] The civilians recommended that Westmoreland be given no more than a token increase in troops and that existing limits on military operations be retained. They went further and once again proposed a shift from search and destroy to population security. U.S. forces would be deployed to protect the major population centers, and the South Vietnamese would be forced to assume greater responsibility for the war. The object of the new approach would be a negotiated settlement rather than military victory. U.S. goals should be scaled down to a "peace which will leave the people of SVN free to fashion their own political institutions."[78]

This first major strategic assessment produced little in the way of results. As had been the case so often in the past, Clifford recommended against the military's proposals without resolving the strategic issues. No longer a hawk but not yet a dove, he leaned toward the population-security strategy and a scaling back of U.S. objectives, but he seems to have felt that the proposed changes would be more than Johnson could accept. He may have sought to prepare the president for change gradually rather than confront him immediately. Clifford's formal report thus kept the strategic issue alive by calling for continued study of the alternatives. But the secretary would go no further than to recommend the immediate deployment of 22,000 troops, a reserve call-up of unspecified magnitude, and an approach to get the Saigon government to do more.[79]

Johnson's subsequent post-Tet decisions, however dramatic in some particulars, also represented more a perpetuation of the old approach than a dramatic new departure. He approved only 13,500 new ground troops, less than Clifford had recommended, and he endorsed an early form of what would later be called Vietnamization. To pacify a restive home front, he brought Westmoreland back to Washington as army chief of staff, cut the bombing back to the area below the 20th parallel, and proposed a new peace initiative. Most dramatic of all, on March 31, 1968, Johnson announced that he would not run for reelection. But he did not change the ground strategy, and, indeed, in April he quietly authorized the military to "fight vigorously while negotiating."[80]

Johnson's decisions did not even get near the heart of the problem. Success in the battles of Tet reinforced the conviction of some U.S. officials that an independent, noncommunist South Vietnam could yet be salvaged from the war. The president's post-Tet decisions appear to have been designed to buy time to attain that result, but they seem to have derived from wishful thinking. Militarily, the means were scaled back without modifying the ends. In retrospect, it is impossible to see how U.S. officials hoped to achieve their thus far elusive aims with the application of less force. The United States had taken over the war in the first place because of the nonperformance of the South Vietnamese, and the concept of Vietnamization was illusory. Negotiations were desirable from a domestic political standpoint, but in the absence of a military advantage that the United States did not have and concessions that it was not prepared to make, negotiations could achieve nothing. Moreover, the mere fact of negotiations could soften U.S. resolve and limit the administration's ability to prosecute the war.

An already complicated war became much more complex after March 31, 1968. The profound political impact of the Tet Offensive in the United States combined with the other stunning events of the year and the presidential campaign to make the home front an even more vital and volatile factor in the war. The opening of negotiations in Paris in May added a new and uncertain element to an already bewildering mix. Thus anything that was done or not done in Vietnam had to be calculated in terms of its possible impact in Paris and the United States. That stage of the war the North Vietnamese called "fighting while negotiating" required the most delicate, fine-tuned strategy and the most careful and precise implementation.

The dilemmas of this new phase of the conflict were quickly apparent. Seeking to apply lessons learned from Tet, Clifford insisted that the military publicly minimize the extent and significance of the losses inflicted on the enemy. Otherwise, the American people might begin to expect an imminent victory as they had in 1967 and be vulnerable to another major shock if the North Vietnamese mounted a new offensive. The military obliged but protested that the public-relations field would be left to the "prophets of doom."[81] To establish the strongest possible position prior to negotiations, the administration had authorized "all-out" ground operations in South Vietnam. When the press revealed in April the largest allied operations to date, code-named *toan than* (total victory) by the South Vietnamese, critics charged the United States with reckless escalation of the war and sabotaging possible negotiations. Wheeler advised Westmoreland not to use provocative code names and not to draw attention to operations. Otherwise, restrictions might be imposed "which none of us wants and which could be adverse to our negotiating posture." Westmoreland agreed to comply but he worried about leaving the impression that the war was winding down and that the United States was doing nothing.[82]

Once negotiations got under way, the problems heightened. In May, when Westmoreland proposed a large-scale offensive against retreating North Vietnamese units, U.S. negotiator Cyrus Vance protested that such operations would appear to be a major escalation of the war and might have adverse effects in Paris and at home. Chief negotiator Averell Harriman worried, on the other hand, that the administration's policy of "full-scale fighting while negotiating" would make it impossible for the North Vietnamese to reduce the level of violence, thereby preventing mutual deescalation and a negotiated settlement.[83]

Not surprisingly, divisions within the government grew even sharper in this new phase of the war. The central issue was interpretation and implementation of the president's March 31 speech. Was it intended to extricate the United States from a war now considered unwinnable or to achieve the original goal at a lower cost? On the one side were Secretary of State Rusk, national security adviser Walt Rostow, ambassador to South Vietnam Ellsworth Bunker, and the military. Dubious about the prospects for negotiations and certain that Tet had given the United States the upper hand, they were not inclined to make concessions and sought instead to keep heavy military pressure on a battered enemy. "We can afford . . . to be tough, patient and not too anxious in our negotiating stance," Bunker insisted.[84] Clifford, Harriman, Under Secretary of State Nicholas Katzenbach, and Defense Department civilians Paul Nitze and Paul Warnke, on the other side, had all long since abandoned hope of military victory and had concluded that Vietnam was undermining the nation's global security posture. They therefore sought mutual deescalation and disengagement through the Paris negotiations.[85]

The internal battle raged throughout 1968. The two sides fought bitterly over the negotiating position to be taken in Paris, the scale and intent of ground operations, and resumption or curtailment of the bombing. The stakes were high, the participants exhausted, and nerves frayed. Clifford remembered 1968 as a year that lasted five years, and Rusk recalled only a "blur." The secretary of state later described surviving on a heavy daily regimen of aspirin, Scotch, and cigarettes.[86] Personal attacks descended to unprecedented levels. Harriman found Rusk's behavior in one battle "contemptible." Rusk charged that Clifford had lost his nerve.[87] "The pressure grew so intense that at times I felt that the government itself might come apart at the seams," the secretary of defense later observed. "There was, for a brief time, something approaching paralysis, and a sense of events spiralling out of control of the nation's leaders."[88]

Johnson was no more able than before to extract a workable strategy from the conflicting positions of his advisers. He had always abhorred conflict in his official family, and he literally pleaded with Rostow on one occasion to get Rusk and Clifford together.[89] He too was exhausted and dispirited from four years of an exceedingly frustrating war, and his impending retirement from the presidency may have removed an element of urgency. Although finding occasional "flashes" of the "old vigor," *Time* also reported an "unfamiliar atmosphere of tranquility" in the White House, even signs that Lyndon Johnson had "placed himself in the past tense."[90] He veered erratically between a hard line and a softer position. Of the only time he worked with Johnson, Assistant Secretary of State William P. Bundy later recalled that he was unsure "what [Johnson's] line was," what "he was really trying to do."[91]

Although he seems to have leaned toward the Rusk-Rostow position emotionally, the president refused to adopt either position. He was unwilling to escalate the war to break the military stalemate or to make concessions to break the diplomatic deadlock. He killed by deferral Rusk's proposal to resume bombing north of the 19th parallel. Yet he later denounced as "mush" a Harriman proposal for a complete bombing halt, complaining bitterly that "the enemy is using my own people as dupes."[92] In late October 1968, under extreme pressure from Democratic politicos, he finally backed a bombing halt as a way to salvage Hubert Humphrey's faltering presidential campaign. He continued to act, Clifford later observed, more like a "legislative leader, seeking a consensus among people who were often irreconcilably opposed than like a decisive Commander-in-chief giving his subordinates orders."[93]

The inevitable result was perpetuation of the military-diplomatic stalemate through the end of the Johnson presidency. After nearly six months of verbal shadow-boxing, U.S. and North Vietnamese diplomats, in the aftermath of the October 31, 1968, bombing halt, finally agreed to open substantive negotiations. But a nervous and intransigent South Vietnamese president, Nguyen Van Thieu, blocked the opening of talks and then delayed their progress. Resolution of the conflict was left to the Republican administration of Richard M. Nixon.

Much of the criticism of Lyndon Johnson's leadership in Vietnam is misplaced. The strategy of graduated escalation, if indeed it can be called a strategy, was doomed to failure. It is by no means clear, however, that the all-out approach advocated by Johnson's critics would have produced victory at acceptable cost. Such an approach ran the huge risk of leading to the general war that Johnson and his advisers were seeking to prevent by taking a firm stand in Vietnam. Other critics rightly charged that the administration's proposals to negotiate did not include terms that were likely to bring about successful negotiations. Still, given the persisting military stalemate and the positions taken by North Vietnam, there is little to suggest that short of an immediate and total withdrawal from Vietnam, which could have had fatal repercussions for the administration at home, a negotiated settlement was within reach.

Johnson's leadership is vulnerable to criticism on other grounds. Korea and especially the Truman-MacArthur controversy had stimulated a veritable cult of limited war in the 1950s and 1960s. The major conclusion was that in a nuclear age where total war was unthinkable, limited war was essential. Robert McNamara, McGeorge and William Bundy, and Dean Rusk, along with Johnson, were deeply imbued with limited-war theory, which was crucial in their handling of Vietnam. Coming of age in World War II, they were convinced of the essentiality of deterring aggression to avoid a major war. Veterans of the Cuban Missile Crisis, they lived with the awesome responsibility of preventing nuclear conflagration, and they were thus committed to fighting the war in "cold blood" and maintaining tight operational control over the military. They also operated under the mistaken assumption that limited war was more an exercise in crisis management than the application of strategy, and they were persuaded that gradual escalation offered the means to achieve their limited goals without provoking the larger war they so feared. Many of these notions turned out to be badly flawed.

To an even greater extent, Lyndon Johnson's own highly personalized style indelibly marked the conduct of the war and contributed to its peculiar frustrations: the reluctance to provide precise direction, define a mission, and set explicit limits; the unwillingness to tolerate any form of intragovernmental dissent or to permit a much-needed debate on strategic issues; the highly politicized approach that gave everybody something and nobody what they wanted, that emphasized consensus over results, whether on the battlefield or in diplomatic councils. All these were products of a thoroughly political and profoundly insecure man, a man especially ill at ease among military issues and military people. The determination to dupe or co-opt advisers and the public rather than confront them candidly and forcefully was another clear manifestation of the Johnson style, as was the tendency to personalize the domestic debate. Johnson repeatedly denied that Vietnam was his war. It was "America's war," he insisted, and "if I drop dead tomorrow, this war will still be with you."[94] In one sense, of course, he was right. But in terms of how the war was fought and the agony it caused, Vietnam was far more his than he was prepared to admit or even recognize.

Notes

1. Quoted in Brian VanDeMark, *Into the Quagmire: Lyndon Johnson and the Escalation of the Vietnam War* (New York: Oxford University Press, 1991), 178.

2. "The Talk of the Town," *New Yorker*, October 13, 1986, 35.

3. Robert A. Caro, *The Years of Lyndon Johnson: Means of Ascent* (New York: Knopf, 1990), 35–53.

4. Quoted in Doris Kearns, *Lyndon Johnson and the American Dream* (New York: Harper & Row, 1976), 251.

5. Caro, *Means of Ascent*, 4.

6. *Time*, August 6, 1965, 17–18.

7. Emmette Redford and Richard T. McCulley, *White House Operations: The Johnson Presidency* (Austin: University of Texas Press, 1986), 66–67.

8. Art McCafferty memos for Robert Komer, March 24, 25, 1966, National Security File, Country File, Vietnam, box 29, Lyndon Baines Johnson Papers, Lyndon Baines Johnson Library, Austin, Tex.

9. See, for example, James Bishop, *A Day in the Life of President Johnson* (New York: Random House, 1967), 78.

10. *Time*, January 8, 1968, 9–16, February 9, 1968, 10–11.

11. Volney Warner oral history interview, U.S. Army Military History Institute, Carlisle Barracks, Pa.

12. Quoted in C. L. Sulzberger, *Seven Continents and Forty Years* (New York: Quadrangle, 1977), 443.

13. *Time*, August 6, 1965, 19.

14. Thomas Moorer oral history interview, Johnson Library.

15. *Time*, August 6, 1965.

16. George McGovern, *Grassroots* (New York: Random House, 1977), 104–5.

17. Entry, March 7, 1965, Lady Bird Johnson, *A White House Diary* (New York: Holt, Rinehart and Winston, 1970), 248.

18. Henry Fowler oral history interview, Johnson Library.

19. Stephen Rosenfeld, "Fathers, Sons and War," *Washington Post*, April 19, 1985.

20. Fowler oral history interview, Johnson Library. For Johnson and Lincoln, see Allan Nevins to LBJ, April 20, 1967, and LBJ to Nevins, April 28, 1967, Confidential File, box 73, Johnson Papers.

21. Tom Johnson notes on meeting, August 9, 1967, Tom Johnson's Notes on Meetings, box 1, Johnson Library.

22. Powell Allen Moore oral history interview, Richard B. Russell Papers, Richard B. Russell Library, Athens, Ga. I am indebted to Professor Frank Mitchell of the University of Southern California for bringing this document to my attention.

23. William S. White, *The Making of a Journalist* (Lexington: University Press of Kentucky, 1986), 216.

24. Record of meeting, July 19, 1965, National Security File, Country File, Vietnam, box 15, Johnson Papers; Busby to LBJ, July 21, 1965, Busby Files, box 3, Johnson Papers; Kathleen J. Turner, *Lyndon Johnson's Dual War: Vietnam and the Press* (Chicago: University of Chicago Press, 1985), 149.

25. Bundy memorandum for LBJ, June 30, 1965, "France in Vietnam, 1954, and the U.S. in Vietnam, 1965—A Useful Analogy," National Security File, NSC History: Deployment of Major U.S. Forces to Vietnam, July 1965, box 43, Johnson Papers.

26. Bill Moyers, "One Thing We Learned," *Foreign Affairs* 46 (July 1968): 662.

27. Memorandum of conversation, Rusk and Harold Holt, April 28, 1965, "Asia and the Pacific: National Security Files, 1963–1969," Frederick, Md., 1988, reel 1, frame 152.

28. Quoted in William Conrad Gibbons, "The 1965 Decision to Send U.S. Ground Forces to Vietnam," paper given at the International Studies Association, April 16, 1987.

29. VanDeMark, *Into the Quagmire*, 211–17.

30. Rusk's statement is in Michael Charlton and Anthony Moncrief, *Many Reasons Why: The American Involvement in Vietnam*, 2d ed. (New York: Hill & Wang, 1989), 115.

31. Notes on National Security Council meeting, July 27, 1965, Meeting Notes File, box 1, Johnson Papers.

32. Quoted in Barbara Tuchman, *The March of Folly* (New York: Ballantine, 1984), 326.

33. Notes on National Security Council meeting, July 27, 1965, Meeting Notes File, box 1, Johnson Papers; Turner, *Dual War*, 149, 151.

34. Chester Cooper memorandum, September 10, 1965, National Security File, Country File, Vietnam, box 22, Johnson Papers; Melvin Small, *Johnson, Nixon and the Doves* (New Brunswick, N.J.: Rutgers University Press, 1988), 46–48.

35. See, for example, *Time*, May 20, 1966, 10.

36. *Time*, May 24, 1968, 17.

37. Clark Clifford, "Annals of Government: Serving the President—The Vietnam Years, I," *New Yorker*, May 6, 1991, 72–73.

38. *Time*, June 17, 1966, 9, January 13, 1967, 8, February 3, 1967, 12, August 25, 1967, 9.

39. Harold Johnson memorandum for the record, July 20, 1966, Harold Johnson Papers, U.S. Army Military History Institute.

40. Walt Rostow to LBJ, May 9, 1966, Walt Rostow memos, vol. 2, Johnson Papers; Moyers to Arthur Krock, September 15, 1966, Moyers Office Files, Johnson Library.

41. Entry, October 4, 1966, in David Lilienthal, *The Journals of David Lilienthal*, 7 vols. (New York: Harper & Row, 1964–1983), 6:296.

42. Notes on meeting, August 19, 1967, Meeting Notes File, box 1, Johnson Papers.

43. Tom Johnson notes on meeting, October 3, 1967, Tom Johnson's Notes on Meetings, box 1, Johnson Papers.

44. Entry, January 5, 1967, Lady Bird Johnson, *A White House Diary*, 469.

45. Andrew Goodpaster oral history interview, Johnson Library.

46. Henry Brandon, *Anatomy of Error* (Boston: Gambit, 1969), 164.

47. Stephen Peter Rosen, "Vietnam and the American Theory of Limited War," *International Security* 7 (Fall 1982): 96.

48. Robert A. Caro, *The Years of Lyndon Johnson: The Path to Power* (New York: Knopf, 1982), 494.

49. Rosen, "Vietnam," 96.

50. See especially Mark Clodfelter, *The Limits of Air Power: The American Bombing of North Vietnam* (New York: Macmillan, 1989), particularly chapters 3

and 4; and Earl H. Tilford, Jr., *Setup: What the Air Force Did in Vietnam and Why* (Maxwell Air Force Base, Ala.: Air University Press, 1991), particularly chapter 3.

51. Gen. Victor Krulak to Gen. Wallace Greene, July 19, 1965, box 1, Victor Krulak Papers, Marine Corps Historical Center, Washington, D.C.

52. Mark Perry, *Four Stars* (Boston: Houghton Mifflin, 1989), 156-58.

53. See, for example, Krulak to Robert Cushman, May 25, 1967, box 1, Krulak Papers.

54. See, for example, John McNaughton to McNamara, May 6, 1967, in Neil Sheehan et al., *The Pentagon Papers as Published by the New York Times* (New York: Bantam Books, 1971), 534; and McNamara draft presidential memorandum, May 19, 1967, National Security File, Country File, Vietnam, boxes 74-75, Johnson Papers.

55. Clifford, "The Vietnam Years, III," *New Yorker*, May 20, 1991, 59.

56. "I don't want loyalty. I want loyalty," Halberstam reports him saying. "I want him to kiss my ass in Macy's window at high noon and tell me it smells like roses." Halberstam, *The Best and the Brightest* (New York: Random House, 1972), 434. See also Caro, *Means of Ascent*, 111.

57. George Ball oral history interview, Johnson Library.

58. Dean Rusk as told to Richard Rusk, edited by Daniel Papp, *As I Saw It* (New York: Norton, 1990), 435, 474.

59. Paul Miles interview with Westmoreland, January 7, 1971, Paul Miles Papers, U.S. Army Military History Institute.

60. Westmoreland historical briefing, July 12, 1967, William C. Westmoreland Papers, U.S. Army Military History Institute.

61. Wheeler to Westmoreland, June 2, 1966, Wheeler to Westmoreland and Admiral U.S. Grant Sharp, February 13, 1967, and Wheeler to Sharp and Westmoreland, March 6, 1967, Backchannel Messages, Westmoreland/CBS Litigation File, boxes 15, 16, 17, U.S. Federal Records Center, Suitland, Md.

62. *Public Papers of the Presidents of the United States: Lyndon Baines Johnson, 1967* (Washington, D.C.: GPO, 1968), 2:816-17.

63. Katzenbach to Johnson, November 16, 1967, quoted in Larry Berman, *Lyndon Johnson's War* (New York: Oxford University Press, 1989), 106-7.

64. George C. Herring, *America's Longest War: The United States and Vietnam, 1950-1975*, 2d ed. (New York: Knopf, 1986), 183-84.

65. McPherson to LBJ, October 27, 1967, Harry McPherson Office Files, box 53, Johnson Library.

66. Bundy to LBJ, November 10, 1967, Diary Backup, box 81, Johnson Papers.

67. Handwritten notes on McNamara memorandum to Johnson, November 1, 1967, National Security File, Country File, Vietnam, box 75, Johnson Papers.

68. Johnson memorandum for the record, December 18, 1967, in Lyndon B. Johnson, *The Vantage Point* (New York: Holt, Rinehart and Winston, 1971), 800-801.

69. Herring, *America's Longest War*, 182-83.

70. Ibid.

71. *Time*, November 17, 1967, 23.

72. *Public Papers: Johnson, 1967*, 2:1045-55.

73. *Time*, November 24, 1967, 7.

74. For the upswing in popular support of the president and the war, see Fred Panzer to Jim Jones, December 28, 1967, Confidential File, box 73, Johnson Papers.

75. Johnson, *Vantage Point*, 392–93.

76. Clifford, "Vietnam Years, II," *New Yorker*, May 13, 1991, 62–66.

77. Herring, *America's Longest War*, 196.

78. Ibid.

79. Ibid.

80. Wheeler to Westmoreland, April 12, 1968, Backchannel Messages, Westmoreland/CBS Litigation File, box 20.

81. Wheeler to Westmoreland, March 8, 1968, Backchannel Messages, Westmoreland/CBS Litigation File, box 20; Gen. Dwight Beach to Sharp, April 12, 1968, box 32, Westmoreland Papers.

82. Wheeler to Westmoreland, April 12, 1968, Backchannel Messages, Westmoreland/CBS Litigation File, box 20; Westmoreland to Wheeler, April 12, 1968, box 32, Westmoreland Papers.

83. Wheeler to Westmoreland, May 28, 1968, Backchannel Messages, Westmoreland/CBS Litigation File, box 20; Harriman to Rusk, May 11, 1968, box 553, W. Averell Harriman Papers, Manuscript Division, Library of Congress.

84. Bunker memorandum, "Viet-Nam Negotiations: Dangers and Opportunities," April 8, 1968, box 521, Harriman Papers.

85. Clifford, "Vietnam Years, III," 63–64.

86. Ibid., II, 45; Rusk, *As I Saw It*, 417.

87. Harriman memorandum, "General Review of the Last Six Months," December 14, 1968, box 521, Harriman Papers.

88. Clifford, "Vietnam Years, II," 45.

89. LBJ note, November 21, 1968, National Security File, Rostow Files, Vietnam, July–December 1968, box 6, Johnson Papers.

90. *Time*, May 3, 1968, 14, June 28, 1968, 12–13.

91. William Bundy oral history interview, Johnson Library.

92. Clifford, "Vietnam Years, III," 73–75.

93. Ibid., 59.

94. Quoted in Berman, *Lyndon Johnson's War*, i.

6

Lyndon Johnson
and the Vietnamese

Sandra C. Taylor

Lyndon Baines Johnson came to the presidency as the result of the assassination of John F. Kennedy, and the conflict he inherited in Southeast Asia was not of his choosing. Yet in deciding to keep the majority of the Kennedy team intact, he hitched himself to a policy and a war that engulfed his administration and destroyed his plans for domestic reform—the Great Society. The reasons for Johnson's failure are complex, but one factor that sheds light on his conduct of the war as well as on his personality and presidency is the way he viewed the Vietnamese as a people.

The Vietnamese were difficult for Americans, including their presidents, to understand. Several authors have even advanced the notion that the roots of the U.S. war in Vietnam were cultural misunderstanding and conflict produced by American ethnocentrism, racism, and technological arrogance.[1] That the enemy and the ally in Vietnam were the same people complicated the matter but did not change its essence. Cross-cultural blindness can be blamed for American and Vietnamese views of each other and American conceptions of both the South and North Vietnamese. In an analysis of U.S. relations with South Vietnam, George Herring concluded: "From the outset, neither nation really understood the other, and the interaction between them hindered the advance of goals that, at least for much of the war, they shared."[2] As the president who dramatically escalated U.S. involvement in Vietnam to hundreds of thousands of troops and thousands of bombing sorties, Johnson faced the task of articulating U.S. purposes to the Vietnamese, his fellow Americans, and himself.

What Johnson really thought of the Vietnamese had profound consequences for the course of the war. It shaped decisions on how to conduct military actions, how much to "punish" the enemy, and how to estimate the likely consequences of particular strategies. Americans have a well-known inability to distinguish foreign cultures from their own, and they tend to be blind to the differences of other peoples. This solipsistic view, as Loren Baritz has shown, has led Americans to assume that all peoples want to be like them and would be if they could.[3] Given this attitude, a logical question is whether a president as quintessentially American as Johnson could understand the Vietnamese, distinguish what drew some of them to communism, and comprehend why those opposing it fought—or did not fight—as they did. Frances FitzGerald has written that in entering Vietnam the United States "was entering a world qualitatively different from its own. . . . To find the common ground that existed between them, both Americans and Vietnamese would have to re-create the whole world of the other, the whole intellectual landscape."[4]

What was Lyndon Johnson's conception of the Vietnamese people and their leaders? Did he ever move beyond stereotypes and racial prejudices to perceive them as individual human beings who were culturally distinct but not inferior? Johnson's many critics at the time found him guilty of "imperialism, landlordism and racism . . . compound[ing] miscomprehension with bravado."[5] Is there evidence in his words that Johnson was guilty of such a charge?

Johnson was not a simple man. In his memoirs, he presents the world as a place of good versus evil, but this apologia was written after the fact with an eye to the long view of history. Those around him knew better. George Reedy, his press secretary, has expressed doubt about "whether the president himself knew why he was behaving the way he did" with respect to Vietnam.[6] The vast documentary collection in the Lyndon Baines Johnson Library provides a wealth of information to which the president had access, but it is difficult to determine which of the numerous memos now open to the public Johnson read or to which he responded. He wrote few memos himself and only occasionally made notations on those prepared for him by others; many of the diaries and papers of those closest to him are open only in part or are still closed.[7] Johnson is an easy man to caricature, for he was emotional, at times crude, given to wild outbursts of calculated rage, and very quick with his tongue.[8] Like the South Vietnamese leaders and officials who dealt with the Americans, he could be his own worst enemy, but understanding the man beneath the rhetoric is a complicated task.

Johnson had no more understanding of the Vietnamese, North or South, than he did of the man in the moon. In part this was the result of his provincialism, a trait he shared with most Americans. It was also the product of ignorance; Johnson prided himself on having read no more than six books since he graduated from college in San Marcos, Texas.[9] A latent racism entered into the mix as well. In Vietnam both the allies and the enemies were Asian, culturally unlike Americans in almost every way. The temptation to dismiss the South Vietnamese as insignificant "others" haunted the U.S. effort throughout the war, it inclined the president to discount their abilities and their power, and it led to a great temptation to patronize. At times Johnson did just that, manifesting an unconscious racism in his attitudes and actions toward both allies and enemies. He treated the latter with a cruelty that would have been unlikely had they been white, while betraying a scarcely concealed contempt for his South Vietnamese allies.

Johnson's only prior experience with Australasia had been during the Second World War. The first U.S. congressman to enlist, he joined the navy the day after Pearl Harbor. His tenure was abruptly terminated when President Franklin D. Roosevelt recalled all senators and congressmen to their duties on Capitol Hill. But his little adventure in what he called the "Far Pacific" netted him a Silver Star for participation in an overseas tour in Australia. Although details of the mission were "ambiguous," he wore that battle ribbon for the rest of his life.[10] Whatever his assignment actually was, it helped convince him of the dangers of appeasement and the need to check aggression. He probably learned nothing of Asia, its cultural heritage, or the burdens of colonialism left behind by the British, Dutch, and French. Johnson experienced far less of war itself than his immediate White House predecessors, which may have made it easier for him to engage in it. Once in, however, he found that he "had a bear by the tail and could not let go."[11]

Johnson's picture of communism emerged from the early 1950s and the first days of the Cold War. Global and monolithic, all communist movements were directed from the Kremlin; they were atheistic, evil, and a menace to the security and very existence of the United States. By the late 1950s the communists had begun a new strategy, fighting so-called wars of national liberation, of which the war in Vietnam was a major test case. In Johnson's view, this policy cloaked naked expansionism in the guise of a benevolent nationalism, especially in the Third World. The war in Vietnam might appear to the naive as an indigenous insurrection, but it was part of a worldwide conspiracy. Such upheavals had to be recognized for what they were and checked whenever they appeared.[12] Communists must be taught that, in his words, "aggression should not, must not, succeed."[13] The line had been drawn in Vietnam, and it was the United States' duty to assist these people so they would be "free to settle their own future."[14] The United

States just needed to "get the boys in Vietnam to do their own fighting with our advice and with our equipment."[15] The United States would take "all necessary measures in support of freedom and in defense of peace in southeast Asia."[16] Americans must be, as Lyndon Johnson said in 1965, the "guardians at the gate."[17]

Frenzied anticommunism was one sentiment to which many Americans subscribed in the 1950s and 1960s, but its Asian manifestations brought out a peculiar racism as well. John Dower has demonstrated how easy it was for Americans fighting Japanese in the Pacific during the Second World War to become enmeshed in what was truly a race war; its stereotypes and racial epithets were, like the term "gook" itself, easily revived for another Asian conflict.[18] Personal histories, memoirs, novels thinly disguised as fiction, and films demonstrate that many soldiers applied derogatory racial terms such as gooks, dinks, slopes, or zipperheads to all Vietnamese, whether enemy or ally; they all looked alike, especially when dead, which of course made them all Vietcong.

Lyndon Johnson's experience with the Vietnamese was far more limited. He met the South Vietnamese leaders only a few times, and they were the governing elite, not peasants in the jungle. But their intransigence may have led him to draw conclusions about their character. He may not have been able to pronounce "Veet-nam" correctly, and he knew little of its history before "Dinbin-foo," but he did not slur the South's leaders in public. He just treated them as if they were Americans. Johnson was certainly given to colorful phrases and "bizarre personal conduct," as many have noted, but even the sharply critical historian Gabriel Kolko has concluded that "the case that his boorish manners were crucial to policy has yet to be made."[19] It may be even harder to determine whether his pithy phrases contained a latent racism that influenced his war policies.

Johnson had no firsthand knowledge of Vietnam prior to assuming the vice-presidency in 1961, but as vice-president he made one trip to Saigon for President John F. Kennedy. Although Johnson's stay was extremely brief, it created certain impressions in his mind about the South Vietnamese leader Ngo Dinh Diem, whom he met, and the Vietnamese people as well. With characteristic rhetorical exaggeration, the vice-president praised Diem, calling him the "Winston Churchill of Asia," and he was extravagant in his promises of aid to the South Vietnamese leader in his fight against communism.[20] Johnson's Eurocentric depiction of the so-called nation builder of Southeast Asia as a Western-style democrat clearly betrayed his ignorance of Vietnam, but it was a view widely shared in the American press as well. For example, *Life* magazine labeled Diem a man of "deep religious heart" who had "halted the red tide of Communism in Asia."[21] This was a far cry from the derogatory epithets that American soldiers would apply to the Vietnamese people five years later, and certainly miles away from the role the United States would play in Diem's eventual fall from power.

Johnson had no direct interaction with the North Vietnamese or the Vietcong. He viewed them entirely through an ideological lens as misguided dupes of international communism and a danger to all that the "free world" stood for. To Johnson, their leader Ho Chi Minh was just another tinhorn dictator who was "willing to use force to realize his dreams: Communist control over all of Vietnam as well as Laos and Cambodia."[22] According to Johnson's public words, race and ethnicity had nothing to do with America's image of its allies and enemies in Vietnam; ideology was everything. At a time when anticommunism was a national obsession and the civil rights movement could not be ignored, it was inevitable that Johnson would publicly depict the conflict and the protagonists in such terms.

When Vice-President Johnson made his first visit to Saigon on May 11, 1961, the United States had already committed itself to defend South Vietnam. Over 3,200 military advisers and billions of dollars in aid had been advanced; yet victory was nowhere in sight. Johnson's trip was, in fact, part of a "series of high level conferences" to devise more effective responses to the communist challenge. The vice-president's journey, according to the *Pentagon Papers*, was designed to "reinforce the U.S. commitment to RVN [Republic of Vietnam] and to improve the image of President Ngo Dinh Diem's government." The ebullient Johnson "swept into Saigon . . . acting as if he were endorsing county sheriffs in a Texas election campaign," in Stanley Karnow's words, and his purpose was indeed to endorse Diem, not to judge him.[23] After exchanging greetings and gifts, Diem and Johnson worked on a message from President Kennedy. A joint communique was issued the next day that stipulated increased U.S. aid, referred vaguely to greater Vietnamese attention to pacification and civic action, and promised an enlargement of the South Vietnamese armed forces.[24]

The two men also sized each other up. Johnson saw Diem as a "hard bargainer and a proud man," if not the Winston Churchill of Asia.[25] In such a brief visit, the vice-president could see and understand little of Saigon, let alone the rest of the country, and his image of the capital city was centuries away from the traditional world in which most of the population lived. Diem was also atypical. He spoke English and French, and his devout Catholicism set him apart from his primarily Buddhist countrymen. To him

Americans were "impatient, naive, and childlike, to be humored but never to be heeded."²⁶ Johnson thought Diem had been duly elected to office. The visiting American knew little of Diem's brother Nhu, the tactics of Nhu's police against political opposition, or of Nhu's wife—the infamous Madame. Johnson likely perceived Saigon as comparable to any southern U.S. city. It was sticky, more crowded, and a bit tackier, but not substantially different in culture from San Marcos, Texas. As Hubert Humphrey once remarked in reference to rivers in Indochina and Texas, Johnson thought that "the Mekong and the Pedernales were not that far apart."²⁷

On this 1961 trip, Johnson also traveled to several other Asian countries, among them South Korea. There he was impressed with the crowds that came to cheer him. He recalled "little brown people . . . packed as close as you could pack sardines."²⁸ That was his view of the Asians on America's side in the global struggle: little brown (or yellow) folk, packed into their overcrowded nations as tight as sardines, yearning for the message of freedom the benevolent Americans were bringing them. It was not unlike the Great White Father dispensing justice and mercy to the Indians on the American frontier.

When Johnson briefed Kennedy on the trip, he stressed the need for American leadership in Southeast Asia. Advisers, not combat troops, were preferable, because of Vietnam's colonial heritage. He later recalled: "We can't pick other people's governments. We have enough trouble picking our own."²⁹ He rapidly lost that insight, however, as the communist threat intensified. The question was, he noted, "whether we are to attempt to meet the challenge of Communist expansion now in Southeast Asia by a major effort . . . or throw in the towel." He clearly favored the former, even at the expense of Asian sensitivities about colonialism and their desire to create their own type of government.³⁰

Johnson appeared to like Diem, whatever the Vietnamese leader's flaws, but he later realized that Diem's government would need top-level administrative reform to succeed. Reflecting on this period in his memoirs, he concluded that the United States should have pushed harder for change, but it did not and, as a result, "paid a heavy price for that failure later."³¹ He assumed that even if Washington could not directly select other people's governments, it was entitled to reform South Vietnam's. He probably did not talk to or even see a Buddhist during his whirlwind tour, yet he doubted that their opposition to Diem warranted concern, despite the monks' self-immolations in protest of government repression. Johnson's conception of freedom for South Vietnam did not include the right to petition the government for redress of grievances or to take to the streets to protest its authoritarian behavior—but of course he also disapproved of the latter in the United States. The Kennedy administration's "hasty and ill-advised message [warning Diem to reform or risk loss of U.S. aid] was a green light to those who wanted Diem's downfall," Johnson believed, and this American move was a "serious blunder" that led to Diem's overthrow.[32]

Succeeding to the presidency in November 1963, Johnson stuck with the South Vietnamese through the chaos that followed Diem's assassination. When the government headed by Nguyen Khanh asked for more aid, Johnson told Congress that he shared with Ambassador Henry Cabot Lodge "the conviction that this new government can mount a successful campaign against the Communists," and he reiterated his pledge to "stand with the free people of Vietnam."[33] But Khanh was only one of seven prime ministers to rotate in and out of that office in the chaotic year that followed Diem's assassination, and Johnson privately lost patience with the inability of our "democratic" allies to resolve the problems of self-government peacefully. He quietly put out the word that there were to be "no more coups," recalled Barry Zorthian, who served as director of the United States Information Service in Saigon at the time.[34] In his memoirs, Johnson put his concerns more diplomatically: South Vietnam's leaders had a "strong impulse toward political suicide"; they wanted to run their own lives but had great difficulty cooperating to govern themselves. In moments of discouragement, Johnson felt that the South Vietnamese leaders were "their own worst enemies," yet he favored giving them "understanding and patience, not constant vilification."[35] In these words Johnson displayed patience born of a hindsight that he did not have at the time, but he also showed a misunderstanding of both Saigon politics and traditional Asian ideas about government. "American boys," he said, should not "do the fighting that Asian boys should do for themselves," but they "would find us at their side if they wanted and needed us." Johnson would not "pull up stakes and run."[36] His benevolent paternalism was patronizing if not racist.

One cannot fault the president too much for the narrowness of such an approach, since those who advised him also had limited knowledge of the Vietnamese. Civil and military officials such as Dean Rusk, McGeorge Bundy, Maxwell Taylor, Walt W. Rostow, and William Westmoreland drew upon European and American imagery, and their historical analogies were drawn from Munich and the Second World War, as John Stoessinger has noted. They did not understand the facts that they confronted, and they "simply superimposed their own misperceptions on Asian realities."[37]

Even the Americans working in Saigon had difficulty understanding their allies. When Zorthian was asked who had advised him on "Vietnamese psychology" and ways to appeal to them, he recalled receiving only "some conventional wisdom anyone would get when they got in the field about the Confucian mind and oriental thinking." He gathered information from South Vietnamese in his employ, which was sometimes very useful, but he recognized that each person he spoke to represented a particular viewpoint: "a northerner living in the city [Saigon], a southerner living in the city. [There was] very little communication with the village, with the hamlet dweller, with the peasant."[38] Zorthian's position might have given him the opportunity to assess the Vietnamese from their own soil, but he was tied to Saigon and had little insight into the world of the peasant. Those military and civilian individuals who did possess special insights into the nature of the Vietnamese people did not have the opportunity to brief the president directly. Moreover, the United States had a very small number of Vietnam specialists when the war broke out, and they were primarily people whose opposition to the conflict cut them off from the president.

That the enemy and the ally in Vietnam were the same people further obscured matters for the president, as it did for the troops. The Vietnamese had a sense of racial identity that had survived a thousand years of Chinese domination as well as fifty years of French colonialism, when even the use of the name "Vietnam" was prohibited. To love the South while hating the North was complicated by their shared appearance, language, culture, and tradition and further confused by the fact that many southerners supported the Vietcong. The only clearly defined point of differentiation was ideology, and that, as U.S. military practices made abundantly clear, was very hard to determine when the supposed "enemy" could be a bunch of peasants in black pajamas and straw hats working in their rice paddies. Soldiers often simplified it by considering any dead Vietnamese a communist. At times Lyndon Johnson, like his secretary of state, Dean Rusk, also simplified the problem by linking the communist enemy with their northern neighbors, the Chinese. When the president escalated the war by landing marines at Danang in 1965, he informed the public that "the confused nature of this conflict cannot mask the fact that it is the new face of an old enemy. Over this war—and all Asia—is another reality: the deepening shadow of Communist China." That this "old demon," as James William Gibson termed it, should be perceived as the puppet master pulling the strings of a docile Ho Chi Minh showed a misunderstanding of both the nature of Vietnamese communism and the very real differences separating the Vietnamese and

Chinese peoples, who had been enemies for hundreds of years longer than they had been comrades.[39]

Johnson's first encounters with Ho Chi Minh gave little indication that he would be able to move beyond stereotypes to understand the man behind Vietnam's revolution. Ho and his advisers clearly hoped that the anarchy in Saigon would provide the opportunity to reunite their divided homeland. Johnson's advisers sought to dispel this illusion by informing Hanoi through Canada that the war was now a test case of American resolve, and if they did not cease aggression the United States would bomb.[40] Johnson thought that the North Vietnamese simply did not understand America's determination, but he completely misgauged Hanoi's resolve. He mused that "perhaps a sudden and effective air strike would convince the leaders in Hanoi that we were serious."[41] If Ho knew what force the United States could bring to bear, and if he were assured that the United States did not intend to overthrow his regime or to remain permanently in the South, perhaps then he could be persuaded to "keep . . . [his] men inside their own territory and stop sending military supplies to the South."[42] But Hanoi was unwilling to stop while the United States escalated, and its spokesmen called Johnson's offer "trickery."[43] An exchange of letters illuminated the gulf that separated the two leaders. Johnson would talk if Ho would stop infiltrating men into the South, but Ho demanded that the United States first cease its aggression against Vietnam, including the bombing. To Ho, Americans had intervened and brought war and destruction to his land; what had the Vietnamese people done to warrant that? The gulf was miles deep.[44]

Lyndon Johnson created a mental image of Vietnam in order to convince himself that the North and South Vietnamese could be persuaded to do what he wanted. Surprisingly, for one who held such rigid views of communism, he thought that the two political systems were "different but negotiable." War was after all just politics in a different form, and he kept seeking the "rules of the game," as he had understood them from his days in the Senate, where compromise and agreement were possible. He could not conceive of a culture in which that would not work. Given sufficient inducement or relentless punishment, Ho Chi Minh would be reasonable and settle the war once he realized that victory and reunification under communism were impossible for such a small, ill-equipped nation facing the mighty American war machine. This conceptualization contrasted sharply with Johnson's other beliefs about Ho, which were shaped by his stereotypical notions of the communist world. Ho was a man who could sit in his "quiet and peaceful capital giving orders that resulted in the killing of Americans and South Vietnamese every day." Oddly enough, Johnson did not see himself as doing the same thing. Ho mistakenly viewed the United States as a "paper tiger," yet Johnson thought that such a man should either be amenable to reason or pummeled until he said "ouch."[45] Ho, in contrast, realized that "the Americans are much stronger than the French, though they know us less well."[46] His strategy was to weaken that strength as the tiger does on the back of the elephant, and to get at Johnson by draining the endurance of the American people.

Johnson, grasping for some kind of inducement for peace, devised a $1 billion project for the social and economic betterment of Indochina through the development of the Mekong River Valley. This vision first appeared in a presidential speech at Johns Hopkins University on April 7, 1965. Despite Hanoi's aggression and the United States' determination to stop it, after the war "the task . . . [would be] nothing less than to enrich the hopes and the existence of more than a hundred million people."[47] Aide Hugh Sidey recalled this announcement as Johnson's happiest moment: "He dispatched agriculture and economic experts to South Vietnam with far more joy than he did more troops." The Mekong development plan made him "more ecstatic" than anything else he ever desired for the country.[48] In another speech in 1966, Johnson incorporated development into a wider vision: "I want to leave the footprints of America in Vietnam. I want them to say when the Americans come, this is what they leave—schools, not long cigars. We're going to turn the Mekong into a Tennessee Valley."[49] But Ho would not be bribed, and his determination and willingness to suffer were inconceivable to Johnson. The president told Senator George McGovern (D-S.Dak.), "I'm going up old Ho Chi Minh's leg an inch at a time"; but he had no idea that the man was ten feet tall.[50]

The men around him recognized the president's problem. Bill Moyers of the White House staff said that Johnson could not understand why Ho Chi Minh would not jump at a $1 billion project; he knew American labor leader George Meany would have. Robert Komer of the CIA said that Johnson had no real grasp of foreign cultures: "He was a people man, and he thought people everywhere were the same. He saw the Vietnamese farmer as being like the Texas farmer or the Oklahoma farmer. 'We're going to provide them with rural electricity. We're going to provide them with roads and water, and we're going to improve the rice crop.'"[51] To aide Jack Valenti, Johnson exclaimed: "Damn it, we need to exhibit more compassion for these Vietnamese plain people."[52] He could not understand the allure of communism or the effect of the awesome destructiveness of U.S. warfare on the hearts and minds of the Vietnamese people. The terror of a B-52 bombing run was far more real to them than promises of future development.

Generals Nguyen Cao Ky and Nguyen Van Thieu brought a measure of stability to Saigon in 1965, but, according to Assistant Secretary of State William Bundy, Johnson's advisers looked upon the military directorate as "the bottom of the barrel."[53] Soon, however, Johnson was praising the generals' leadership. He met them in Honolulu in February 1966 and perceived them as "brave and determined young men." He tried in his patronizing way to give Ky a compliment: "Boy, you speak just like an American."[54] These leaders of the new generation in South Vietnam "know and we know that this revolutionary transformation cannot wait until the guns grow silent and until the terrorism stops," Johnson declared. But at the same time he emphasized that he wanted more than "phrases, high-sounding words." He demanded "coonskins on the wall."[55]

At a Guam conference with South Vietnamese leaders in March 1967, Johnson praised the constitution that Thieu had drafted and Saigon's plans to hold an election. That magic word, "election," captivated him. He was very impressed when Ky decided to be Thieu's running mate rather than to challenge him for the presidency. This "act of statesmanship" went unrecognized at the time, wrote Johnson later, but it was one that Ky knew would "benefit his country." The election was, Johnson added, hard fought but clean.[56]

By 1967 the election hardly mattered, however, because it was Lyndon Johnson's war. The South Vietnamese were barely holding up their end of it. Johnson did not publicly subscribe to the common view that their army was "inept, cowardly, and lazy." In his memoirs he stated that "some . . . units were excellent, some were bad; but most were good—and getting better."[57] When the South Vietnamese delegation at Guam departed, they were apparently convinced, however, that Johnson "wanted concrete results and he wanted them soon."[58]

Saigon's ambassador to the United States, Bui Diem, who was also at the Guam meeting, provided another insight into Johnson's understanding of the South Vietnamese. It seemed that Johnson had finally begun to recognize the human dimension of the war. The fact that the president's staff had thoroughly researched the backgrounds of the Vietnamese delegation impressed Diem, who concluded that the president was "someone who instinctively saw problems in human terms."[59] Diem was invited to return from Guam to Washington on Air Force One. He was flattered, but afterward he concluded that Johnson's Vietnam policy "did not accord its allies their requisite dignity as human beings. . . . Vietnam was regarded primarily as a geopolitical abstraction, a factor in the play of American global interests."[60] Diem's postwar reflections were more on the mark than were Johnson's.

President Johnson visited Vietnam on October 24, 1966, but the stop was squeezed out of a trip to Manila and was solely to visit and cheer on the American troops at Cam Ranh Bay. What most impressed him on this journey to Asia (where he also visited Thailand, Malaysia, and South Korea) was "the vision of a new Asia," one in which U.S. aid would play a big part.[61] Noticeably lacking was any comprehension of what kind of people would lead this new world. Bui Diem described how the Vietnam flyby appeared to Thieu, who learned of the president's intentions informally from Philip Habib, the minister-counselor in the U.S. embassy in Saigon. "Johnson's visit to Cam Ranh was like a slap in the face," Diem recounted. "The president of the United States was taking the time to tour six Asian capitals, and yet he would not visit Saigon, the capital of an allied country where more than 300,000 of his countrymen were fighting." Johnson had been advised to avoid the South Vietnamese capital for security reasons, and similar reasons apparently ruled out informing the Vietnamese leaders of his visit. "Still, the open lack of confidence in our ability to protect him was humiliating," Diem remarked bitterly, and it was part of the "price we would pay for our overdependence on the United States."[62]

Johnson visited Vietnam again in December 1967 after attending the funeral of Prime Minister Harold Holt of Australia. It was another whirlwind tour; he spoke briefly with Thieu in Canberra and then, on his way home via Rome, stopped in Cam Ranh Bay to greet the troops. Again he sidestepped Saigon and a formal visit to the government that the United States was doing so much to support. Apparently no one had told him of Asian notions of "face."[63]

Not only did Johnson misunderstand the North and South Vietnamese, he misunderstood the nature and effects of the war. Clark Clifford, who became secretary of defense in 1968, realized that Johnson wanted to believe those U.S. officials in Saigon who told him that the war was not excessively destructive and that it was being won. Johnson disregarded information to the contrary. As FitzGerald concluded, the president had "very little latitude to alter his public stance and little interest in discovering the gloomy truths." Those truths involved the extent of the corruption of the Saigon regime and its minions. Bureaucratic inertia and the unwillingness to be a messenger of bad tidings militated against sending such information up the line.[64] Johnson thought that his tactics were humane; he refused to destroy part of the system of dikes in the Red River delta to avoid the "heavy civilian casualties" that would result, and he would not widen the war.[65]

In part because of his own desire to see the war contained, the size, scope, and timing of Hanoi's Tet Offensive early in 1968 shocked Johnson. He could not believe that the communists would "so profane their own people's sacred holiday" by launching the attack then.[66] It was as if, during the American Civil War, Sherman had marched on Georgia on Christmas Day. This action, and the civilian massacres at Hue following the Tet attacks, no doubt helped dehumanize the enemy in Johnson's eyes, but he did not see U.S. actions in the same light. He pronounced himself willing to give the South Vietnamese troops the "best equipment we can," but he worried that those "Asian boys" were just letting "American boys" do the fighting for them.[67] This inequity troubled him as his own two sons-in-law were preparing to go to Vietnam. When Thieu announced that he would raise 100,000 to 125,000 more fighting men over the next six months, Johnson was gratified, and Thieu soon raised this number to 135,000. South Vietnam was lowering the draft age to eighteen, civilians were forming self-defense groups, and Thieu urged people to do even more. Johnson was elated, for this demonstrated to him that the South Vietnamese had not only stood up to the communists at Tet, but had finally started to defend themselves. They were at last beginning "to carry a heavier share of the burden of fighting for their country," something that had troubled Johnson throughout the conflict.[68] It was their Alamo; why would they not do more to defend it?

On March 31, 1968, shortly after the Tet Offensive, Lyndon Baines Johnson announced that he would not run for reelection, he would limit the bombing, and he would begin negotiations for peace. His term still had almost a year to go, during which time Vietnamization began to replace Americanization of the war, but the long-hoped-for negotiations got nowhere. The March speech ended Johnson's obsession, however. Finally, he was letting it become South Vietnam's war again, whatever Saigon's leaders could do with it.

Lyndon Johnson was a southerner raised in a racist society, in which, for example, the word "nigger" could be part of his vocabulary. He sold property with a racial covenant against Negroes in 1948, supported states' rights in 1957, yet endorsed equal opportunity in 1964.[69] He made the long journey from racism against blacks to sponsorship of the Civil Rights Bill of 1964, and he clearly recognized the evils of discrimination in American society. The Vietnamese were not blacks, but they were foreign—a people of color whose culture was totally outside the president's purview. Johnson was ethnocentric, woefully ignorant of the outside world, and had no experience at all with traditional peasant societies. He could talk in the abstract about the effects of colonialism on people, but he had little understanding of what that really meant in Vietnam. He patronized South Vietnam's leaders, glossed over their real defects, and showed what he really thought of their abilities by taking over their war. He imposed an American solution on a government that would have had difficulty standing alone in the best of circumstances. He did not call the Vietnamese gooks and slopes to their faces, but one can only speculate that he shared much of the mind-set of those who did.

Notes

1. Jeffrey P. Kimball, ed., *To Reason Why: The Debate about the Causes of U.S. Involvement in the Vietnam War* (Philadelphia: Temple University Press, 1990), 21–22.

2. George C. Herring, " 'Peoples Quite Apart': Americans, South Vietnamese, and the War in Vietnam," *Diplomatic History* 14 (Winter 1990): 21–22.

3. Loren Baritz, *Backfire: A History of How American Culture Led Us into Vietnam and Made Us Fight the Way We Did* (New York: Morrow, 1985), 30–32.

4. Frances FitzGerald, *Fire in the Lake: The Vietnamese and the Americans in Vietnam* (New York: Vintage, 1972), 8–9.

5. Eric Goldman, *The Tragedy of Lyndon Johnson* (New York: Knopf, 1969), 442.

6. George Reedy interview by Melvin Small, Milwaukee, January 25, 1984, quoted in Melvin Small, *Johnson, Nixon and the Doves* (New Brunswick, N.J.: Rutgers University Press, 1988), 2. See also Lyndon Baines Johnson, *The Vantage Point: Perspectives on the Presidency, 1963–1969* (New York: Holt, Rinehart and Winston, 1971).

7. David C. Humphrey, "Searching for LBJ at the Johnson Library," *Society for Historians of American Foreign Relations Newsletter* 20 (June 1989): 1–18; John P. Burke and Fred I. Greenstein, *How Presidents Test Reality: Decisions on Vietnam, 1954 and 1965* (New York: Russell Sage Foundation, 1989), 238–39.

8. George Reedy, *Lyndon B. Johnson: A Memoir* (New York and Kansas City: Andrews and McMeel, 1982), especially chapters 6 and 15.

9. John G. Stoessinger, *Crusaders and Pragmatists: Movers of Modern American Foreign Policy* (New York: Norton, 1979), 197.

10. Doris Kearns, *Lyndon Johnson and the American Dream* (New York: Signet, 1976), 99.

11. Reedy, *Johnson*, 149. Reedy said that Johnson was fond of this old frontier story, which fit neatly with the dilemma in which he found himself in Vietnam.

12. Address to the Detroit Economic Club, "Present Objectives and Future Possibilities in Southeast Asia," April 19, 1965, in House Committee on Armed Ser-

vices, *United States-Vietnam Relations, 1945-1967: Study Prepared by the Department of Defense* (Washington, D.C.: GPO, 1971), 7:D-33 (hereafter cited as *U.S.-Vietnam Relations*).

13. Johnson, *Vantage Point*, 472.

14. Address by Dean Rusk before the American Society of International Law, April 23, 1965, "The Control of Force in International Relations," citing President Lyndon Johnson, *U.S.-Vietnam Relations*, 7:D-37.

15. Johnson speech in Manchester, N.H., September 28, 1964, in *Quotations from Chairman LBJ* (New York: Simon & Schuster, 1968), 66.

16. Radio and television report to the American people following renewed aggression in the Gulf of Tonkin, August 4, 1964, *Public Papers of the Presidents of the United States: Lyndon B. Johnson, 1963-1964* (Washington, D.C.: GPO, 1965), 927-28.

17. Johnson, *Vantage Point*, 422. He used the phrase in a televised news conference July 28, 1965, *Public Papers: Johnson, 1965* (Washington, D.C.: GPO, 1966), 794.

18. John Dower, *War without Mercy: Race and Power in the Pacific War* (New York: Pantheon, 1986), 10-13, 152.

19. Gabriel Kolko, *Anatomy of a War: Vietnam, the United States, and the Modern Historical Experience* (New York: Pantheon, 1985), 168.

20. Reedy, *Johnson*, 147.

21. Quoted in FitzGerald, *Fire in the Lake*, 96.

22. Johnson, *Vantage Point*, 52-53.

23. Stanley Karnow, *Vietnam: A History* (New York: Viking Press, 1983), 250. Reedy, *Johnson*, 24-25, suggests that Johnson got along well on a person-to-person basis with poor people in developing nations (better than with their leaders), but the examples offered are more illustrations of Johnson's populist instincts and well-practiced political style than of any particular cultural understanding.

24. "The Strategic Hamlet Program, 1961-1963: An Appraisal," *U.S.-Vietnam Relations*, 3:4-5.

25. Johnson, *Vantage Point*, 54.

26. Arthur Schlesinger, *The Bitter Heritage* (Boston: Houghton Mifflin, 1967), 20.

27. Baritz, *Backfire*, 33.

28. Merle Miller, *Lyndon: An Oral Biography* (New York: G. P. Putnam's Sons, 1980), 456.

29. Speech in Louisville, Ky., October 9, 1964, in *Quotations from Chairman LBJ*, 70. See also paper prepared by Johnson, undated, and report by Johnson, undated, Department of State, *Foreign Relations of the United States, 1961-1963*, vol. 1, *Vietnam 1961* (Washington, D.C.: GPO, 1988), 149-57. Johnson told Henry Cabot Lodge that "we had spent too much time and energy trying to shape other countries in our own image," and they knew better than we what sort of nations they wanted. We should just help them establish peace and order. Johnson, *Vantage Point*, 44-45.

30. Johnson, *Vantage Point*, 53-54. See also *U.S.-Vietnam Relations*, vol. 2, part B, 53-57.

31. Johnson, *Vantage Point*, 57.

32. Ibid., 60–61.

33. "Special Message to the Congress Transmitting Request for Additional Funds for Viet-Nam," May 18, 1964, in *Public Papers: Johnson, 1963–64*, 692–93.

34. Barry Zorthian interview by Ted Gittinger, May 26, 1982, Oral History Collection, 3:33, Lyndon Baines Johnson Library, Austin, Tex. (hereafter cited as LBJ Oral History Collection).

35. Johnson, *Vantage Point*, 64–65.

36. Ibid., 68.

37. Stoessinger, *Crusaders and Pragmatists*, 197.

38. Zorthian interview, 3:12.

39. James William Gibson, *The Perfect War: Technowar in Vietnam* (Boston and New York: Atlantic Monthly Press, 1986), 94. Johnson's words are from his Johns Hopkins University speech, April 7, 1965, *Public Papers: Johnson, 1965*, 394–99.

40. Kolko, *Anatomy of a War*, 124.

41. Johnson, *Vantage Point*, 125.

42. Ibid., 67.

43. Ibid., 267.

44. "President Ho Chi Minh Answers President L. B. Johnson" (Hanoi, 1967), in William Appleman Williams, Thomas McCormick, Lloyd Gardner, and Walter LaFeber, eds., *America in Vietnam: A Documentary History* (New York: Norton, 1989), 259–62.

45. Johnson, *Vantage Point*, 122, 124, 134.

46. Bernard Fall, *Vietnam Witness, 1953–66* (New York: Praeger, 1966), 105.

47. Kearns, *Johnson*, 277–79. Quotation from the Johns Hopkins University Speech, April 7, 1965, *Public Papers: Johnson, 1965*, 394–99.

48. Miller, *Lyndon*, 465.

49. Ibid., speech before AFL-CIO, March 22, 1966.

50. George McGovern, *Grassroots: The Autobiography of George McGovern* (New York: Random House, 1977), 104–5.

51. Miller, *Lyndon*, 466.

52. Jack Valenti, *A Very Human President* (New York: Norton, 1975), 133.

53. William Bundy interview, LBJ Oral History Collection.

54. Nguyen Cao Ky, *How We Lost the Vietnam War* (New York: Stein & Day, 1984), 81.

55. Transcript of Johnson briefing, February 8, 1966, National Security File, International Meetings File—Honolulu, box 2, Lyndon B. Johnson Papers, Johnson Library. See also Walt W. Rostow interview, January 22, 1990, LBJ Oral History Collection.

56. Johnson, *Vantage Point*, 263.

57. Ibid., 259–61.

58. Bui Diem, *In the Jaws of History* (Boston: Houghton Mifflin, 1987), 188.

59. Ibid., 189.

60. Ibid., 341.

61. Johnson, *Vantage Point*, 362–63.

62. Diem, *In the Jaws of History*, 174.

63. Miller, *Lyndon*, 494.

64. FitzGerald, *Fire in the Lake*, 486–89.

65. Ibid., 369.

66. Ibid., 384.

67. Ibid., 400.

68. Ibid., 413–14, 423.

69. For Johnson's growth on this sensitive political issue see Robert Dallek, *Lone Star Rising: Lyndon Johnson and His Times, 1908–1960* (New York: Oxford University Press, 1991), 138, 519–20.

7
Containing Domestic Enemies: Richard M. Nixon and the War at Home

Melvin Small

During the interval between his election in November 1968 and his in-auguration in January 1969, Richard M. Nixon had little time to savor his hard-won triumph. The United States confronted an unprecedented series of crises. War raged in Southeast Asia with victory apparently beyond reach, cities were aflame in massive urban rebellions, and young protesters, often from elite campuses, were spouting revolutionary rhetoric and adopting violent tactics. These crises had brought down Lyndon Johnson. Nixon was determined to avoid his predecessor's fate.[1]

Fortunately, he had time to work things out. Even the eastern media, which he despised, talked about a new Nixon—a moderate statesman who deserved the honeymoon period accorded new presidents. In addition, he had run for office with a veiled hint, albeit not a "secret plan," that he could bring the Vietnam War to an honorable conclusion at least as fast as the Democratic standard bearer, Hubert H. Humphrey.

Whether they believed him or not, the leaders of the antiwar movement were in no position to launch a new campaign. Licking their wounds from the failed presidential candidacies of Robert F. Kennedy and Eugene Mc-Carthy, antiwar activists were hampered as well by factional disputes, particularly among increasingly violent splinter groups of the New Left. The movement was momentarily resigned to giving the new president a breathing spell.

Nixon was relatively certain that he would not need much time. He confided to Congressman Donald Riegle (R-Mich.) that he thought he could end the war six months after taking office.[2] And, of course, American diplomats were talking to their communist enemies at the negotiations in Paris.

Nixon visits with U.S. troops in Vietnam in July 1969. (U.S. Army, courtesy National Archives)

Indeed, because of those talks, the television networks had shifted their nightly war reports from jungle combat in Vietnam to the negotiating rooms in Paris, reinforcing the notion that the war was winding down.[3]

Nixon had a window of opportunity, and he planned to make the most of it. The new president arrived in Washington with the outlines of bold foreign policy initiatives, all of which depended on ending the Vietnam War or at least neutralizing its effects. He was disturbed by the way the war had consumed the attention of Lyndon Johnson and his foreign policy advisers. Nixon hoped to launch programs to take advantage of new opportunities in Europe, the Middle East, and Asia that had been virtually ignored because of the war.[4] His soon-to-emerge policy of détente toward the Soviet Union and his effort to open a dialogue with the People's Republic of China depended on winding down the war in Vietnam, the major irritant in East-West relations.

Like all presidents since Franklin D. Roosevelt, Nixon realized that he had the best chance of making his mark on history in the area of foreign affairs. He was bored with many of the nation's intractable social and economic problems, which were difficult to solve under most circumstances and impossible to solve with a Democratic Congress. In addition, he was personally interested in foreign affairs, an area in which he had exceptional experience and expertise. Finally, a believer in a strong presidency, Nixon found that in the international sphere he could work with secrecy and dispatch without being sabotaged by the entrenched Washington bureaucracy, much of which he perceived to be supportive of the Democratic party.[5]

To combat that bureaucracy and especially the prying eyes of a hostile Congress, he centralized policymaking in the White House. His national security adviser, Henry Kissinger, and an enlarged National Security Council staff completely overshadowed Secretary of State William Rogers. This system controlled not just the planning and coordination of U.S. foreign policy but sometimes, as was the case with Kissinger's secret talks with the North Vietnamese, its execution as well. Although Kennedy and Johnson had also enhanced the importance of their national security advisers, Secretary of State Dean Rusk had retained much of his traditional role and power during those years.[6]

Aside from establishing tight control over policymaking in the White House, Nixon had to demonstrate to friend and foe alike that he would not be hobbled by protesters in the streets or by media criticism.[7] His initiatives depended on his ability to prove that the United States was back and that it could project its power abroad without fear of major domestic political opposition. He believed that a forced precipitous withdrawal from Vietnam, without the requisite peace with honor, would weaken the United States in the eyes of other major international players.[8] No doubt an early departure from Vietnam might also lead to the overthrow of the Saigon government before Nixon had to stand for reelection in 1972, but at this juncture domestic considerations were less important than those involving matters of *Weltpolitik*.

Nixon's policies in Vietnam were based on three premises: (1) that the public had to be prepared for something less than a complete military victory, (2) that the South Vietnamese could not be abandoned, and (3) that the war should be brought to an end "as quickly as was honorably possible."[9] When he was unable to achieve the quick breakthrough he had promised Riegle, he was stuck with Vietnamization for the long haul. That process included the slow but steady withdrawal of American troops and an increase in matériel and training for the South Vietnamese forces so that they would be able to shoulder an ever larger share of the combat. In essence, Vietnamization was a return to 1964, when Lyndon Johnson declared that "the boys of Asia" should do the fighting for themselves.[10]

Implicit in Vietnamization was a willingness to use U.S. air power to counter any new offensives launched by Hanoi before Saigon's forces were prepared to meet them on their own. But Americans, who had endorsed deescalation in the polls, would be nervous about any apparent reescalation. Thus, central to Vietnamization's success was winning the hearts and minds of the American people, who, Nixon believed, had been adversely affected by the dovish media and the antiwar movement.

From January through the spring of 1969, he vacillated on how to deal with the media and the dissenters.[11] At times he tried reasoning with them; at other times he took up the cudgels against them, offering a glimpse of a later strategy. Before attacking them in earnest, however, he began working to improve his image, to control the "spin" that print and electronic journalists put on his actions. Few presidents have been so concerned with image, and even fewer have devoted so many hours to working on the public-relations aspects of the presidency.[12] Nixon saw nothing wrong with this. To the contrary, he wrote: "In the modern presidency, concern for image must rank with concern for substance."[13] And changing one's image was no easy task, since, according to the president, the media were the most powerful institution in the United States. Interestingly, although he later admitted how important image was, when he was president he often proclaimed disingenuously that he did not care about his image and was not bothered by what the media said about policies he had promulgated in the national interest.[14]

To enhance his image, Nixon ordered—very early in his administration—the organization of an unprecedented network of Republican operatives around the country who, at a moment's notice, could be mobilized to barrage offending media with letters either applauding the president or denouncing biased editorials and columns. This same cadre also sent letters of support to the White House after presidential speeches.[15] The latter operation was an important one. A White House announcement that it had received thousands of letters at a ratio of five to one in support of the president helped convince fence sitters to leap on the bandwagon with the majority. That leap could show up in public-opinion polls that followed news of the "spontaneous" outpouring of support for Nixon. And the publication of these favorable polls, influenced by the covert letter-writing campaigns, could produce even more shifts of support toward the Nixon camp.[16] It appears that the president occasionally forgot about the fabricated campaigns and privately took pride in the support he received from letter and telegram writers.

Although Nixon tried to woo regional, nonestablishment print and electronic media, he was convinced that seven key institutions set the news and opinion agenda and that all of them were biased against him to some degree.[17] These were the *New York Times, Washington Post, Time, Newsweek,* and the three television networks, especially their evening newscasts.[18] In general, and in a much less sophisticated way, Lyndon Johnson had also singled out these seven for special attention and occasional intimidation. Johnson had had his morning levee, where he summoned aides to his bedside to be dispatched to assail detractors in the media. Nixon left the details to his Ten O'Clock and Five O'Clock Clubs, two informal task forces within the White House whose job it was to create favorable news flows.[19] Even more important were the instructions Nixon scribbled daily on the elaborate media surveys prepared by Mort Allin, Pat Buchanan, and others.[20] Evidence of the inordinate amount of attention he lavished on the media, and thus his image, can be seen in the thousands of notes he made in the margins of the lengthy daily analyses of newspaper, television, and magazine reportage of his administration's activities.[21] Nixon eagerly read these summaries to see if the media had "turned around" due to his campaigns. He noted that, "while we are not going to be influenced in our policy decisions on what the columnists, commentators, or writers say," there is a need to know what they were saying "to counteract whatever effect they may be having in public."[22] For example, he was distressed by the media's concentration on the lack of democracy in South Vietnam rather than on the totalitarianism of the North.[23]

Nixon's belief that the media favored the Democratic party and supported a dovish policy in Vietnam was buttressed by the publication in 1971 of *The News Twisters*, a pseudo-social-scientific survey of biases in television news. He and his aides were so pleased with the book that they encouraged sales and tried to promote it onto the best-seller lists.[24] To this day, many politicians—and journalists—believe that the media contributed significantly to America's loss of the Vietnam War. Indeed, one reason that antiwar activities received little coverage during the Persian Gulf crisis of 1990–1991 was the media's fear of again being branded as traitors.[25] Despite this widely held belief, recent scholarship suggests that during much of the Vietnam War era the media were supportive of Washington's policies.[26]

Nevertheless, Nixon was absolutely convinced that most print and electronic media were his enemies and that as many as 65 percent of journalists were in that category. His battles with them began as early as 1952 during the vice-presidential campaign, highlighted by his "Checkers speech"; continued through the 1960 campaign, when he felt that Kennedy was coddled by the liberal media; and apparently ended with his famous farewell address to the press in California, when he told them that they would no longer have him to "kick around."

Nixon's media monitors fed his long-standing bias by identifying negative comments amid otherwise favorable newscasts or articles.[27] Moreover, with little knowledge of opinion and communications theory, those operatives went about their task in an unprofessional manner.[28] For example, his television watchers tended to concentrate on the narratives from news anchors Chet Huntley and David Brinkley of NBC and Walter Cronkite of CBS, and not on the pictures that accompanied their voice-overs. As was seen during the Gulf War of 1991, despite what American officials said in defense of their controversial bombing of the command and control center/bomb shelter in Baghdad in February, the gruesome pictures of victims were far more powerful than messages from talking heads.

Media critics were also contained through Nixon's approach to press conferences. He held fewer press conferences than his predecessor—seven per year compared to Johnson's twenty-six. He also knew which reporters were his supporters and tried to call on them more frequently than those on his burgeoning enemies list who were "trying to give us the hook."[29]

Finally, two other lesser-known tactics were employed against the media. First, Nixon helped friendly publishers from large chains by supporting passage of the Newspaper Preservation Act in 1969. He expected that this act, which permitted joint operating agreements, might increase the proportion of favorable editorials in certain cities. Second, he encouraged the development of the Vanderbilt University Television News Archive, hoping that if the networks knew that someone was recording them for posterity, they would be more objective.[30] Despite all this activity devoted to creating a positive image, Nixon was never completely satisfied that he had won the battle with the media.[31] No doubt he remained convinced of the media's antagonism because of their central role in uncovering the Watergate scandal that forced him from office in 1974.

The antiwar movement posed a different sort of challenge for Nixon, although he recognized that the protesters' effectiveness related to the press coverage they received. If reporters did not cover the movement or stressed its violent and radical activities, the president would be free to fashion his peace with honor.[32] He had mixed feelings about the unprecedented scattered acts of violence that greeted his inaugural parade in Washington on January 20, 1969. Although enraged by the way radicals marred the dignity of the event by throwing stones and bottles at official vehicles and by chanting "Ho, Ho, Ho Chi Minh, the NLF is going to win," Nixon knew that such actions also angered many who viewed the inaugural.[33]

Nixon was convinced that the antiwar movement gave aid and comfort to the enemy and that, in turn, international communist organizations gave financial aid and strategic direction to antiwar leaders. Although the CIA had been unable to find evidence of linkages between the movement and communist powers, he was certain that the agency had not looked hard enough.[34]

While the CIA went back to the drawing board for him, Nixon picked up the pace of Lyndon Johnson's more limited campaign of harassment and penetration of the movement. These activities ranged from unleashing the Internal Revenue Service (IRS) on dissenters—bolstered by its new White House–inspired investigative agency, the Special Services Staff—to acts of sabotage by agents provocateurs. The activities of the CIA, FBI, National Security Agency (NSA), military intelligence, and various ad hoc programs were meant to uncover the radical links within the movement and, more important, to render it ineffective through harassment and dirty tricks. Two thousand FBI agents alone were assigned to the New Left. The FBI's Cointelpro, the CIA's Operation Chaos, and the NSA's Operation Minaret, among other programs, produced more than 100 grand jury investigations in 84 cities with more than 2,000 witnesses subpoenaed to testify. Whether or not they found any smoking guns, the intelligence agencies kept Nixon's critics busy defending themselves against serious charges.[35] In addition to these official investigations, Nixon's aides employed their own private detectives to surveil putative enemies.[36]

Finally, certain that the antiwar protesters who were not dedicated ideologues were motivated primarily by fears of "getting their asses shot off," Nixon moved swiftly to allay their fears.[37] The draft lottery was announced in May 1969, and controversial General Lewis B. Hershey of the Selective Service System was retired in September of that year. The complete end of the draft was in sight.

Some of the programs and practices that Nixon instituted against antiwar critics were clearly illegal. Others, especially the assault against the media, violated the spirit if not the letter of the Constitution. Yet in 1969, Nixon was not alone in viewing the United States as in the midst of its worst crisis since the Civil War. These were extraordinary times, with sober commentators suggesting the possiblity of the imminent end of the American experiment in some sort of violent revolution. Nixon and his defenders have contended that extraordinary times demanded extraordinary measures to protect national security.[38]

Some antiwar and New Left activities also involved illegal acts that ranged from simple trespass to the trashing of buildings and even firebombings.[39] Nixon worried that academic and even political leaders, cowed by unlawful demonstraters, were dangerously "vulnerable to mob rule."[40] All major American institutions—especially the presidency—were under attack from violent, seditious radicals. Thus, when Nixon took actions that some interpreted as defending his own political career, he saw himself as defending the hallowed institution of the presidency.[41]

Nixon always played political hardball, and his methods were not always new. Some of the illegal and extralegal actions he authorized had also been used by his predecessors. Presidents from Roosevelt through Johnson had ordered such actions as wiretapping, secretly recording Oval Office conversations, or the use of intelligence agencies for partisan political purposes— and they had gotten away with them.[42] Thus, Nixon could maintain that he had merely used the same sort of hard-hitting methods employed by all successful American politicians. It was only the unprecedented animus of the press, he charged, that led to his getting caught and punished, in effect, for practicing his craft. Of course, although all his predecessors did some of the things Nixon did some of the time, none of them did as many of those things so much of the time.

Nixon's efforts to contain the media and the antiwar movement were part of his secret strategy, albeit not a secret plan, to end the war. He wanted to demonstrate to Hanoi that he could escalate the air war without arousing domestic opposition. Thus, he sent a signal to the communists in March

1969 with his secret bombing campaign of the Ho Chi Minh Trail in Cambodia. He had been angered by a communist offensive that was launched in February, an action that he interpreted as a direct challenge to his Vietnam policies. Hanoi had apparently thrown down the gauntlet to test the mettle of the new president.

Although *New York Times* reporter William Beecher broke the story on May 9, it created little interest and little follow-up, a commentary on the state of the antiwar movement and media critics at that time. The most important aspect of the Beecher story was Nixon's search to find the leak in his administration, to find out who blew the whistle on the bombing to the reviled *New York Times*. That search ultimately led to the infamous campaign of wiretapping of White House aides and journalists, which later became one of the major crimes of Watergate.[43]

Like all modern presidents, Nixon was bedeviled by leaks. Clearly they made it more difficult for him to operate an effective diplomacy, since other leaders were not pleased to find their private conversations on the front page of the *Washington Post*. Naturally, when the president himself leaked a story in order to make a point in the press—a not uncommon happening—that was another matter.[44]

Despite the Beecher leak, Nixon got away with the bombing of Cambodia. Further, he stepped up ground action in South Vietnam to the point that combat in the first half of 1969 resulted in the second largest number of American battle deaths during any six-month period of the war. At this point, according to chief aide H. R. Haldeman, Nixon was employing his "madman" theory; he hoped to capitalize on his legendary anticommunist image to convince North Vietnam to shape up at the bargaining table soon or face irrational overkill.[45]

Nixon's relative domestic strength was reflected in the turnout for the fifth annual series of spring antiwar demonstrations. The April 5–6, 1969, actions in over forty cities drew about 150,000 people, a somewhat disappointing total given the ever larger demonstrations that marked the Johnson years. Antiwar activists, however, could take solace in the fact that during the first six months of the Nixon administration, over 400 college campuses experienced major protests.[46] Of course, since many of those protests involved the trashing of buildings or clashes with police—often captured on television—this intensification of campus activism was a mixed blessing for the movement.

After the Cambodian bombing seemed to make his point, the next part of Nixon's strategy involved the issuance of a secret ultimatum to Ho Chi

Minh in July: Change your negotiating position by November 1 or confront a savage blow. At the same time, White House aides began to work on the feasibility of Operation DUCK HOOK, a series of punishments envisaged for Ho should he fail to heed the ultimatum. These included the mining of Haiphong Harbor, the invasion of the North, or even the bombing of the network of dikes in that country, which could produce catastrophic flooding. Nixon thought his threat to escalate was credible in part because he had contained his critics in the media and the movement.

But the movement was not moribund yet. Hitting upon a new strategy, its leaders put together the largest and most dramatic protest ever—the Moratorium. In over 200 cities, as many as 4 million Americans (who did not know about Nixon's ultimatum) paused in their daily routines on October 15, 1969, to participate in an activity aimed at convincing the president to withdraw from Southeast Asia more rapidly. The turnout—which included many middle-class adults as well as luminaries such as Lyndon Johnson's former negotiator in Paris, W. Averell Harriman—helped convince Nixon of the unwisdom of escalating after the November 1 deadline. Although he had announced a troop withdrawal of 60,000 in September, canceled draft calls for November and December, relieved General Hershey of his duty, encouraged a hyperpatriotic campaign to support American POWs, announced that he would not be influenced by the demonstrations, and leaked information to the press about radicals in the Moratorium, the unique protest succeeded in capturing almost universal positive attention from the most influential media.[47] The coverage of the gentle, genteel, and unique event was so favorable that Nixon was probably more angry at the media than he was at the demonstrators.[48]

The television networks devoted almost their entire newscasts on the evening of October 15 to the Moratorium. All three covered the sizable protest at Nixon's alma mater, Whittier College; a dignified ceremony in the heartland of America in Bethel, Kansas; and innumerable church services and graveside vigils from New York's Wall Street to the Golden Gate Bridge. The most moving coverage appeared on NBC where, for nine minutes, brief vignettes took viewers to protests from sunup to sundown across the country without one word of narrative from reporters or anchors.

The exact relationship of the Moratorium to Nixon's failure to call Hanoi's bluff after November 1 is unclear. He felt that it "undercut the credibility of the ultimatum."[49] Also important were the conclusions of Operation DUCK HOOK planners, who were not certain that anything short of making North Vietnam a parking lot could convince the communists to accept U.S.

negotiating proposals. And Ho Chi Minh's death in September contributed to the clouding of the situation.

Whatever the impact of the Moratorium, it no doubt encouraged Hanoi as it discouraged Nixon. He had to neutralize antiwar critics before Henry Kissinger's worst fear was realized—foreign policy made by impassioned mobs in the streets. According to the national security adviser, the United States had to "withdraw fast enough to ease public concerns but slowly enough to give Hanoi an incentive to negotiate. . . . The persistent domestic pressures . . . turned this task into an ordeal."[50]

Nixon began working on his defense against antiwar crowds—his Silent Majority speech—almost immediately after the Moratorium. During a three-week period, he labored over twelve drafts of the message.[51] The nationally televised address of November 3, which he claimed was the most important speech of his career, appealed to the alleged majority to rally around the flag and his program of Vietnamization against noisy and unrepresentative demonstrators. He recognized correctly that although most Americans wanted a speedy end to the war, a majority strongly disliked what appeared to them to be radical, unkempt hippies who were fundamentally unpatriotic and un-American.[52] He called on "the great silent majority of my fellow Americans" to understand that "North Vietnam cannot defeat or humiliate the United States. Only Americans can do that."[53] The speech was not just a cynical plan of "positive polarization"; Nixon believed it when he depicted the opposition as unpatriotic radicals who were a threat to national security.[54] It was during this period that Nixon and his supporters began to wear tiny American flags in their lapels.

The Silent Majority speech did the trick in terms of public opinion. The White House received more than 50,000 telegrams and 30,000 letters that favored the speech. Moreover, over 300 representatives and 58 senators expressed support for it, and a Gallup poll recorded a 68 percent approval rating for the president.[55] Nixon was pleased with this support. He told an aide that the "White House Press Corps is dying because of that television speech. . . . You can get across your point of view without having what you say strained through the press and that drives the press right up the wall."[56] Of course, some of this outpouring of support was self-generated. The president had given orders to prepare special "strike forces" to retaliate against the networks and the *New York Times, Washington Post, Time,* and *Newsweek.*[57]

In a clear case of overreacting to negative comments, the president and his aides were outraged at what they thought was unfair "instant analysis" in network commentary immediately following the speech.[58] Nixon ordered Federal Communications Commission (FCC) Chairman Dean Burch to request transcripts of the instant analyses from the networks for possible commission action. What the transcripts revealed was that although Nixon's opponents had their say on those roundtables, the networks carefully balanced them with his supporters.[59]

Despite his anger at the networks, Nixon had to be encouraged by the general tone of the print media and the positive response from the public and Congress. The widespread support for the speech did not, however, keep more than one-quarter of a million Americans from turning out in Washington for the Moratorium-Mobilization protests of November 13–15, 1969. Although the demonstrations were dignified and huge, the media coverage was not as extensive or as favorable as the coverage for the October Moratorium.[60] The movement needed more than just large crowds to maintain the momentum from the Moratorium—it needed adequate attention from the media.

Unfortunately for protest organizers, the media had responded to the message of the Silent Majority speech as well as to Vice-President Spiro T. Agnew's parallel assault against them, highlighted by his November 13 speech in Des Moines.[61] Targeting the alleged dangerous concentration of power among a handful of ultraliberal journalists and editors in that most un-American of cities, New York, Agnew's attack helped convince network executives to limit coverage of the largest single-city demonstration in movement history.[62] They feared antagonizing Agnew, whose message was apparently accepted enthusiastically by the public. Americans sent more favorable mail to the White House in response to Agnew than they had after Nixon's November 3 speech.[63]

The new media offensive had originated in a memo drafted by White House aide Jeb Stuart Magruder entitled "The Rifle and the Shotgun." Writing on October 17 just after the Moratorium, Magruder argued that previous media containment programs were too scattered—the "shotgun." What was needed was a more carefully aimed "rifle" approach. Included in this plan were FCC monitoring of unfair media reports, threats of antitrust actions against the networks, use of the IRS to investigate possible tax frauds, and favoring of proadministration editors and journalists.[64]

Elected on a pledge to bring a disintegrating country together, Nixon and Agnew further polarized the nation with a successful appeal to the majority that supported the administration's foreign policy, distrusted the media that seemed so critical of American institutions, and abhorred the cultural and political revolutionaries of the youthful left.[65] Indeed, Nixon's strategy depended on the encouragement of "dissensus," with the majority uniting in its hatred of domestic enemies.[66]

The movement and the media were quieted for a while. After the very bloody first six months of 1969, casualty figures began to decline, troops were coming home, peace talks were going on, and the public seemed relatively confident that Nixon was making slow but steady progress to end the war. The movement, which had threatened monthly protests increasing in length and extent until the war ended, could not deliver on its promises. The annual spring antiwar activities on April 15, 1970, were lifeless and comparatively small. In fact, the antiwar front was so tranquil and relatively unpopular that Nixon thought it safe to invade or, as he put it, to launch an incursion into Cambodia to destroy COSVN, Hanoi's central command and control infrastructure for the war in the South.

He expected a good deal of criticism in the media, in Congress, and on the campuses for the perceived escalation, and he even delayed telling his secretaries of state and defense about the move until the eleventh hour because he knew that they would think it politically unwise. As Secretary of State Rogers commented upon finally hearing about it, it would "make the students puke."[67]

Perhaps Nixon could have ridden out the initial storm of criticism that the invasion provoked. All bets were off, however, after four students were killed by the Ohio National Guard at Kent State University on May 4.[68] This brutal act, which inflamed college students and some of their parents like no other event during the war, created the most serious domestic political crisis for the president during his first administration. Hundreds of colleges and universities closed down for several days, and some never resumed the semester. Hundreds more experienced strikes and violent protests against the Kent State murders and the invasion that Nixon maintained was not an escalation of the war.[69] He hunkered down in a barricaded White House that, to one aide, resembled a beseiged presidential palace in a small Latin American country.[70] Nixon felt "utterly dejected" and wrote later that "those few days after Kent State were among the darkest of my presidency."[71]

As movement leaders hastily planned a demonstration in Washington on May 9–10, the administration worried about the prospect of mobs of angry young people trying to storm the White House. After he realized that his initial official responses to the Kent State tragedy were insensitive, the president, in effect, folded before the movement. He met with critics and college presidents and, most important, announced on May 8, in response to agitation on Capitol Hill, that he would withdraw the troops from Cambodia by the end of June. In addition, he made a spontaneous visit to the Lincoln Memorial in the middle of the night before the demonstration to meet young people who were camping out there. Although his conversations with the startled students received a mixed reception from the media, he did try to demonstrate that he understood and sympathized with their idealism—a far cry from his previous attacks against them.

Nixon would not soon forget the reaction to his Cambodian invasion. At least for a while, he would have to tread cautiously in Southeast Asia and refrain from another move that looked like an escalation. At the same time, upon reflection, many students, the foot soldiers of the movement, became worried about another paroxysm on campus. This one had interfered with graduation and careers in the uncertain economic environment termed "stagflation." Although Nixon would be leery of another Cambodia in the near future, his opponents in the antiwar movement would be leery of another such reaction to a presidential demarche.

After the dust had settled from the May crises and the students had left the campuses, Nixon launched a new Silent Majority type of offensive. This effort included an endorsement of hard-hat counterdemonstrators who had roughed up antiwar protesters in New York and an appearance in late May in Knoxville, Tennessee, in a large stadium with the Reverend Billy Graham.[72] He even dared to venture onto a college campus with a speech at Kansas State University that drew approval from Hubert Humphrey.[73]

In addition, support groups such as the Tell It to Hanoi Committee and the Committee to Support the President for Peace in Vietnam stepped up their activities on his behalf, as did the intelligence services. In early June, in the wake of the Cambodia invasion, Nixon began working on the abortive Huston Plan (later revealed by the Watergate investigation) to place control over domestic intelligence activities in the White House. The troops continued to come home. Force strength in the combat theater dropped from 414,000 in June to 334,000 by the end of the year. As the war became Vietnamized, American casualties decreased. On the diplomatic front, Nixon repackaged a peace plan in October to make it appear that the talks in Paris might begin moving at last.

According to the polls, Americans continued to express impatience with the pace of withdrawal, but they generally preferred Nixon's options to those posed by the unruly antiwar movement. Yet when he escalated the rhetoric against the movement on the eve of the congressional elections in November 1970, he went too far. After a speech in San Jose, California, on October 29, he taunted a heckling crowd and found himself a target for stones and other

missiles. Using that incident, he took to the airwaves with a fierce denuncia-
tion of the mobs in the streets. Speaking for the Democratic party, Senator
Edmund S. Muskie (D-Me.) responded with a gentle speech urging the cool-
ing of passions on all sides. Pollsters suggested that Muskie had struck the
right note of calm and, incidentally, had catapulted himself to the forefront
of candidates for the 1972 nomination. He also leaped to the top of Nixon's
political enemies list and became the target of a variety of dirty tricks meant
to deny him the Democratic nomination in favor of a weaker candidate. In
any event, Nixon's attempt to purge Congress of liberal Democrats failed—
in part because of the harshness of his antiradical line.[74]

Although the antiwar movement was in disarray in the fall of 1970, the
president still feared its power. When planning a raid on the Son Tay prisoner of war camp in North Vietnam in November, he worried about public
reaction if it failed. Allegedly he said: "Christ, they surrounded the White
House, remember? This time they will probably knock down the gates and
I'll have a thousand incoherent hippies urinating on the Oval Office rug.
That's just what they'd do."[75]

Nevertheless, Nixon felt strong enough at home in February 1971 to
launch an incursion into Laos. This time the protests were limited, in good
measure because this was a South Vietnamese operation of brief duration
and also because it took place during a season not conducive to outdoor ral-
lies. Nixon was aided as well by the general fatigue of antiwar activists and
their relative inability to produce large and enthusiastic crowds at a time
when the public grudgingly accepted the pace of withdrawal. Moreover, as
Nixon expected, some young protesters were no longer so personally involved in the war once the draft lottery began to operate in December 1969.

In addition, Nixon the peacemaker announced in July 1971 his upcoming
spectacular visit to China. That announcement was later matched by his
January 1972 revelation that Henry Kissinger had been engaged in secret
talks with the North Vietnamese since 1969. Although Nixon himself was
obviously an object of scorn for many Americans, his national security adviser was seen as almost a closet peacenik, exercising a positive influence on
his boss. Kissinger cultivated this reputation through innumerable leaks and
off-the-record comments ("backgrounders") to influential friends in the
media.

There was activism aplenty in the period from 1971 through 1973, but
nothing that threatened Nixon's power base as long as he did not escalate
precipitously or halt the troop withdrawal program. Moreover, the media
had decided that antiwar protests were no longer very newsworthy.[76] In es-

sence, Nixon had won the domestic war by the end of 1970 after some shaky moments during the first two years of his presidency.

It cannot be emphasized enough how important the ending of the draft was to that victory, as was the decline in American battle deaths from 4,200 in 1970 to 1,300 in 1971. When Nixon ran for the presidency in 1972, his campaign took out advertisements in newspapers proclaiming that, under his guidance, casualties in the war had declined 95 percent. What was omitted from that figure was the modifier "American." By all estimates, Asian battle deaths increased during his first term, including new and larger tallies in Cambodia and Laos, but this detail mattered little to most Americans.[77]

The victory at home, however, did not give him a completely free hand to prosecute the war to a successful conclusion. He could escalate the air war in response to North Vietnamese offensives, as was the case in the spring of 1972, but he had to continue to make steady progress toward that day when the last American soldier would leave Vietnam. Opponents of the war in the movement, the media, and Congress had won that point with the general public by 1969.

Paradoxically, Nixon's policy in Vietnam was hamstrung by the same factor that crippled the antiwar movement after 1969. The slow but steady withdrawal pacified the public and made it harder for doves to attract popular support. At the same time, that withdrawal meant that the United States would soon reach a point when it would no longer pose a military threat to North Vietnam. Why should Hanoi give Nixon his negotiated peace with honor when the end of U.S. military intervention was in sight?

Nixon's crushing of his domestic enemies, along with a variety of dirty tricks, helped him coast to a stunning victory in the 1972 presidential election. The seamy legal as well as blatantly illegal means he used to obtain that victory, however, contributed significantly to the bill of charges that led to the greatest loss of his life in the summer of 1974.

Although the Watergate scandal began as a break-in at the Democratic party headquarters at the Watergate complex in Washington, it ultimately came to encompass an unprecedented series of crimes and misdemeanors committed by the president and his aides. Some of the activities that became part of the indictment against the Nixon administration related to his attempt to contain domestic enemies. The use of the intelligence services, the IRS, and wiretapping for the illegal surveillance, harassment, and sabotage of political rivals—including those in the antiwar movement and Edmund Muskie, following his stirring televised response to Nixon's inflammatory rhetoric—were some of the more serious charges leveled against Nixon's

White House. In addition, his massive programs to intimidate the media contributed to the journalistic feeding frenzy that occurred after the *Washington Post*, *New York Times*, and others began to take the Watergate break-in seriously in the spring of 1973. In a sort of self-fulfilling prophecy, Nixon's enemies in the media, made more hostile by his four-year campaign against them, leaped enthusiastically into the investigative journalism that turned up more and more Watergate crimes.

In Vietnam, the United States won almost all the battles but ultimately lost the war. The same description could be applied to Nixon's war at home.

Notes

An earlier version of this chapter was presented at the Society for Historians of American Foreign Relations meeting in Washington, D.C., June 20, 1991. I am indebted to Joan Hoff-Wilson, Jeffrey Kimball, and H. Bruce Franklin for their comments at the session.

1. Of course, Nixon thrived on crises. See his triumph over adversity in Richard M. Nixon, *Six Crises* (Garden City, N.Y.: Doubleday, 1962). See also Joan Hoff-Wilson, "Richard M. Nixon: The Corporate Presidency," in Fred I. Greenstein, ed., *Leadership in the Modern Presidency* (Cambridge, Mass.: Harvard University Press, 1988), 167–68.

2. Donald S. Riegle, *O Congress* (Garden City, N.Y.: Doubleday, 1972), 20. Riegle confirmed this incident in a letter to the author, November 20, 1990.

3. Av Westin, *Newswatch: How TV Decides the News* (New York: Simon & Schuster, 1982), 96–97; Godfrey Hodgson, *America in Our Time* (New York: Vintage, 1978), 378.

4. Richard M. Nixon, *RN: The Memoirs of Richard Nixon* (New York: Warner Books, 1978), 354.

5. Stephen E. Ambrose, *Nixon: The Triumph of a Politician, 1962–1972* (New York: Simon & Schuster, 1989), 233.

6. Walt Whitman Rostow, who was Lyndon Johnson's powerful national security adviser from 1966 to the end of his term, never tried to usurp Rusk's position. Rostow likes to show interviewers a photograph of his relatively small staff, which was dwarfed by the staff Kissinger put together. Rostow interview with author, May 20, 1983, Austin, Tex. Nixon's NSC was twice the size of the Kennedy-Johnson NSCs. See John Prados, *Keepers of the Keys: A History of the National Security Council from Truman to Bush* (New York: Morrow, 1991), 282.

7. Nixon's other major perceived enemies, members of Congress and the Washington bureaucracy, will not be discussed in detail here.

8. Tom Wicker, *One of Us: Richard Nixon and the American Dream* (New York: Random House, 1991), 572.

9. Nixon, *Memoirs*, 349.

10. Theodore Draper, *Abuse of Power* (New York: Viking, 1967), 67.

11. Charles DeBenedetti with Charles Chatfield, *An American Ordeal: The Antiwar Movement of the Vietnam War* (Syracuse, N.Y.: Syracuse University Press, 1990), 246.

12. See, for example, H. R. Haldeman to Pat Buchanan, July 10, 1969, in Bruce Oudes, ed., *From the President: Richard Nixon's Secret Files* (New York: Harper & Row, 1989), 411; John Ehrlichman, *Witness to Power* (New York: Simon & Schuster, 1982), 266; and Stephen E. Ambrose, *Nixon: Ruin and Recovery* (New York: Simon & Schuster, 1991), 27. It is true, of course, that the nature of the presidential materials sequestered by the government for the Watergate hearings, and now used by historians, may lead some to overemphasize Nixon's concern with the media and his image.

13. Nixon, *Memoirs*, 354. See also David Frost, *I Gave Them a Sword: Behind the Scenes of the Nixon Interviews* (New York: Morrow, 1978), 191.

14. Stanley I. Kutler, *The Wars of Watergate: The Last Crisis of Richard Nixon* (New York: Knopf, 1990), 167.

15. For information on the campaign, see Nixon to John Ehrlichman, February 5, 1969, and Charles Colson to Ehrlichman, August 16, 1971, in Oudes, *From the President*, 310; Haldeman to Jeb Stuart Magruder, February 4, 1970, in Joseph Spear, *Presidents and the Press: The Nixon Legacy* (Cambridge, Mass.: MIT Press, 1984), 101; and Raymond Price, *With Nixon* (New York: Viking, 1977), 181-82. For an example of the pleasure taken in the planting of College Republican letters in *Newsweek* in October 1969, see Herbert Klein to Nixon, October 30, 1969, Klein Files, White House Special Files, Staff Members' Office Files, box 3, Nixon Presidential Materials Project (NPMP), Alexandria, Va. (hereafter cited by individual file name only). This system did not always work. During one week in August 1971, only six of the many letters sent to the print media were published. See Colson to Ehrlichman, August 16, 1971, in Oudes, *From the President*, 310.

16. On the media creating opinion by reporting it, see Michael Parenti, *Inventing Reality: The Politics of the Mass Media* (New York: St. Martin's Press, 1986), 89.

17. On Nixon's "obsession" with media bias, see Ambrose, *Nixon*, 325-26. See also DeBenedetti, *An American Ordeal*, 239; Jeb Stuart Magruder, *An American Life: One Man's Road to Watergate* (New York: Atheneum, 1974), 58-59; and Wicker, *One of Us*, 438-40.

18. Nixon himself thought that television was more important in affecting opinion than newspapers and magazines, but realized that the networks' news agenda often came from the newspapers. Richard M. Nixon, *In the Arena* (New York: Simon & Schuster, 1990), 138. On his relative success with television compared to print, see Marilyn A. Lashner, *The Chilling Effect in TV News: Intimidation by the Nixon White House* (New York: Praeger, 1984).

19. These groups were so named because of the timing of their meetings just before the important noon and 6 P.M. deadlines for the electronic media.

20. Johnson did not routinely ask for such analyses. On the sloppiness of the me-

dia analysis in his administration, see Peter Benchley oral history interview, 35, Lyndon Baines Johnson Presidential Library, Austin, Tex.

21. For typical summaries, many of which ran thirty single-spaced pages, see Alexander Butterfield to Nixon, October 7, 1969, November 1969 folder, Memos for the President, Haldeman Files, box 138, NPMP. On Nixon's reading habits, see Haldeman to Pat Buchanan, October 23, 1969, Memos to Buchanan, box 53, ibid. See also Ehrlichman, *Witness to Power*, 332; Spear, *Presidents and the Press*, 67; William E. Porter, *Assault on the Media: The Nixon Years* (Ann Arbor: University of Michigan Press, 1976), 57–59; and Daniel Schorr, *Clearing the Air* (Boston: Houghton Mifflin, 1977), 33.

22. Nixon to Haldeman, November 24, 1969, President's Personal File (PPF), box 1, NPMP.

23. Nixon, *Memoirs*, 350.

24. Edith Efron, *The News Twisters* (Los Angeles: Nash, 1971); Herbert S. Parmet, *Richard Nixon and His America* (Boston: Little, Brown, 1990), 586–88.

25. See, for example, the limited coverage in the *New York Times* and on the networks of the January 26, 1991, rally in Washington that drew more than 75,000 participants.

26. See Todd Gitlin, *The Whole World Is Watching: The Mass Media in the Making and Unmaking of the New Left* (Berkeley: University of California Press, 1980); Daniel C. Hallin, *"The Uncensored War": The Media and Vietnam* (New York: Oxford University Press, 1986); and William M. Hammond, *Public Affairs: The Military and the Media, 1962–1968* (Washington, D.C.: GPO, 1988).

27. Ambrose, *Nixon*, 249–51, 455.

28. For an example of the misreading of the media, see Herbert Klein, *Making It Perfectly Clear* (Garden City, N.Y.: Doubleday, 1980), 197. See also Spear, *Presidents and the Press*, 67. Charles Colson disagreed with those who challenged the accuracy and objectivity of the summaries. Colson to Jack Anderson, April 12, 1971, Pat Buchanan Files, box 1, NPMP.

29. Kutler, *The Wars of Watergate*, 173–74.

30. Colson to Haldeman, April 5, 1972, Haldeman Files, box 95.

31. Kutler, *The Wars of Watergate*, 93.

32. Nixon was pleased when the networks framed their movement stories in terms of violence. Ibid., 107.

33. These protests reinforced Nixon's image of antiwar dissenters and led to administration plans to tighten up defenses in the capital. See Egil Krogh to Ehrlichman, January 24, 1969, President's Handwriting (PH), President's Office Files (POF), box 1, NPMP.

34. For Johnson's attempts to find the linkage, see Richard Helms to Johnson, September 1968, and George McGhee to Johnson, January 17, 1969, National Security File, White House Central Files, box 3, Johnson Library. See also Charles DeBenedetti, "A CIA Analysis of the Anti-Vietnam War Movement, October 1967," *Peace and Change* 9 (Spring 1983): 31–42. For Nixon's attempts, see Ambrose, *Nixon*, 262, 264.

35. For information on these activities, see DeBenedetti, *An American Ordeal*, 246–47, 293; Kutler, *The Wars of Watergate*, 105; Athan G. Theoharis and John Stu-

art Cox, *The Boss: J. Edgar Hoover and the Great American Inquisition* (Philadelphia: Temple University Press, 1988), 408–14; and Ambrose, *Nixon*, 265.

36. Len Colodny and Robert Gettlin, *Silent Coup: The Removal of a President* (New York: St. Martin's Press, 1991), 94–96.

37. Curt Smith, *Long Time Gone: The Years of Turmoil Remembered* (South Bend, Ind.: Icarus, 1982), 217.

38. On the national security argument, see Frost, *I Gave Them a Sword*, 184–86.

39. Kutler, *The Wars of Watergate*, 79.

40. Nixon, *Memoirs*, 354.

41. Of course, as Tom Wicker points out in *One of Us*, 678, Nixon sometimes confused his own political interests with those of the nation.

42. Victor Lasky, *It Didn't Start with Watergate* (New York: Dial, 1977). For a recent look at some of John F. Kennedy's actions in this vein that Nixon later learned about, see Michael R. Beschloss, *The Crisis Years: Kennedy and Khrushchev, 1960–1963* (New York: HarperCollins, 1991), 346–47.

43. For a defense of wiretaps, see Nixon, *Memoirs*, 389–90.

44. For an example of a Nixon-calculated leak, see Ambrose, *Nixon*, 301.

45. H. R. Haldeman with Joseph Dimona, *The Ends of Power* (New York: Times Books, 1978), 83.

46. DeBenedetti, *An American Ordeal*, 242–43.

47. Ibid., 258; Ambrose, *Nixon*, 300.

48. Spear, *Presidents and the Press*, 40. See also Nixon, *Memoirs*, 403.

49. Nixon, *Memoirs*, 405.

50. Henry Kissinger, *Years of Upheaval* (Boston: Little, Brown, 1982), 87–88. It is interesting to note that the word "ordeal" is used in the title of the best book on the antiwar movement, DeBenedetti, *An American Ordeal*, as well as in the title of one of the best texts on the war, George Donelson Moss, *Vietnam: An American Ordeal* (Englewood Cliffs, N.J.: Prentice-Hall, 1990).

51. Parmet, *Richard Nixon*, 581.

52. DeBenedetti, *An American Ordeal*, 259.

53. Nixon, *Memoirs*, 409.

54. Parmet, *Richard Nixon*, 577, 464–66. For Nixon's own views on the speech, see Nixon, *Memoirs*, 409–12.

55. Ambrose, *Nixon*, 311.

56. Nixon to Keogh, November 5, 1969, Memoranda for the President, POF, box 79, NPMP.

57. Nixon to Haldeman, October 26, 1969, Haldeman Files, box 229.

58. Nixon, *In the Arena*, 216. See also News Summaries, November 4, 1969, folder and personal note of November 3, 1969, Haldeman Files, box 40.

59. Some of Nixon's aides now admit that their boss overreacted to network biases that simply were not there. See James Keogh, *President Nixon and the Press* (New York: Funk & Wagnalls, 1972), 138; and Magruder, *An American Life*, 57. For the transcripts of the instant analyses on November 3, see Keogh, *President Nixon and the Press*, 171–90. For a while in 1973, CBS decided to end the practice of instant analysis. Sally Bedell Smith, *In All His Glory: The Life and Times of William S. Paley* (New York: Simon & Schuster, 1990), 493.

60. Fred Powledge, *The Engineering of Restraint: The Nixon Administration and the Press* (Washington, D.C.: Public Affairs Press, 1971), 31–32.

61. On the speech, see William Safire, *Before the Fall: An Inside View of the Pre-Watergate White House* (Garden City, N.Y.: Doubleday, 1975), 352; Klein, *Making It Perfectly Clear*, 168; and John R. Coyne, Jr., *The Impudent Snobs: Agnew vs. the Intellectual Establishment* (New Rochelle, N.Y.: Arlington House, 1972), passim.

62. CBS President William S. Paley denies that he was intimidated by Nixon, Agnew, and later, Charles Colson. William S. Paley, *As It Happened: A Memoir* (Garden City, N.Y.: Doubleday, 1979), 335, 341. Colson was the point man for the administration on the media. Twenty years later, even after being "born again," he maintained that the biased coverage on television made him "go up the walls." Charles Colson oral history interview, NPMP.

63. William Hopkins to Larry Higby, December 1, 1969, mail operations folder, Haldeman File, box 129.

64. Magruder to Haldeman, October 17, 1969, Haldeman Files, box 141. On that same day, Herbert Klein reported that he had warned the heads of NBC and CBS that the White House and the FCC were watching them carefully because of their unbalanced coverage of the war. Klein to Nixon, October 17, 1969, White House Action Memos, Klein Files, box 5. A less organized campaign against the media had begun even before the circulation of Magruder's memo. See Spear, *Presidents and the Press*, 42; and Lashner, *Chilling Effect*, appendix A.

65. On the success of the media campaign, see Gitlin, *Whole World*, 278–79. Another campaign aimed at increasing support for the administration revolved around the prisoner of war issue. November 9 had been proclaimed a national day of prayer for POWs and MIAs by Congress in a resolution endorsed by Nixon operatives.

66. Richard A. Melanson, *Reconstructing Consensus: American Foreign Policy Since the Vietnam War* (New York: St. Martin's Press, 1991), 42.

67. Seymour Hersh, *The Price of Power: Kissinger in the Nixon White House* (New York: Summit, 1983), 191. Three of Kissinger's NSC aides resigned in protest of the invasion, as did more than 100 foreign service officers.

68. Although two black students were killed at Jackson State University on May 15, the original furor about Kent State had begun to subside by then.

69. As many as one-fifth of all U.S. colleges and universities closed down for some time during the crisis. DeBenedetti, *An American Ordeal*, 279–80.

70. Charles W. Colson, *Born Again* (New York: Bantam, 1976), 36–37. See also Nixon, *Memoirs*, 457–66.

71. Nixon, *Memoirs*, 457.

72. On another occasion in 1971, Nixon took pleasure in the way teamsters had beaten up antiwar demonstrators. Kutler, *The Wars of Watergate*, 107.

73. Safire, *Before the Fall*, 288. For an eyewitness account of the speech and a new Nixon strategy of confronting hecklers aggressively, see Ambrose, *Nixon*, 376–77.

74. On these and other elections, see Stephen E. Ambrose, "Nixon and Vietnam: Vietnam and Electoral Politics," in George Donelson Moss, ed., *A Vietnam Reader* (Englewood Cliffs, N.J.: Prentice-Hall, 1991), 203–16.

75. Benjamin F. Schemmer, *The Raid* (London: Macdonald & Jane's, 1977), 164.

76. By not paying attention to movement activities, the media may have made the antiwar position more acceptable to the public, which had always been nervous about supporting the views of the radical hippies they saw on television. DeBenedetti, *An American Ordeal*, 656.

77. When the author sent a letter to the *New York Times* pointing out that the Nixon campaign ad was misleading, its editors chose not to run the "correction."

8
"Peace with Honor": Richard Nixon and the Diplomacy of Threat and Symbolism

Jeffrey P. Kimball

In the beginning of the 1968 presidential campaign, candidate Richard Nixon promised that he would achieve "peace with honor" in Vietnam. After four more years of war, the spectacular bombing of Hanoi and Haiphong in December 1972, and the compromise Paris Agreement of January 1973, President Nixon and his chief negotiator, Henry A. Kissinger, claimed that they had accomplished an honorable peace, a diplomatic victory, and a reaffirmation of the United States' global credibility. But the reality was continued war in Vietnam, diplomatic defeat for the United States, and a legacy of tragedy, deception, and misunderstanding in Vietnam.

In 1968, Nixon seemed an unlikely peacemaker. With a mixture of political opportunism, ideological conviction, and personal temperament, he had launched his political career in 1946 as a right-wing Republican, an anticommunist, and a Red-baiter. Until the start of his victorious presidential campaign in 1968, he had been an outspoken hawk on the war, almost always espousing more militant strategies than had presidents Dwight Eisenhower, John Kennedy, and Lyndon Johnson. As vice-president, he had insistently urged a resistant Eisenhower to authorize unilateral U.S. air strikes—including use of atomic bombs—against the Vietminh at Dienbienphu in 1954. He also advocated sending American troops in the event of a French defeat, supported the formation of the Southeast Asia Treaty Organization (SEATO), and agreed with Eisenhower's decision to back Ngo Dinh Diem's presidency of the Republic of Vietnam (RVN). After his loss in the 1960 presidential election, Nixon had fully endorsed Kennedy's deepening involvement in Vietnam. With Diem's assassination in 1963, however, he lamented Kennedy's apparent abandonment of the South Vietnamese strongman. Although supporting Johnson's escalations from 1964 to 1968, Nixon was critical of Johnson's alleged "go-slow" strategy and advocated more aggressive military steps. He also maintained that Johnson had mishandled the war politically at home and abroad and, in particular, had allowed himself to become prisoner to the criticisms of congressional doves and antiwar protesters, both of whom Nixon loathed.[1]

Nixon's conception of the Vietnam crisis was conventional but with right-leaning accents. He portrayed the war as part of a global struggle against communist aggression, which the Union of Soviet Socialist Republics (USSR) and the People's Republic of China (PRC) carried out in Asia through local proxy agents by means of covert revolutionary "subversion."[2] One of the original proponents of the domino theory, he continued to argue during the 1968 campaign and throughout his presidency that the U.S. effort in Vietnam was necessary to prevent Southeast Asia from falling to Soviet and Chinese expansion. From Nixon's perspective, the threat of falling dominoes was real, particularly in the psychological sense. The United States had to preserve its credibility as a guarantor against subversion. Otherwise, revolutionary movements in the Third World would be encouraged, and Washington's client regimes might realign their foreign policies.[3]

Credibility was the symbolic linchpin of a broad U.S. policy that included interconnected economic, military, political, and psychological elements. It was a code word for describing the United States' leading role in the formation of and provision of security for a global "private enterprise" system, in which republicanism was desirable but not always necessary. In the Third World, the greatest threat to this system came from anticolonial and anticapitalist revolutions. Whether these revolutions erupted from indigenous conditions or were the product of Soviet and Chinese machinations mattered little to Nixon and other policymakers. More important was the fact that the established communist states provided support to revolutionary movements and made the U.S. task of containing socialist challenges to international capitalism more difficult. Furthermore, the success of revolutions in small countries like Vietnam enhanced the global influence of the USSR and the PRC. Thus the United States needed to be in, stay in, and win in South Vietnam. If it pulled out of or lost in Indochina, Nixon maintained, its own trustworthiness in opposing aggression would be destroyed, not only in Asia but also in Europe and elsewhere around the world. Dredging up the politically sinister term "appeasement" to describe diplomatic and political compromise, Nixon had unswervingly opposed negotiations with Vietnamese communists, Geneva-like agreements, and neutralist or coalition government solutions in South Vietnam. He insisted that any settlement must begin with the withdrawal of the military forces of the Democratic Republic of Vietnam (DRV) from the South.[4]

Early in 1968, however, Nixon moderated his tone. On March 5 he proclaimed to a New Hampshire audience that he could "end the war and win the peace in the Pacific." Repeating the promise elsewhere but contending that premature disclosure would doom prospects for diplomacy, he refused to be explicit about the steps he would take to bring the Vietnam War to a "successful conclusion." He denied concealing a "secret plan" and instead emphasized his ability to provide better "leadership." On balance, the attention he received and the confusion about whether he had a plan or not served him well in the campaign; his withholding of details obviated the necessity of explaining how he would negotiate without giving anything away.[5]

Despite his apparent about-face, Nixon had not fundamentally revised his pre-1968 positions. In his public statements he qualified the word "peace": "win" the peace, peace with "honor," and the closely related "successful" conclusion to the war. These formulas obscured his unaltered, hard-line conception of peace while raising the hopes and expectations of many war-weary voters. To much of the public, peace vaguely meant "no war," an "end to the fighting," or, primarily, an "end to American involvement" even if a war between the Vietnamese continued. So-called hawks preferred a peace won through quick military victory; doves wanted an end to the war through some sort of diplomatic compromise. At a minimum, both doves and hawks wanted American ground troops out of Vietnam, and Nixon's conservative constituency in particular hoped that this could happen without "cutting and running," "defeat," or "dishonor." Nixon discovered that he could tap the yearnings of many Americans by proposing a phased withdrawal of American troops. Delivered against the backdrop of a commitment to an honorable peace, it was his most popular slogan.[6]

A peace with honor meant, Nixon wrote in 1967, either "winning the peace" or, if that were not possible, at least extricating U.S. forces while avoiding the reality or appearance of military or political defeat. In a narrow sense, the maximum goal of winning the peace meant ensuring the survival of a viable, anticommunist government of an independent South Vietnam. In a broader sense, Nixon viewed the preservation of an anticommunist South Vietnamese state as essential in retaining the United States' global counterrevolutionary credibility. This, in turn, was a prerequisite to his vision of a postwar American-led economic, political, and military association of "free" Pacific Rim states, with South Vietnam at the apex of an arc curving from New Zealand to Japan.[7]

By early 1968, however, Nixon concluded that *military* victory in Vietnam was infeasible as long as the United States insisted on employing the conventional search-and-destroy strategy of General William Westmoreland and President Johnson. The Tet Offensive, which began at the end of January, implied the failure of big-unit sweeps in destroying the southern Vietcong guerrillas of the People's Liberation Armed Forces (PLAF) and the northern regulars of the People's Army of Vietnam (PAVN). Moreover, the erosion of political consensus at home limited the government's ability to continue mobilizing large numbers of America's youth. Nevertheless, Nixon had not abandoned hope of *political* victory through military means. He thought that several other military options remained available: intensified and expanded air bombardment throughout Indochina; a naval blockade of the DRV; accelerated counterinsurgency and pacification programs; and greater reliance on the Army of the Republic of Vietnam (ARVN) to replace U.S. forces.[8]

An important part of his optimism was faith in the efficacy of coupling these military steps with diplomatic and political strategies. To the poker-playing Nixon, his ace in the hole was his ability to bluff the enemy with the threat of ruthless, massive, retributive violence. The secret to making it work was the credibility of his "irrationality"—his psychological inclination to exceed reasonable norms of international behavior. In the fall of 1968 he explained his version of this brinkmanship or big-stick diplomacy to longtime aide H. R. Haldeman: "I call it the Madman Theory, Bob. I want the North Vietnamese to believe I've reached the point where I might do *anything* to stop the war. We'll just slip the word to them that, 'for God's sake, you know Nixon is obsessed about Communism. We can't restrain him when he's angry—and he has his hand on the nuclear button'—and Ho Chi Minh himself will be in Paris in two days begging for peace.'"[9] The predictable irrationality of the madman theory was to be built into all adversarial relationships. But if an adversary called his bluff, Nixon believed that, despite the risks, he must be prepared to gamble and use massive force. "When you bite the bullet," he exclaimed, "bite it hard—go for the big play."[10]

In addition to "jugular diplomacy," as Kissinger termed it, Nixon counted on secret diplomacy and "linkage"—the linking of progress on détente with the Soviets and the Chinese to their compliance on other matters, such as persuading their alleged North Vietnamese clients to make diplomatic concessions. Secret and back-channel diplomacy was preferable to public diplomacy, Nixon thought, because the latter hampered freedom of action, raised public expectations, involved other players (such as Congress and the Saigon government), and ran the risk of provoking the enemy. In any case, he believed that the public neither cared about nor was capable of understanding diplomatic details.[11]

Nixon intended to control his elaborate foreign policy scheme from the White House, which meant bypassing the State and Defense Departments. He believed that their bureaucracies, staffed with liberal Democrats, hampered effective executive leadership because of their turf-protecting, rule-obeying, compromise-prone nature. And because of its susceptibility to press leaks, the bureaucracy negated secret diplomacy. Nixon also wanted to neutralize antiwar critics and produce at least a semblance of political consensus that would enhance his bargaining position with Vietnamese adversaries. He intended to use government agencies to harass antiwar groups, and he favored installing an all-volunteer system in place of the draft, which he cynically believed was at the heart of the antiwar movement. His campaign pledge of a phased withdrawal of U.S. troops was another step in this direction. Recognizing the political necessity of de-Americanizing the ground combat, he leaned toward "Vietnamization" of the war—strengthening the firepower, training, and leadership of the ARVN to enable it to fight alone to contain the PAVN and PLAF.[12]

In South Vietnam, everything would hinge on the political legitimacy and vitality of President Nguyen Van Thieu's Saigon government. If he could survive as the leader of a viable, independent South Vietnam, then the war would have been won. If that objective could not be achieved, the withdrawal of U.S. forces under honorable conditions would still require a South Vietnamese government strong enough to avoid defeat during U.S. disengagement and to continue the struggle after the U.S. departure. Nixon elevated this Vietnamization approach to a global policy in his Nixon Doctrine declaration of July 25, 1969, wherein the United States would expect client nations to handle more of the burden of internal security with their own troops backed up with U.S. military, political, advisory, and economic aid.[13]

Meanwhile, during his presidential campaign against Vice-President Hubert Humphrey, Nixon carried out a back-channel conspiracy with President Thieu. Kissinger, who was then working as a consultant for the Democratic administration, informed Nixon that Johnson was preparing to call a halt to the bombing of North Vietnam and enter into negotiations with the DRV and the National Liberation Front (NLF)—the political coalition of south-

ern guerrillas. Concerned that Johnson would succeed in pulling off a public-relations "October surprise" that would boost Humphrey's chances for
election, Nixon sought to persuade Thieu to "hold on" by resisting Johnson's entreaties to cooperate. Nixon assured Thieu that his own policies on
Vietnam would be more supportive of South Vietnam than Humphrey's.
Thieu was receptive because he had concluded at a 1967 meeting with the
vice-president that Humphrey would soften the U.S. position on the role
and legitimacy of the NLF if elected president. In any case, he believed that
Nixon's election would at least buy some time by derailing the apparent
Democratic momentum toward a settlement. Nixon's lobbying succeeded.
On November 1, four days before the election, Thieu announced that he did
not support the bombing halt and negotiations, which Johnson had revealed
on October 31. The bubble of voter support for Humphrey that had followed Johnson's news burst with Thieu's rejection of the peace initiative.[14]

Nixon's own plan for achieving peace in Vietnam was not a detailed blue-
print for action but a collection of guidelines that would help steer his strategic improvisations over the rocky road of the next four years. Except for the
influence of his personal style, there was little, if anything, that was substantively new in Nixon's rudimentary "secret plan" for achieving peace. It resembled Eisenhower's approach of economic and military aid to Ngo Dinh
Diem coupled with a threat of direct U.S. military action. Other elements
paralleled methods that Johnson had tried: back-channel talks, bombing escalations, overtures to the Soviet Union, and the search for a Vietnamese
strongman. What Nixon intended to do, Johnson had already pursued—a
two-track policy of fighting and talking. Starting the process of negotiation
in Paris and calling a halt to the bombing of North Vietnam in the fall of
1968, Johnson dramatically increased bombing in Laos and South Vietnam.
Beginning to consider a move away from big-unit war and toward counterinsurgency and de-Americanization, Johnson kept his options open for other
military escalations.[15]

Neither Johnson nor Nixon was willing to abandon the essential goal of
U.S. policy—a viable, anticommunist government of an independent South
Vietnam. If Nixon doubted that search-and-destroy missions could bring it
about, he still sought it as a political goal. Johnson, Humphrey, and even
Nixon may have wanted Thieu to move toward an accommodation with the
NLF, but that accommodation did not include the acceptance of real com-
promise—a coalition government including the NLF. What Nixon defined
as a minimum political settlement to avoid a dishonorable American de-

feat—namely, an anticommunist, pro-American regime with a good chance to survive—was itself a defeat for the DRV and NLF.[16]

Nixon still wanted a political victory of sorts in Vietnam, and so did his Vietnamese adversaries. Within the Politburo in Hanoi, there were differences over strategy, the nature and pace of revolution, the direction of agricultural policy, the relationship between North and South, and the degree of acceptable Western influence. But there was unanimity about the ultimate terms of a diplomatic settlement with the United States: Vietnam must be unified and independent, free of colonial or neocolonial control. For the communists in the North and the South, Vietnam must also be socialist. The noncommunists in the NLF, who may have had nonsocialist visions of Vietnam's future, were nevertheless firmly committed to national unity and independence. In post-Tet 1968, the DRV-NLF position was realistic: Although negotiations could safely take place under conditions of battlefield indecision, a desirable diplomatic settlement was possible only if the military situation was favorable. They sought the removal of Thieu, but they would accept U.S.-RVN recognition of the NLF in a coalition government in South Vietnam. Essential to the achievement of favorable military conditions, they believed, was the viability of the PLAF, the continued presence of the PAVN in the South, a halt to the bombing of the North (which affected military conditions in the South), and a withdrawal of U.S. troops.[17]

At the time of Nixon's inauguration in January 1969, therefore, none of the usual historical conditions necessary for war termination existed.[18] The influence of "hawks" outweighed "doves" at the decision-making level on both sides. Despite the military stalemate, both retained the view that the military balance on the field of battle could be changed in their favor. Although both remained optimistic about military prospects and tenacious concerning political goals, neither was confident of its own prospects following a cease-fire and a political compromise. In different ways, the leadership on each side continued to be tolerant of the suffering of its own country and especially of the Vietnamese people.

Although priding himself on his realism, Nixon was ardently optimistic and hence unrealistic about his chances for bringing immediate peace to Vietnam on his own terms.[19] His illusions were nurtured by necessity: "I'm not going to end up like LBJ," he observed in November after his electoral victory, "holed up in the White House afraid to show my face on the street. I'm going to stop that war. Fast."[20] Henry Kissinger, whom Nixon appointed special assistant for national security affairs, shared Nixon's optimism, but they were an improbable pair. Nixon was anti-intellectual, partisan, combative, distrustful, moody, and alternately conceited and insecure. He tended toward feelings of persecution, was prone to rage, and had a strange and limited sense of humor. Kissinger was a confident, charming, and witty Ivy League intellectual. Associated with the establishmentarian Council on Foreign Relations, he had served as a consultant on Vietnam to the Johnson administration and to Nelson Rockefeller, Nixon's centrist Republican rival for the presidential nomination. Nixon was an old-stock Anglo-American who thought that his rise to power from humble beginnings exemplified the saga of the self-made man. Kissinger was an immigrant Jew with a heavy German accent whose family had fled Nazi rule. His rise to fame and prestige rested on his intellectual talents as well as his ability to cultivate influential patrons.[21]

Despite their differences, both were crafty and ambitious men who needed and complemented one another. Kissinger, the courtier, needed Nixon, the president, in order to gain access to power. Nixon, the right-wing, southern California outsider, needed Kissinger's help in appeasing moderate Republicans and forming links and credibility with the eastern foreign policy establishment. Kissinger convinced Nixon that he was a hawk but persuaded others, including his own aides, that he was a dove, or at least more temperate and tactful than Nixon. Kissinger's scholarly, political science view of foreign policy supplemented Nixon's grand goals; his reputation for diplomatic skill counterbalanced Nixon's renowned militancy. He agreed with Nixon on the advantages of top-down decision making and suggested an administrative means of accomplishing it—making the National Security Council (NSC), not the Cabinet, the principal forum on interagency coordination for foreign policy. Both fancied themselves as practitioners of realpolitik, shared visions of a revised world structure, and feared that defeat in Vietnam would, in Kissinger's words, "unloose forces that would complicate prospects for international order." Originally questioning whether U.S. intervention in Vietnam was in its vital interest, Kissinger now genuinely worried that, having committed itself, U.S. credibility was at risk.[22]

Nixon and Kissinger agreed on the essential strategy for ending the Vietnam War on their terms. Although accounts differ about the degree of his support for the use of maximum force, Kissinger was eager—backed as he would be by Nixon's reputation for ruthlessness—to play the game of "good cop–bad cop." The good cop Kissinger would communicate the bad cop Nixon's irrational threats to the DRV, thus intimidating them into giving in through negotiations with the rational diplomat rather than facing the awful consequences to be dealt out by the mad president.[23] Kissinger was cynically contemptuous of the Vietnamese, unable to comprehend that "a little fourth-rate power like North Vietnam does not have a breaking point."[24] Both he and Nixon believed that their approach differed from Johnson's simple pursuit of military victory. They would employ diplomatic, political, and psychological strategies to initiate secret negotiations, begin a dialogue, and reach an honorable agreement. At a minimum, the settlement would extricate U.S. forces without the actuality or appearance of military and political collapse. Kissinger may have been more willing than Nixon to settle for the pretense of a "decent interval" between the time of the U.S. pullout and the fall of the South Vietnamese government, but it was more likely that neither he nor Nixon believed at the outset that they would have to resort to this ruse. They were counting on the leverage of military threat to achieve their diplomatic ends, and they believed that their commitment to *irrational* "compellence" strategy (the actuality or threat of sudden, dramatic escalation) as compared to Johnson's *rational* compellence strategy (gradual escalation) would be more effective.[25]

In the first several months of 1969, "Nixon and Kissinger set out to end the war," one historian wryly commented, "with that sublime self-confidence common among men new to power."[26] In March they began to employ military options not used by Johnson and to apply "irresistible military pressure," as Nixon put it. An aerial campaign using B-52 heavy bombers began against PAVN-PLAF bases in Cambodia near the border with South Vietnam. In April and into the summer, they moved to isolate North Vietnam by opening diplomatic back channels to the Soviet Union and China, linking progress on détente to progress on a Vietnam settlement and warning of escalation in the war if North Vietnam did not cooperate. To the DRV they proposed that negotiations move along two paths: The United States and DRV could talk about mutual withdrawal of forces from the South while the DRV and RVN discussed political questions. In June, after meeting with Thieu at Midway Island, Nixon kicked off de-Americanization with the announcement of the recall of 25,000 troops. U.S. battlefield tactics also shifted from big-unit sweeps to small-unit patrols. Simultaneously, Vietnamization proceeded with accelerated arms transfers to the ARVN and intensified pacification programs that included rural construction, amnesty for NLF defectors, assassination of NLF cadres, and peasant land reforms.

If Nixon originally intended to ignore domestic constraints while he applied irresistible military pressure against the enemy, he deviated from the plan. Constantly worried about public reaction, he resorted to a gradual escalation of the air war in Cambodia—as opposed to a dramatic return to the bombing of North Vietnam—and then tried to conceal the operation from public view. The Cambodian bombing was also partly an improvised reaction to a PAVN-PLAF offensive in February. Contradicting his preference for secrecy, Nixon occasionally turned to public diplomacy in an effort to influence public opinion, counter moves by the other side, or send signals to the Vietnamese. Responding in May, for example, to the NLF's public unveiling of a ten-point peace proposal, Nixon publicized his private call for negotiations and mutual withdrawal and then tried to put his domestic critics on the defensive by defining the war as a test of national will.[27]

The Nixon-Kissinger plan failed to bring an end to the war in the "matter of months" Kissinger had once assured his former Harvard colleagues he required.[28] In large part the failure resulted from the reality that in diplomacy, as in war, one's adversaries behave both rationally and in unanticipated ways. Little things go wrong and accumulate; plans go awry. Karl von Clausewitz, the nineteenth-century military philosopher who would be in vogue among the Monday-morning quarterbacks of the postwar era, figuratively referred to these phenomena as the "fog" and "friction" of war. Although the Soviets acquiesced in the expansion of the air war into Cambodia and advised the North Vietnamese to negotiate, they continued to supply material aid to the DRV and, in June, recognized the Provisional Revolutionary Government of the Republic of South Vietnam (PRG), which the DRV and NLF had formed in May in order to establish a southern negotiating entity. U.S. détente with China progressed slowly, and although Mao Zedong would eventually use his influence to try to persuade the southern NLF-PRG to soften its position on Thieu, China, like the Soviet Union, did not want to see a U.S. victory, had limited leverage with the Vietnamese, and continued its material support.[29]

Although worried about relations with the USSR and the PRC, the Hanoi Politburo regarded the Nixon-Kissinger proposal for a mutual withdrawal as a nonstarter and the U.S. suggestion to recognize the Demilitarized Zone (DMZ) as the boundary between two independent Vietnams as a farce. Moreover, Hanoi would not accept the separation of military and political discussions in the negotiating process. Confronted by the opportunity of de-Americanization and the challenges of the expansion of the air war, pacification, and Vietnamization, the DRV responded with its own military steps. The PAVN began to enhance its overland supply routes through Laos and adopted a defensive disengagement strategy of withdrawing some troops across the DMZ, avoiding big battles, and, with the PLAF, turning to protracted war.[30]

Nixon was increasingly frustrated and angered by his own lack of success and a resurgence of antiwar activism and congressional criticism. In July he began to improvise a "go-for-broke" strategy. Through French intermediaries he warned Ho Chi Minh of "measures of great consequence and force" unless diplomatic progress took place by November 1. Through Kissinger he alerted Ambassador Anatoly Dobrynin, the Soviet back-channel contact, that the wheels of dramatic escalation were now in motion. In early September, Kissinger had convened a special National Security Council group to prepare a plan for "savage, punishing blows" against the DRV. Code-named DUCK HOOK, it included the strategic bombing of Hanoi and other population centers, a naval blockade of North Vietnamese ports, the mining of ports and rivers, the bombing of dikes, a land invasion of North Vietnam, and the possible use of nuclear weapons in North Vietnam. Adding the weight of public commitment, Nixon leaked word of these possibilities to Congress and the press.[31]

Meanwhile, on August 4, Kissinger met privately in Paris with North Vietnamese diplomat Xuan Thuy and initiated what would be a long series of intermittent secret meetings. Except for this procedural accomplishment, the Nixon-Kissinger plan faltered. Thuy held firm on maximum DRV-PRG negotiating terms, calling for U.S. withdrawal and Thieu's removal. On August 15, two weeks before his death, Ho Chi Minh, the spiritual and organizational leader of the Vietnamese revolution, formally rejected Nixon's ultimatum. Although the DRV leaders were concerned about Nixon's threatened savage blows, after twenty-five hard years of war they were prepared to continue the struggle from the jungles and mountains if need be rather than abandon South Vietnam and the goal of a unified nation.[32]

Nixon also met domestic resistance to his go-for-broke approach. Secretary of Defense Melvin Laird and Secretary of State William Rogers advised against provoking domestic opposition with new, major escalations. An NSC staff paper cautioned that expanded air strikes and a blockade would probably not be decisive, and B-52 losses over Hanoi would be heavy. Outside the government, the largest number of people to demonstrate against war in American history participated in teach-ins, memorial services, and suspensions of business as usual in cities and towns across the country on October 15.

Nixon countered with a televised speech on November 3 in which he set the tone for future attacks on his domestic opposition. He appealed to the

"silent majority" to support the war until an honorable peace through negotiations could be achieved, excoriating the "minority" of "divisive" critics at
home, and warning of "bloodbaths" in Vietnam and a "collapse of confidence" abroad if the United States were to precipitously withdraw from
Vietnam. North Vietnam could not "defeat or humiliate America," he proclaimed; only his critics could do that by undermining the American will to
persist. Thus was born the stab-in-the-back legend, which Vice-President
Spiro Agnew played to the hilt, attacking intellectuals, liberals, the peace
movement, the eastern establishment, and the press for betraying the war effort. To most Americans the nation's vital interests did not seem to be in
jeopardy; the purposes of this ugly war were not tangible. Nixon's counterattack attempted with some success to transform this intangibility into an
asset. He tried to convert the struggle with domestic critics from a debate on
the wisdom and morality of the war into a battle of national symbols, which
he portrayed as a battle for honor, pride, loyalty, the flag, the return of
American prisoners of war (POWs), and the old notion of global credibility.[33]

The peace movement invoked other symbols. In a March against Death
memorializing the 45,000 Americans who had died in Vietnam, tens of
thousands of protesters carried candles and name placards through cold
wind and rain in the nation's capital from the night of November 12 through
November 14. In what was by some estimates the largest single antiwar demonstration, 800,000 people gathered near the Washington Monument on
November 15 and called for U.S. withdrawal, peace in Vietnam, and justice
at home. Polls indicated, however, that Nixon's November 3 speech had
been well received by the broad citizenry and that he was more popular than
the antiwar protesters. Nevertheless, in the months that followed, congressional and elite opposition to Nixon's policies generally rose, and the public's
approval of his handling of the war fluctuated. Precisely what the American
people thought and how Nixon's and Kissinger's decisions were affected by
public opinion were difficult to measure. It was clear in November 1969,
however, that the country was divided and war weary, and Nixon's plan for
peace on U.S. terms was in shambles.[34]

Unwilling to make realistic compromises in the negotiations, Nixon persisted in waging political campaigns at home and military campaigns in Indochina. For the rest of 1969 and into 1970, he produced mixed results with
Vietnamization, de-Americanization, pacification, counterinsurgency, and
high levels of bombing in South Vietnam, Laos, and Cambodia. The withdrawal of U.S. troops in particular, while defusing home-front opposition to

the war, created enormous problems for Nixon in Vietnam and Paris. The morale of U.S. troops who remained in Vietnam to fight what seemed an abandoned and lost cause deteriorated rapidly and profoundly. This problem and fewer U.S. combat units in the field eroded Nixon's military leverage in negotiations and encouraged the other side to hold out. In March 1970 he announced the removal of another 150,000 troops during the next year. According to the withdrawal plan, U.S. combat troops were to be out by November 1972. He was walking a tightrope, and he knew it.[35]

Then, on March 18, neutralist Prince Norodom Sihanouk of Cambodia was overthrown by Lon Nol and other pro-American generals. Nixon seized the opportunity for a big play, sending U.S. and ARVN units into border regions of Cambodia northwest of Saigon on April 28 and 29. (Earlier in April he had resumed the bombing of North Vietnam up to the 20th parallel in what were called "protective reaction" strikes.) Speaking to a national television audience on April 30, he confessed his frustration: "If when the chips are down, the world's most powerful nation . . . acts like a pitiful, helpless giant, the forces of totalitarianism and anarchy will threaten free nations and free institutions throughout the world."[36] The invasion achieved several successes: The enemy's coastal logistics network from North Vietnam through southern Cambodia was uncovered, bunkers and large caches of supplies were destroyed, and moderate casualties were inflicted on enemy forces. But for Nixon's purposes the big play flopped. The ostensible objective of the thrust, the destruction of the PAVN-PLAF headquarters and supply network, was not accomplished. Even though the military situation called for pursuit into Cambodia, U.S. troops withdrew into South Vietnam on June 29, leaving ARVN units in Cambodia to continue operations near the border. Despite the withdrawal, Nixon now had a much wider war on his hands, with ultimately tragic results for Cambodia.[37] At home the invasion sparked widespread and angry demonstrations, climaxing in the killings of students at Kent State and Jackson State Universities by National Guardsmen and police and the closing of hundreds of colleges and universities around the nation. Congress edged toward restricting presidential war powers. Infuriated and feeling besieged, Nixon initiated an elaborate and illegal plan of domestic surveillance, infiltration, and disinformation. In Paris, Kissinger had held his first meeting with Politburo member Le Duc Tho on February 21, but following the Cambodian incursion, secret discussions were suspended and not resumed until September. DRV and PRG delegates boycotted the public talks.

Nevertheless, Nixon was encouraged by the invasion and more confident that Thieu's regime could survive a proposal Kissinger tendered to Tho at a secret meeting on September 27. It called for a cease-fire, a bombing halt throughout Indochina, an immediate prisoner release, an international conference to guarantee the agreement, a negotiated withdrawal of U.S. troops, and the cessation of PAVN infiltration into the South. On October 27, just before the congressional elections, Nixon made the terms public, eagerly denigrating his domestic critics' call for a cease-fire. Hanoi rebuffed the proposal because it did not include provisions for the withdrawal of both U.S. troops from Vietnam and U.S. support for President Thieu and because it failed to provide for a coalition government and a political role for the NLF-PRG in South Vietnam.[38]

The year 1971 began badly for Nixon. Unemployment was up, the value of the dollar was down, members of the Senate called for a specific withdrawal date, his public approval rating declined, and antiwar protests continued. A military court found First Lieutenant William Calley, Jr., guilty of multiple murders at My Lai village in 1968, lending public credence to the charge that Americans had committed war crimes in Vietnam. The *New York Times* began publishing the *Pentagon Papers*, which provided evidence that the U.S. government had lied about the war for years.

In Indochina, Nixon persevered in his strategy of Vietnamization and military pressure through pacification, air attacks, and occasional big plays. On February 8 he launched an ARVN invasion code-named LAM SON 719 into Laos. The operation's aim was to disrupt a PAVN supply buildup, buy time for Thieu, and test the ARVN's capabilities. It ended on March 24 with heavy ARVN losses and an ignominious retreat into South Vietnam. Although inflicting large casualties on the PAVN and temporarily disrupting its preparations, LAM SON 719 proved the failure of Vietnamization, and, significantly, it demonstrated to the PAVN that it could beat the ARVN in head-to-head battle. Nixon publicly claimed that the operation was a success and blamed the press for misrepresenting the whole affair.[39]

On May 31, Nixon and Kissinger put forward a seven-point plan at a new round of secret meetings in Paris, initiating what Kissinger considered the first real negotiations since the process began. Like their proposal of September 1970, it called for a cease-fire in place but contained two new ideas: the withdrawal of U.S. troops six months after an agreement was signed and the resignation of President Thieu thirty days before a plebiscite on the political future of South Vietnam. Although adhering to their long-standing requirement that no specific date for withdrawal could be set until the safety of U.S. troops was assured, prisoners were released, and the Thieu government had a reasonable chance of surviving, Nixon and Kissinger had abandoned their 1969 demands for a mutual withdrawal and their 1970 suggestion for a negotiated U.S. withdrawal after an agreement. They had also begun to accept the linking of military and political issues.[40]

On June 26, Le Duc Tho offered the DRV's nine-point counterproposal, which also represented significant movement. In the past, the DRV had expressed willingness to negotiate a POW release only after a U.S. withdrawal; now Tho proposed a POW release concurrent with a U.S. withdrawal by the end of 1971. Instead of demanding Thieu's removal, the proposal called on the U.S. government to "stop supporting" Thieu. At the public Paris talks on July 1, the PRG submitted its own seven-point proposal. It applied only to South Vietnam but complemented the private DRV plan. Coming as it did three months before scheduled presidential elections in South Vietnam, it signaled DRV-PRG willingness to allow free elections to decide whether Thieu would remain in power or a more moderate government would replace him. This latter eventuality could provide an honorable exit for the United States and lead to internal Vietnamese negotiations on the political future of the South.[41]

Nixon and Kissinger backed away from this apparently momentous opportunity to end U.S. involvement with honor in 1971. Unable to ignore or deny the PRG's public proposal, they portrayed it as propaganda intended to manipulate public opinion in the United States, and they misrepresented the other side's position on Thieu as demanding his removal. Instead of ending active support of Thieu, the CIA and the American embassy in Saigon cooperated with Thieu to sabotage open and free elections. American money was used to bribe the South Vietnamese legislature into disqualifying one of the candidates, Nguyen Cao Ky, while Thieu's province chiefs prepared to defraud the upcoming vote. Rejecting a tax-free, $3 million American bribe to stay in the rigged race and provide it with a veneer of legitimacy, the other candidate, Duong Van Minh, withdrew on August 2. In the voting of October 3, Thieu won a 94.3 percent majority.[42]

In Paris on September 13, the DRV delegation, noting the withdrawal of opposition candidates, declared that the U.S. pledge of neutrality in the election was meaningless. On October 11, after Thieu's reelection, the U.S. delegation proposed another peace plan. It called for a cease-fire, the withdrawal of U.S. troops, the release of POWs, a mixed electoral commission that would include the PRG, and the resignation of Thieu one month before elections. With Thieu firmly in power, the North Vietnamese continued to adhere to their nine-point proposal of June. Although neither side had formally rejected the other's proposal, the private talks had reached an impasse, and no new meetings were scheduled.

Nixon and Kissinger turned to renewed emphasis on Vietnamization and its military correlates. In October the president ordered "reinforced" protective reaction strikes against the North, and just before Christmas he intensified the bombing of North Vietnam. There was now also a new element in their calculations—the hope that triangular diplomacy would solve the riddle of Vietnam. On July 15, Nixon disclosed that he would visit China in early 1972; on October 12 came the announcement that he would travel to the USSR following his return from China. Nixon and Kissinger thought that extending the carrot of détente to both China and the Soviet Union would enable them to play one power off against the other. By inducing the Chinese and the Soviets to put pressure on or withdraw support from the North Vietnamese, they could then use the stick of linkage to score a diplomatic victory in Indochina. Détente would also distract attention from their floundering diplomatic approach to the war. In January 1972, still seeking to rebut domestic criticism and the PRG's public diplomacy, Nixon revealed to the nation that he was conducting secret talks with the DRV, and he released the text of his last proposal. It was well received by many in the United States but contributed nothing to the negotiations.[43]

In the fall of 1971, meanwhile, the Hanoi Politburo had resolved to make 1972 the year of decisive victory. Nixon's obdurate support for Thieu in the October 1971 election had tipped the balance in the Politburo in favor of a military offensive during the spring dry season of 1972. There were several other, related considerations in Hanoi's shift from a defensive strategy of protracted war to an offensive one of mobile war. By the end of 1971, U.S. troop strength would be down to approximately 160,000, with only a small percentage of combat infantry, and their numbers would continue to decline rapidly into 1972. Even though the ARVN had more than 1 million men and the PAVN had fewer than 200,000 in the South at the end of 1971, the northern army was confident. An escalation of the fighting accompanied by ARVN defeats would demonstrate to the Soviets and Chinese the hollowness of Nixon's military credibility in Vietnam. In any event, despite Nixon's wooing, the USSR concluded a comprehensive arms assistance agreement with the DRV in October, providing assurance of continued Soviet support—for the time being at least. The Chinese continued their material aid as well. But the Politburo reasoned that if U.S. triangular diplomacy were eventually to influence USSR and PRC aid to the DRV, the dry spring season of 1972 was an opportune time to achieve military and political gains.[44]

At a minimum, an offensive would move additional PAVN troops from the North to the South in anticipation of a military cease-fire and diplomatic compromise. It would draw the ARVN into battle and away from pacification, thus allowing for the return and rebuilding of the NLF in its former territories. Success on the battlefield would produce territorial gains and demonstrate that the PAVN could always fight above the level of the ARVN. At best, the offensive would force the ARVN's military collapse, Thieu's political collapse, and the United States' diplomatic collapse.[45]

The DRV's big play, the Spring or Easter Offensive of 1972, began at dawn on March 30. Three PAVN divisions using tanks and heavy artillery attacked into Quang Tri province from southern Laos and across the DMZ. Additional multidivision attacks followed northwest of Saigon and in central South Vietnam. Making rapid initial progress, the offensive stalled in June in the face of massive U.S. B-52 and fighter-bomber attacks, heavy artillery fire, and the PAVN's difficulties with mobile pursuit. Thus aided, the ARVN, which had seemed on the verge of disintegration, recovered, and the war devolved once more into stalemate. Both Vietnamese armies lost heavily; more fields were cratered and hundreds more villages were leveled; a million more refugees were on the road; and North and South Vietnam approached exhaustion. But the territory held by the PAVN had been enlarged; the NLF had reorganized, especially in the Mekong Delta; the ARVN's weaknesses had again been exposed, with desertions on the rise; and the U.S. Congress slowly moved closer to cutting off funding for the war.

Meanwhile, the offensive stirred the caldron of war and diplomacy. In early April, in addition to accelerated air support for the ARVN in South Vietnam, Nixon authorized expanded U.S. bombing into North Vietnam, striking targets that had been on a restricted list since 1967. B-52s attacked the DRV for the first time since 1968, flying 700 sorties by the end of the month, including raids on April 15–16 against Hanoi and Haiphong. Despite the U.S. aerial counteroffensive, which included bombing Soviet ships in Haiphong harbor, détente moved forward. Kissinger went to Moscow that month to prepare the way for Nixon's trip in May. He pressed the Soviets to rein in the North Vietnamese, warned of greater escalations, and again linked progress in détente to progress in Vietnam negotiations. In the United States, Nixon leaked hints of the possible mining of harbors and bombing of dikes. The Soviets agreed to transmit Kissinger's new negotiating concessions to the DRV: a cease-fire in place, the release of all POWs, and a unilateral U.S. withdrawal from Indochina four months later. On May

2, a day after the PAVN took Quang Tri City—a major defeat for the ARVN—Kissinger met with Tho and communicated his revised proposal.[46]

Six days later, Nixon announced to a national television audience that he had ordered the mining of North Vietnamese ports, including Haiphong, and the bombing of rail lines, communications, and logistics facilities. From Nixon's point of view, these latest dramatic escalations, code-named Operation LINEBACKER, served several purposes. They would likely have a military impact on the PAVN's ability to sustain an offensive and thus help prevent the ARVN's defeat. Equally if not more important they were symbolic. They would make credible earlier threats delivered to the Soviets, Chinese, and North Vietnamese; the mining in particular seemed to fulfill a madman's scenario. They would serve home-front political ends as well. Explaining the escalations to Americans as necessary in order to force the enemy to seek a political rather than a military solution pleased the hawks at home but provoked no large-scale protests. Military and political moves by both sides were, of course, intertwined, and the fighting was all about political issues. But the latest LINEBACKER escalations obscured U.S. diplomatic concessions, producing the impression that progress made in the negotiations was the result of Nixon's defensive, but militarily decisive, actions.[47]

In Moscow on May 22 for the scheduled summit, Nixon and Kissinger transmitted revised terms to the North Vietnamese via the Soviets. Their major new concession—willingness to respond constructively to the DRV's insistence on combining political and military issues—created the basis for a breakthrough agreement. Specifically, Kissinger told Foreign Minister Andrei Gromyko that the United States would accept a tripartite commission to govern South Vietnam after the war. Although the suggestion was ambiguous about whether the commission would be a real government, it was, nevertheless, an innovation that addressed previous DRV-PRG calls for a three-segment "government" or "administration" of "national concord" for South Vietnam that would work toward "general elections."[48]

As the fighting continued through the summer, the United States and the DRV assessed the situation. The DRV was disappointed that the USSR and the PRC had not vigorously protested the mining of Haiphong; the United States was disappointed that they had not exerted more pressure on the DRV by cutting off material aid. By late summer, the Politburo envisaged three possible settlements: a political agreement with a coalition government replacing Thieu; a cease-fire, Thieu remaining, and formal recognition of the PRG; or a continuing war after U.S. withdrawal. The last two, though less desirable than the first, were becoming more acceptable.

At the same time, Nixon and Kissinger had resolved that the war should be ended before the next dry-season opportunity for fighting. Thieu's persistent objections to the PAVN's presence in the South, the surrender of territory, and the recognition of the PRG would be ignored. He would be presented with a fait accompli rather than be given an opportunity to sabotage an agreement.[49] As far as the forthcoming U.S. presidential elections were concerned, Nixon was uncertain until the last moment whether a settlement would be advantageous, but in any case he wanted the war over before he began his next term in January. Kissinger was eager for a settlement too. Other global problems awaited both men. The Politburo, for its part, decided that since Nixon would win the election, there was no point in waiting and more to gain in settling now, either because Nixon would be more willing to sign before the election or because he might be more difficult to deal with afterward. In sum, neither side judged the military situation as favorable; both considered their overall prospects to be better with a cease-fire than without one; and the costs of the war had become intolerable to both sides. Neither the United States nor the DRV-PRG had relinquished their political goals, but both had shifted to practical, minimum solutions.

At a secret meeting on September 26, Le Duc Tho offered his concession by translating Kissinger's call for a tripartite commission into a tripartite National Council of Reconciliation and Concord (NCRC). It was more likely to be acceptable to Thieu than Kissinger's proposal because it would not be a government and it did not call for Thieu's removal. It would, however, recognize the PRG and operate on the basis of unanimity, thus giving the PRG an equal voice. When Tho met Kissinger again on October 8, he presented the English-language version of his breakthrough proposal. Key provisions were an immediate cease-fire before the formation of the NCRC; the ending of hostile acts against the DRV, including bombing and mining; a prisoner exchange; the withdrawal of U.S. forces from South Vietnam within sixty days; two Joint Military Commissions (JMCs) to supervise the cease-fire, one including the U.S. and all Vietnamese parties, the other including only the South Vietnamese parties; an International Commission of Control and Supervision (ICCS) to oversee the agreement; and the reunification of Vietnam. On October 12, Kissinger headed for Washington with a draft agreement. The understanding was that the initialing would take place in Hanoi before the month was out and before the U.S. presidential election.[50]

Events that followed were fast-moving and complex. Nixon gave Kissinger his full support for the agreement, regarded it as "RN's settlement," raised no objections, and sent Kissinger back to Paris to tighten up the language and put it in final form.[51] After Paris, Kissinger flew to Saigon, arriving on October 19. Thieu and his staff challenged Kissinger's view that the agreement provided his government with a good chance to survive. Meanwhile, between October 19 and 21, the Politburo agreed to U.S. demands to separate the release of U.S. POWs from the release of Vietnamese civilian detainees. On October 23, as Kissinger was leaving for Washington, Thieu objected to the presence of the PAVN in the South after a cease-fire, called the NCRC a disguised coalition government, complained about the release of civilian prisoners, and demanded that the DMZ be made secure. The following day, he leaked portions of the agreement and effectively and publicly rejected it.[52] Kissinger consulted Nixon in Washington and cabled Hanoi that the bombing halt would apply only north of the 20th parallel. He postponed the signing, pleading difficulty with his ally. On October 25, Radio Hanoi responded by broadcasting details of the agreement, reviewing the history of negotiations and the agreed-upon timetable, and charging Nixon with sabotaging the chance to end the war. The next day, disappointed and embarrassed, Kissinger declared to the press that "peace was at hand" as he tried to explain why an already negotiated agreement could not be signed. Essentially, his message was that after careful scrutiny the U.S. government had determined that nuances, technicalities, and ambiguities had to be clarified.[53]

In reality, Kissinger had arrived in Washington on October 24 to discover that Nixon had had second thoughts. Some political critics were viewing the agreement as a cynical electioneering ploy. Hard-liners on both Kissinger's and Nixon's staffs, believing that the enemy was on the run, opposed the compromise, which they viewed as a sellout.[54] Thieu and the U.S. press were referring to the NCRC as a coalition government, which implied that Nixon was caving in to one of the key demands of the other side, abandoning Thieu, and bugging out. The basic problem for Nixon was the appearance, not the reality, of the agreement. Although the NCRC did give de jure recognition to the de facto PRG, thus acknowledging that Thieu's was not the only lawful administration in South Vietnam, the NCRC was not a coalition government.[55] Nixon continued to support the agreement and regarded it as his, but he wanted to "knock down" the "code word" of "coalition government."[56] Confronted by his ally's opposition and the appearance of cutting and running, Nixon believed that politically he could not afford to sign the October treaty.

Thieu remained in power, but the PAVN was still in the South and the

Americans were on the way out. The last U.S. combat unit had been with-drawn in August, and by the end of 1972 only 24,200 American personnel would remain in South Vietnam. Nixon had grudgingly accepted these reali-ties and expected both sides to cheat on an agreement after the U.S. with-drawal. Nixon and Kissinger now believed, or had convinced themselves, that with U.S. aid the struggle would continue at a reduced level, the enemy could be contained, and Thieu could survive—either for a long time or at least for a decent interval. It was the best and only honorable thing to do. Nixon's difficulty was establishing credibility at home and around the world. As long as Thieu refused to cooperate, it would seem that Nixon had abandoned him, denying the purpose of having fought the war. The DRV and PRG, however, would not accede to Thieu's demands. This was the pres-ident's new tightrope.[57]

Following his landslide electoral victory on November 7, Nixon con-cocted a plan to bolster Thieu, reestablish U.S. credibility, and end the war with honor before the inauguration. Operation ENHANCE PLUS delivered large amounts of heavy artillery, helicopters, tanks, and aircraft to the ARVN. Secret military agreements were worked out with Thieu for contin-ued cooperation after the war. The U.S. Seventh Air Force in Thailand, for example, would maintain communications with the ARVN, provide target-ing information on the PAVN, and launch tactical and B-52 attacks against North Vietnam if it threatened to topple Thieu. Alexander Haig, a hard-liner on Kissinger's staff whom Thieu liked, was sent to Saigon on Novem-ber 9 to assure Thieu of U.S. support but also to secure his acceptance of an agreement. When talks resumed in Paris on November 20, Kissinger pre-sented Le Duc Tho with a set of what he later referred to as "preposterous" revisions. Their purpose was to improve the provisions of the agreement and placate Thieu. Finally, Nixon believed that his ace in the hole was the threat of ruthless bombing. Walking his tightrope, he noted that "for better or for worse, we are on a course now where we have no choice but to make the very best settlement that we can and then do the best we can to see that it is en-forced."[58]

Although independent information about what took place in Paris is lacking, it appears that several U.S. revisions to the agreement were signifi-cant. Kissinger demanded references to the DMZ that implied that the PAVN's presence in the South was illegal and restricted civilian movement from North to South. He called for a clause requiring PAVN troop with-drawals, proposed language changes that altered the status of the NCRC from a three-party administrative structure to a weakened two-party council, and demanded that all references to the PRG be eliminated. Tho agreed to some minor revisions but rejected the major ones. Then on November 25, Kissinger opened new issues. The ICCS was to be increased significantly in size and would be permitted to carry side arms, which to the DRV took on the trappings of an occupation force. The DRV must designate its points of entry for armaments replacement, which the DRV thought would make the PAVN vulnerable to ARVN attacks. Kissinger also proposed that the two-party JMC, consisting of representatives from the PRG and RVN, determine areas of control by military factors alone, not both military and administrative factors, having the net effect of diminishing PRG territory. In addition, the PRG would have to declare the strength and location of military units. He threatened to intensify the war with savage bombing unless Hanoi yielded.[59] Nixon had authorized Kissinger to suspend the talks for a week for negotiators to consult with their principals "if the Communists remained intransigent," and during the interval he would be prepared to approve a "massive bombing strike" on North Vietnam.[60]

At meetings that began on December 4, Le Duc Tho withdrew previous concessions and introduced new revisions. Kissinger conceded some minor points but held firm on demands concerning restrictions on civilian movement across the DMZ, deletions of references to the PRG, and changes in the NCRC, ICCS, and JMC. Tho reopened the question of the relationship of POW releases to civilian-detainee releases. The Nixon-Kissinger negotiating strategy had backfired. Their threats had not forced concessions but had led the other side to hang tough and counterattack. Now they faced another diplomatic impasse—although Le Duc Tho said that he believed the remaining matters could be resolved. At Kissinger's suggestion, the talks were recessed on December 13 until after Christmas, and he and Tho departed to consult with their governments. Warning of "drastic" steps, Kissinger left Paris on December 14. With clenched fists he later confided to Nixon: "They're just a bunch of shits, tawdry, filthy shits." The Politburo had already begun evacuating children from Hanoi on December 4.[61]

On December 14, Nixon issued the order for U.S. planes to attack north of the 20th parallel three days later. As the bombs began to fall, he told Kissinger and Admiral Thomas Moorer, chairman of the Joint Chiefs of Staff: "The Russians and Chinese might think they were dealing with a madman and so had better force North Vietnam into a settlement before the world was consumed by a larger war."[62] The next day he admonished Moorer: "I don't want any more of this crap about the fact that we couldn't hit this target or that one. This is your chance to use military power to win this war, and if you don't, I'll consider you responsible."[63] The attacks not only re-flected Nixon's and Kissinger's rage but were consistent with the strategy of big-play jugular diplomacy and drew on the perceived success of LINE-BACKER and other big plays of the past. Although Nixon was ready to settle "along the lines of the October 8 principles," the purpose of this "high-risk option" was to make the North Vietnamese more conciliatory on the "ambi-guities" of the agreement, which would both improve the October draft and put him in a better position to force Thieu's acceptance of a settlement.[64] The bombing would hurt North Vietnam, thus helping Thieu in the struggle ahead, and it would make Nixon's threats of using air power in the future more credible to the DRV, the USSR, the PRC, and the RVN. It also sig-naled that Nixon had done all he could, placating right-wing hawks in the United States.[65]

For eleven days from December 18 to 29, with a pause on Christmas Day, the U.S. Air Force, Navy, and Marine Corps carried out unprecedented air raids against the DRV in Operation LINEBACKER II. American crews flew 3,420 bombing and support sorties into the heart of the DRV. Making exten-sive use of B-52s, which flew over 50 percent of the missions, they attacked railroad yards, supply and petroleum depots, radio-communications instal-lations, electrical power and broadcast stations, airfields, surface-to-air mis-sile (SAM) sites, bridges, port facilities, and transshipment points. LINE-BACKER II differed substantially from LINEBACKER I in that it entailed more intense around-the-clock bombing concentrated in and around Hanoi and Haiphong.[66]

This "December Blitz" or "Christmas Bombing" produced a great amount of what the U.S. military called "collateral" damage. In Hanoi, for example, the An Duong, Bach Mai, Ben Chuang Duong, Ben Pha Den, Kham Thien, and other residential areas were heavily damaged; the Bach Mai hospital was destroyed; eight foreign embassies were damaged; 2,196 civilians were killed and 1,577 were wounded.[67] On the other side of the ledger, during what the Vietnamese called the "Twelve Days of Dienbienphu in the Air," SAMs, MiG interceptors, antiaircraft guns, and operational accidents took a heavy toll of American pilots and their planes. By U.S. counts, 121 crewmen were killed, missing in action, or became POWs; thirteen tactical aircraft and fifteen B-52s were shot down.[68] B-52 losses amounted to 12 percent of the 129 big bombers deployed in the raids.

Domestic and international criticism was strong. Press commentators used a long list of derogatory adjectives in describing Nixon's personality—ruthless, deceptive, insecure, paranoid, insensitive, brutal, truculent, cynical, unscrupulous, shameful, monstrous, willful, and arbitrary.[69] Their message to the public was that LINEBACKER II was an unnecessary, irrational act of fury representing the belligerence that Nixon felt toward all his real and perceived enemies, foreign and domestic. Its only rational purpose was to bribe Thieu into accepting the treaty. This interpretation of the bombing by what Nixon deemed his liberal enemies in the media was exactly what he feared. Other doubters and critics included some of his own staff, members of Congress, intellectuals, European allies, neutral governments, the Soviet Union, and China. His public approval rating dropped eleven percentage points.[70] Americans were confused about the purpose of the bombing. The U.S. role in the war had seemed virtually over. Now, at a time of profound public war weariness, Nixon had initiated the most intensive bombing of the long, tragic conflict and had not seen fit to provide a public explanation.

Meeting strong criticism at home and abroad, suffering heavy air losses, and despite earlier hints that the bombing would continue indefinitely, Nixon and Kissinger were ready to compromise and pressed the DRV to resume the negotiations. The Politburo agreed on December 26, the bombing stopped on December 29, and the technical talks recommenced on January 2, 1973.[71] The Kissinger-Tho meetings began on January 8 and concluded on January 13 with a second agreement that reflected compromises by both sides. As the DRV wanted, the PAVN remained in the South, and the DMZ was designated as a provisional demarcation line. The United States dropped demands for specific limitations on civilian movement across the DMZ, but the modalities of movement were subject to negotiation by Vietnamese parties while the PAVN continued to control the DMZ. The NCRC retained its functions, but the term "administrative structure" was omitted in references to it.[72] In line with U.S. wishes, the size of the ICCS was increased, but below the levels previously demanded. The two-party JMC retained its original power to determine who controlled areas of South Vietnam, but how this was to be done would be negotiated within the JMC. For Thieu, mention of the PRG was eliminated, with the phrase "South Vietnamese parties" used to refer to the PRG and RVN. But the PRG was recognized in a compromise worked out for the signing ceremony. There were two documents: One named the PRG in the preamble and was to be signed by the United States and the DRV "with the concurrence" of the PRG and RVN; the other would not mention the PRG anywhere and was to be signed by all four parties.

Pressed relentlessly by Nixon since November to sign the treaty, and given promises of B-52 attacks against the DRV in the future if needed, Thieu reluctantly submitted on January 21, the day after Nixon's inauguration. On January 27, eight years after the massive U.S. combat buildup had begun and twenty-eight years after the United States had become involved in the Indochina fighting, the United States, DRV, RVN, and PRG signed the Paris Agreement on Ending the War and Restoring Peace in Vietnam.[73]

Although Nixon and Kissinger subsequently attached great significance to the changes concerning the NCRC and the ICCS, the January agreement was essentially the same as that reached in October. If the final, slightly revised terms were the ones Nixon and Kissinger had wanted in November, when talks had resumed after Nixon's reelection, it is likely that a more businesslike and less belligerent negotiating approach would have succeeded. LINEBACKER II, intended to force concessions that were not won at the negotiating table, had failed too. Nixon and Kissinger had played poker, bluffed, lost their hand, and thrown in their chips. As one of Kissinger's aides put it: "We bombed the North Vietnamese into accepting our concession."[74]

Realizing as early as January 9, 1973, that they had failed to create a "just and lasting peace," Nixon and his aides discussed the problem of countering skeptics and influencing the verdict of history. Drafted by speech writer Patrick J. Buchanan, the White House plan aimed at portraying Nixon as the leading "peacemaker" in a long war.[75] It would obfuscate details, build on the emerging body of "revisionist" writing that was defending the war, and target the press, scholars, and the public. The plan had four multipart messages. First, with the support of the silent majority and his friends in Congress, the president had had the courage, toughness, and wisdom to make the hard decisions and see them through—despite unprecedented attacks from critics in Congress and the media. Second, no quarter was to be given to opponents, especially those on Capitol Hill, whose criticisms and resolutions against the war had prolonged the conflict. Many in Congress would have simply withdrawn U.S. troops from Vietnam in exchange for POWs, which was nothing more than a plan for cutting and running, the equivalent of abject, dishonorable defeat and surrender. It would also have led to a bloodbath of continued war, in which the 50 million long-suffering people of Indochina would have had to fight on without the United States. The critics were wrong, therefore, and Nixon was right.

Third, "our" peace with a cease-fire was not a "bug out" but one that achieved the major goals of the war: It got our POWs back, won "peace with independence for South Vietnam and peace for the people of Southeast Asia," and assured the right of the South Vietnamese to determine their own future without the communists imposing a government on them. Furthermore, despite the unpopularity of the war and the mistakes made by previous administrations in fighting it, the president's handling of it preserved the credibility of the U.S. commitment, "which is essential not only to our national self-respect but to our continuing role as a force for peace in the world." Fourth, certain misconceptions had to be shot down: It was not possible to settle on a peace in December; the peace agreement signed in January could not have been had earlier; the January agreement was an improvement over the October peace agreement; the NCRC was not a "coalition" government; the Thieu government had not been abandoned; there was never any division between the president and Kissinger. As for the December blitz over Hanoi, Buchanan's document elaborated, it was not "terror bombing" but struck only military targets; it broke the deadlock in negotiations, forced the other side back to the table, and won concessions from them while protecting the sovereignty of South Vietnam and winning the release of U.S. POWs. It had, in other words, won a peace with honor.[76] His diplomacy of threats having failed to achieve a real victory as he had originally defined it, Richard Nixon's Vietnam diplomacy was now aimed primarily at public, scholarly, and international opinion in a battle of symbolism, rhetoric, and interpretation.

Notes

1. Senate Committee on Foreign Relations, "President Nixon's Record on Vietnam, 1954-68," *Legislative Proposals Relating to the War in Southeast Asia: Hearings*, 92d Cong., 1st sess. (Washington, D.C.: GPO, 1971), 295-99; Stephen E. Ambrose, *Nixon*, vol. 1, *The Education of a Politician, 1913-1962* (New York: Simon & Schuster, 1987), vol. 2, *The Triumph of a Politician, 1962-1972* (New York: Simon & Schuster, 1989), and vol. 3, *Ruin and Recovery, 1973-1990* (New York: Simon & Schuster, 1991); Fawn Brodie, *Richard Nixon: The Shaping of His Character* (New York: Norton, 1981); Roger Morris, *Richard Milhous Nixon: The Rise of an American Politician* (New York: Henry Holt, 1990); Herbert S. Parmet, *Richard Nixon and His America* (Boston: Little, Brown, 1990).

2. Nixon had even used the word "aggression" to refer to the Vietminh revolution against French colonialism. Ambrose, *Nixon*, 1:321, 344.

3. Richard M. Nixon, "Asia after Vietnam," *Foreign Affairs* 46 (October 1967): 111; "A Conversation with the President about Foreign Policy, July 1, 1970," *Public Papers of the Presidents of the United States: Richard Nixon, 1970* (Washington, D.C.: GPO, 1971), 546-49.

4. "President Nixon's Record on Vietnam," 295-99; Ambrose, *Nixon*, 2:169; Nixon, "Asia after Vietnam," 111-25. On U.S. foreign policy after World War II,

see Thomas J. McCormick, *America's Half-Century: United States Foreign Policy in the Cold War* (Baltimore: Johns Hopkins University Press, 1989).

5. "President Nixon's Record on Vietnam," 295–99; Ambrose, *Nixon*, 1:141–44; Richard Nixon, *RN: The Memoirs of Richard Nixon* (New York: Grosset & Dunlap, 1978), 298–300.

6. Ambrose, *Nixon*, 2:143–150, argues that Nixon had changed his thinking on Vietnam after Tet 1968. On public opinion, the place to begin is John E. Mueller, *War, Presidents and Public Opinion* (New York: Wiley, 1973).

7. Nixon, "Asia after Vietnam," 111–23.

8. Nixon, *Memoirs*, 298, 347–49.

9. Quoted in H. R. Haldeman with Joseph DiMona, *The Ends of Power* (New York: Times Books, 1978), 82–83. See also Nixon's statements quoted in Thomas L. Hughes, "Foreign Policy: Men or Measures?" *Atlantic*, October 1974, 55. Seymour M. Hersh, *The Price of Power: Kissinger in the Nixon White House* (New York: Summit Books, 1983), 52–53, notes that Daniel Ellsberg lectured to Kissinger's Harvard seminar in 1959 on "The Political Use of Madness" and suggests that Nixon may have gotten the term "madman" from Kissinger. Ellsberg argues that the key element in Nixon's madman theory was the *nuclear* threat (Daniel Ellsberg interview by the author, Washington, D.C., July 15, 1992). Using Theodore Roosevelt's term, Nixon also described his approach as "big-stick" diplomacy. "Brinkmanship" was Eisenhower's and John Foster Dulles's name for this strategy.

10. Quoted in William Safire, *Before the Fall: An Inside View of the Pre-Watergate White House* (Garden City, N.Y.: Doubleday, 1975), 102–3. See also Hughes, "Foreign Policy," 56. Despite evidence from several independent sources and the record of Nixon's actions, some historians doubt that he professed the madman theory. See, for example, Joan Hoff-Wilson, "The Corporate Presidency," in Fred I. Greenstein, ed., *Leadership in the Modern Presidency* (Cambridge, Mass.: Harvard University Press, 1988), 188.

11. The standard study on détente is Raymond L. Garthoff, *Détente and Confrontation: American-Soviet Relations from Nixon to Reagan* (Washington, D.C.: Brookings Institution, 1985). Détente was a goal that the Soviets had long wanted and that other policymakers, including Johnson, sought as well. See also Nixon, *Memoirs*, 726; Ambrose, *Nixon*, 2:168; and George C. Herring, *America's Longest War: The United States and Vietnam, 1950–1975*, 2d ed. (New York: Knopf, 1986), 253.

12. Ambrose, *Nixon*, 2:264–65. For Nixon's and Kissinger's attitudes on bureaucracy and presidential foreign policymaking, see Hersh, *Price of Power*; Roger Morris, *Uncertain Greatness: Henry Kissinger and American Foreign Policy* (New York: Harper & Row, 1977); and Robert D. Schulzinger, *Henry Kissinger: Doctor of Diplomacy* (New York: Columbia University Press, 1989). Charles DeBenedetti with Charles Chatfield, *An American Ordeal: The Antiwar Movement of the Vietnam Era* (Syracuse, N.Y.: Syracuse University Press, 1990), 309, argues that declining morale in Vietnam, mismanagement of the Selective Service System, federal court rulings, and citizen opposition to the draft forced the Nixon administration to introduce a lottery system of determining liability for conscription in 1969 and then to abolish the draft altogether in 1972.

13. "Informal Remarks in Guam with Newsmen," July 25, 1969, *Public Papers: Nixon, 1969* (Washington, D.C.: GPO, 1970), 544–56; "Address to the Nation on the War in Vietnam," November 3, 1969, ibid., 901, 905–6; Nixon, *Memoirs*, 395.

14. Nguyen Tien Hung and Jerrold L. Schecter, *The Palace File* (New York: Harper & Row, 1986), 21–29; Hersh, *Price of Power*, 16–24; Nixon, *Memoirs*, 323–28. Nixon worked the deal through his aides, including John Mitchell. Mitchell was a go-between with Anna Chennault, who was a friend of Thieu, a longtime supporter of Chiang Kai-shek (Jiang Jieshi) and Taiwan, and a staunch Nixon campaigner. Drawing on journalist Theodore H. White's account, Ambrose, *Nixon*, 2:206–17, argues that the Nixon camp, not Nixon, approached Chennault, and that it made no difference, since Thieu would have refused to cooperate with Johnson or Humphrey anyway.

15. Many, if not most, historians, however, deemphasize the continuities between Johnson and Nixon and instead stress Nixon's departures, such as the opening to China and triangular diplomacy. This is true even of his critics. See, for example, Gabriel Kolko, *Anatomy of a War: Vietnam, the United States, and the Modern Historical Experience* (New York: Pantheon Books, 1985), 342–45.

16. Ambrose, *Nixon*, 2:241–42.

17. William J. Duiker, *The Communist Road to Power in Vietnam* (Boulder, Colo.: Westview, 1981), 279–83; Truong Nhu Tang with David Chanoff and Doan Van Toai, *A Viet Cong Memoir* (New York: Vintage, 1985), chapter 12; Kolko, *Anatomy of a War*, 368–76; William S. Turley, *The Second Indochina War: A Short Political and Military History, 1954–1975* (New York: New American Library, 1987), 122–24.

18. For letters of February 20 and March 22, 1991, summarizing her forthcoming publications on war termination, I am indebted to Professor Helena Meyer-Knapp of Evergreen State College.

19. Garthoff, *Détente*, 248–49.

20. Quoted in Haldeman, *Ends of Power*, 81.

21. For Nixon's personality, see biographies cited above. For Kissinger's, see Hersh, *Price of Power*; Marvin Kalb and Bernard Kalb, *Kissinger* (Boston: Little, Brown, 1974), especially pp. 120–21; Morris, *Uncertain Greatness*; Schulzinger, *Kissinger*; and, of course, Henry Kissinger, *White House Years* (Boston: Little, Brown, 1979).

22. Kissinger, "The Vietnam Negotiations," *Foreign Affairs* 47 (January 1969): 218–19, 234.

23. Tad Szulc, *The Illusion of Peace: Foreign Policy in the Nixon Years* (New York: Viking, 1978), 63, uses the phrase, "good guy–bad guy." Kissinger's aides later came to view him as irrational. Hersh, *Price of Power*, 190.

24. Quoted in Hersh, *Price of Power*, 126.

25. Dorothy C. Donnelly, "A Settlement of Sorts: Henry Kissinger's Negotiations and America's Extrication from Vietnam," *Peace and Change* 9 (Summer 1983): 62. See also Allan E. Goodman, *The Lost Peace: America's Search for a Negotiated Settlement of the Vietnam War* (Stanford, Calif.: Hoover Institution Press, 1978), 81–89. There is considerable disagreement about the extent to which Nixon and Kissinger saw eye to eye, and Goodman's book explores their differences.

26. Herring, *America's Longest War*, 225.

27. Nixon, *Memoirs*, 380–82, 391–92. With questionable logic, Nixon maintained that another purpose of secrecy was to provide Prince Norodom Sihanouk of Cambodia the opportunity to be silent on the bombing; that is, if it were not public, he would not have to protest. See also "Address to the Nation on Vietnam," May 14, 1969, *Public Papers: Nixon, 1969*, 369–75; and Gareth Porter, *A Peace Denied: The United States, Vietnam, and the Paris Agreement* (Bloomington: Indiana University Press, 1975), 95.

28. He also told Quaker antiwar activists: "Give us six months, and if we haven't ended the war by then, you can come back and tear down the White House fence." Quoted in Kalb and Kalb, *Kissinger*, 120. Hersh, *Price of Power*, 119, quotes him as having said "three months."

29. Garthoff, *Détente*, chapter 7; Goodman, *The Lost Peace*, 103–4; Kolko, *Anatomy of a War*, 402–30; Porter, *A Peace Denied*, 88–89; Szulc, *Illusion of Peace*, 609–10.

30. The DRV and PRG-NLF consistently adhered to the four points enunciated on April 8, 1965, by Premier Pham Van Dong: "(1) Recognition of the basic national rights of the Vietnamese people: peace, independence, sovereignty, unity, and territorial integrity. . . . (2) . . . While Viet Nam is still temporarily divided into two zones, . . . there must be no . . . foreign military personnel in their respective territories. (3) The affairs of South Viet Nam are to be settled by the South Vietnamese people themselves . . . in accordance with the programme of the South Viet Nam National Front for Liberation. . . . (4) The peaceful reunification of Viet Nam is to be settled . . . without any foreign interference." Reprinted in Goodman, *The Lost Peace*, 27. See also Kolko, *Anatomy of a War*, 368–73.

31. Hersh, *Price of Power*, 120–29. Kissinger suggests in *White House Years*, 283–86, that he was worried about the impact of the withdrawal of U.S. troops on negotiations and urged Nixon to get tougher with North Vietnam. Nixon, *Memoirs*, 394–400, downplays the affair.

32. Robert Shaplen, *Bitter Victory* (New York: Harper & Row, 1986), 181. The Politburo, like Nixon, had to worry about public opinion as the war ground on, especially in the form of peasant support for the NLF and PLAF in the South and general morale in the North. They were confident that their will to continue fighting was greater than the U.S. government's.

33. Nixon, *Memoirs*, 409–12. See also Hersh, *Price of Power*, 128–33; and "Address to the Nation on the War in Vietnam," November 3, 1969, *Public Papers: Nixon, 1969*, 901–9. In a 1970 interview, Nixon used the term "bloodbath" to describe the communist massacre that he claimed would follow a U.S. defeat. "A Conversation with the President about Foreign Policy," July 1, 1970, *Public Papers: Nixon, 1970*, 548.

34. For the history of the antiwar movement, the book to begin with is DeBenedetti, *An American Ordeal*. On Nixon's response to the movement, see Melvin Small, *Johnson, Nixon, and the Doves* (New Brunswick, N.J.: Rutgers University Press, 1988). H. Bruce Franklin argues that Nixon manufactured the POW "issue" to distract attention from the war in "The POW/MIA Myth," *Atlantic Monthly*, December 1991, 45–81.

35. Nixon, *Memoirs*, 446–48.

36. "Address to the Nation on the Situation in Southeast Asia," April 30, 1970, *Public Papers: Nixon, 1970*, 409.

37. The invasion, the continued aerial attacks, and the mistreatment of Cambodians by ARVN forces fostered the growth of the Khmer Rouge, the Cambodian communist resistance movement, which received reluctant but expanded support from the DRV. The classic on the topic is William Shawcross, *Sideshow: Kissinger, Nixon and the Destruction of Cambodia* (London: Andre Deutsch, 1979).

38. Duiker, *Communist Road to Power*, 283–90; Goodman, *The Lost Peace*, 105–11; Nixon, *Memoirs*, 446–69; Porter, *A Peace Denied*, 89–94; Turley, *Second Indochina War*, 137–41.

39. Nixon, *Memoirs*, 497–99.

40. Kissinger, *White House Years*, 1018; Goodman, *The Lost Peace*, 114.

41. The DRV and PRG proposals are reprinted in Goodman, *The Lost Peace*, 111–14. See also Donnelly, "A Settlement of Sorts," 64–66; Porter, *A Peace Denied*, 98; and Marilyn B. Young, *The Vietnam Wars, 1945–1990* (New York: HarperCollins, 1991), 263–64.

42. Donnelly, "A Settlement of Sorts," 64–66; Hersh, *Price of Power*, 423–43; Kissinger, *White House Years*, 1016–37; Young, *The Vietnam Wars*, 264–65. The DRV-PRG view of South Vietnamese elections was that "it is essential to know who will organize them." Hoang Nguyen, "The Paris Agreement on Viet Nam: Its Political and Juridical Implications," in Nguyen Khac Vien, ed., *Indochina: The 1972–73 Turning Point, Vietnamese Studies*, no. 39 (Hanoi: n.p., 1974), 48.

43. Hersh, *Price of Power*, 439–43; Goodman, *The Lost Peace*, 115–17; Nixon, *Memoirs*, 583–86.

44. Nguyen Co Thach, who was a member of the DRV delegation in Paris in 1972–1973, said in a 1988 interview that the offensive's objectives were to combine fighting with talking. Nguyen Co Thach interview by author, Ho Chi Minh City, January 17, 1988.

45. Donnelly, "A Settlement of Sorts," 66–71; Duiker, *Communist Road to Power*, 291–96; Goodman, *The Lost Peace*, 117–23; Kolko, *Anatomy of a War*, 422–24; Porter, *A Peace Denied*, 102–15; Frank Snepp, *Decent Interval* (New York: Vintage, 1978), 18–30; Turley, *Second Indochina War*, 143–49.

46. In addition to sources cited in note 45, see D. W. P. Elliott, "NLF-DRV Strategy and the 1972 Spring Offensive," Interim Report no. 4 (Ithaca, N.Y.: Cornell University, International Relations of East Asia Project, 1974); Arnold Isaacs, *Without Honor: Defeat in Vietnam and Cambodia* (New York: Vintage, 1984), chapter 1; and Neil Sheehan, *A Bright Shining Lie: John Paul Vann and America in Vietnam* (New York: Random House, 1988), 751–90.

47. Donnelly, "A Settlement of Sorts," 70; Nixon, *Memoirs*, 602–8.

48. Goodman, *The Lost Peace*, 113–14, 123; Garthoff, *Détente*, 258–59.

49. Porter, *A Peace Denied*, 116; Goodman, *The Lost Peace*, 125; Kolko, *Anatomy of a War*, 431–35.

50. Porter, *A Peace Denied*, 121–25; Goodman, *The Lost Peace*, 131–33.

51. Nixon's marginal notes, Annotated News Summaries, October 27, 1972,

Presidential Office Files, White House Special Files, Nixon Presidential Materials Project (NPMP), Alexandria, Va. (hereafter cited by individual file name only).

52. Goodman, *The Lost Peace*, 132–35; Hung and Schecter, *Palace File*, 111; Porter, *A Peace Denied*, 124–29. The RVN senate rejected parts of the agreement the next day; the lower house rejected them the following day. Thieu often accused Nixon and Kissinger of giving to the DRV at the bargaining table what they had not been able to win on the battlefield; actually, Thieu wanted to win at the table what he had not won in the political and military arena.

53. Kissinger, *White House Years*, 1392–1401. See also Goodman, *The Lost Peace*, appendix B.

54. The prime hawks were Alexander Haig, Bob Haldeman, and John Erlichman. Goodman, *The Lost Peace*, 131–36.

55. Hersh, *Price of Power*, 563–64; Porter, *A Peace Denied*, 133–34. The NCRC recognized two administrations and three political forces, the third being the neutral party.

56. Nixon's marginal notes, Annotated News Summaries, October 23 and 24, 1972, Presidential Office Files, NPMP; Hersh, *Price of Power*, 604–6.

57. Nixon, *Memoirs*, 732–33; attachments, Kissinger to President, in memos/notes, Kennedy to President, January 9 and 11, 1973, folder "Kissinger Messages Re Vietnam Peace Negotiations—January, 1973," President's Personal Files (PPF), President's Speech File (PSF), 1969–74, box 82, NPMP.

58. Nixon, *Memoirs*, 732. See also Kissinger, *White House Years*, 1417; Porter, *A Peace Denied*, 151; Hersh, *Price of Power*, 606; and Hung and Schecter, *Palace File*, 136–37.

59. Porter, *A Peace Denied*, 146–51; Thach interview.

60. Nixon, *Memoirs*, 722.

61. Kissinger is quoted in Nixon, *Memoirs*, 733. See also Hung and Schecter, *Palace File*, 139; Kolko, *Anatomy of a War*, 432–39; Porter, *A Peace Denied*, 152, 155; and Goodman, *The Lost Peace*, 159.

62. Quoted in Hughes, "Foreign Policy," 56.

63. Nixon, *Memoirs*, 734–36.

64. Ibid., 721–22; Kissinger, *White House Years*, 1462.

65. Nguyen Co Thach said in 1988 that he believed that the United States had four main objectives: to change the terms of the October agreement, to weaken North Vietnam, to gain time in order to deliver more military aid to South Vietnam, and to assure Thieu that the United States would intervene if his government were threatened with collapse. Thach interview. See also Kissinger, *White House Years*, 1449.

66. Mark Clodfelter, *The Limits of Air Power: The American Bombing of North Vietnam* (New York: Free Press, 1989), 194, provides figures for bombs dropped north of the 20th parallel: 15,237 tons by B-52s and 5,000 tons by fighters. Herring, *America's Longest War*, 254, puts the total tonnage of bombs dropped during LINE-BACKER II at 36,000. Karl Eschmann, *Linebacker II: The Untold Story of the Air Raids over North Vietnam* (New York: Ivy Books, 1989), chapter 7, indicates that B-52 bombers flew 742 sorties, fighter-bombers 640, and tactical air support fighters 2,066.

67. Interviews by the author with a Vietnamese witness who requested that his name be withheld, January 1 and 18, 1988, Hanoi and Ho Chi Minh City; Porter, *A Peace Denied*, 158–61; Turley, *Second Indochina War*, 152.

68. Eschmann, *Linebacker II*, 202–6. The Vietnamese claimed 81 U.S. aircraft, including 34 B-52s and 5 F-111s. Vien, *Indochina*, 82. These figures are probably incorrect, but U.S. figures apparently do not include planes lost at sea or those that were damaged and put out of action.

69. Memorandum, "Media Quotes," Larry Higby to Bill Baroody, Jr., February 9, 1973, folder "Vietnam," Alpha Subject Files, H. R. Haldeman Files, NPMP.

70. George H. Gallup, *The Gallup Poll: Public Opinion, 1972–1977*, vol. 1, *1972–75* (Wilmington, Del.: Scholarly Resources, 1978), 79, 87; Nixon, *Memoirs*, 738.

71. The DRV had adjourned the technical talks on December 23 in protest of the bombing. Nixon halted bombing in Vietnam on January 15.

72. Thach argued that the NCRC changes were minor and were the "price paid for peace." Thach interview.

73. The final agreement is in Goodman, *The Lost Peace*, appendix C; Vien, *Indochina*, appendix; and Porter, *A Peace Denied*, appendix. Nixon's letters to Thieu during this period were still classified by the National Archives as of 1991 but are reprinted in Hung and Schecter, *Palace File*, appendix A. See also President to Kissinger, January 11, 1973, "Kissinger Messages," PPF, PSF, NPMP, in which Nixon expressed his intention to conclude an agreement with or without Thieu.

74. John Negroponte quoted in Hung and Schecter, *Palace File*, 146. The DRV view of the agreement can be found in Hoang Nguyen, "The Paris Agreement on Viet Nam," in Vien, *Indochina*, 23–60.

75. According to William Safire, *Before the Fall*, 14, 26, Buchanan was a Nixon "intimate" and "brought a conservative ideology and a punchy prose style" to speech writing. When Nixon wanted a moderate speech he turned to Safire; when he wanted a hard-hitting, right-wing speech he looked to Buchanan.

76. Marginal revisions by RN in memo from Haldeman to Henry A. Kissinger (originally from RN to HRH), January 25, 1973, Alpha Subject Files, folder "Vietnam 2," Haldeman Files; "Key Points to Be Made with Respect to Vietnam Agreement," n.d., Alpha Subject Files, folder "Vietnam Peace Reaction," ibid. Part of the strategy was to "take advantage of the current crest" of public emotion about the return of the POWs. Memo, Ray Price to Haldeman, February 27, 1973, Alpha Subject Files, folder "VN Settlement Euphoria," ibid. Herbert Klein, *Making It Perfectly Clear* (Garden City, N.Y.: Doubleday, 1980), 389, attributes the public-relations plan to Buchanan. Richard Nixon, *No More Vietnams* (New York: Arbor House, 1985), 9–10, provides a long list of "myths of Vietnam," including many of Buchanan's points.

9

Gerald R. Ford and the
Presidents' War in Vietnam

David L. Anderson

When Gerald R. Ford became president of the United States on August 9, 1974, the long agony of the Vietnam War was almost over. More than a quarter century earlier, Harry Truman had begun defining a U.S. strategic interest in Indochina, and each succeeding president had labored to protect that interest. In the years from 1945 to 1974, over 58,000 Americans died in Southeast Asia and billions of U.S. dollars were spent; yet this massive U.S. effort to deny control of South Vietnam to the Vietnamese communists had proved futile. As a member of Congress during most of this period, Ford was not the architect of U.S. policy in Southeast Asia; indeed, he had voiced opposition to Lyndon Johnson's decision to use U.S. ground combat forces in Vietnam. It was Ford's fate, however, to be the man in the White House when the day finally came that his predecessors had all worked to avoid. It was Ford who led the nation at the moment of national humiliation when communist forces marched into the capitals of South Vietnam and Cambodia.

Ford and his foreign policy aides, principal of whom was Secretary of State Henry A. Kissinger, had three major concerns about the "endgame" in Indochina. The first was to "stabilize"—the term most commonly used within the administration—the military confrontation in Vietnam and Cambodia enough to allow for negotiations, elections, or some other orderly resolution of internal authority. The second concern was "credibility"—by now a shopworn concept. But how the United States made its final exit from Indochina would presumably have a far-reaching impact on the effectiveness of U.S. diplomacy in the Middle East, Europe, and elsewhere. Third, Ford and Kissinger sought to preserve as much executive authority as possible in

Ford and Secretary of State Kissinger receive General Frederick C. Weyand's assessment of the situation in South Vietnam in April 1975 at Ford's vacation residence in Palm Springs, California. (David Hume Kennerly, courtesy Gerald R. Ford Library)

shaping the final decisions of the war. Richard M. Nixon had resigned the presidency under threat of impeachment for abusing his authority, and Congress had enacted a number of explicit limits on presidential war powers. The White House was worried that the historic principle of executive power in foreign policymaking was about to be totally undermined.

In the minds of some journalists and legislators, the possibility persisted that the Ford administration might conduct secret bombing or in some other clandestine way reintroduce U.S. forces into Southeast Asia. Although Nixon was gone, the talented and secretive Kissinger remained in his dual role as senior cabinet officer and the president's national security adviser. Regardless of whether Kissinger himself had been chastened by congressional restraints, there was a new president. From the fragmentary national security files available from the Ford White House, it appears that Ford relied heavily on Kissinger. The president had confidence in Kissinger and shared the secretary's concern about military stability in Indochina and diplomatic credibility worldwide. On the question of executive-legislative relations, the president—a twenty-five-year veteran of the House of Representatives—was his own expert. From Ford's ascendancy to the presidency to the surrender of Cambodia and South Vietnam in April 1975, the administration's efforts were a Ford-Kissinger collaboration, not the work of Kissinger alone. In many ways Ford's actions were built on the decisions of his predecessor in the Oval Office, but he, like all chief executives, was ultimately accountable for his administration's policies.[1]

In August 1972, House Minority Leader Ford had declared that, in his view, Presidents Truman, Eisenhower, Kennedy, Johnson, and Nixon had all tried hard to find a solution to the problem of Indochina. Throughout his congressional career, Ford had defined that problem in the same terms as the presidents. He espoused a faith in collective security as the means of defending the "free world" against "atheistic Communist aggressors" and took for granted that the U.S. intervention in Vietnam was an essential part of this defense. "I am unequivocally opposed to retreat and withdrawal from Southeast Asia," he wrote to a constituent in 1965, "which would mean withdrawal to Pearl Harbor."[2] As Johnson escalated the U.S. military presence in Vietnam, Ford championed bipartisan support for the White House: "Knowing that there is no substitute for victory, we [Republicans] will back the President in his every effort to achieve military or diplomatic success."[3]

Despite his acceptance of presidential goals, Congressman Ford often voiced criticism of Johnson's "mismanagement" of the military effort. He charged that the administration was pursuing a "no win" approach that was costing American lives and money with little progress toward success. Early on in the escalation he advocated increased air bombardment and a tight naval blockade of North Vietnam and opposed "getting bogged down in an extended and massive land war in the jungles of Southeast Asia."[4] He joined other Republicans, including former president Eisenhower, in suggesting that the administration cut back its heavy domestic spending program and put more resources into the Indochina war. On August 8, 1967, he made one of the few major floor speeches of his long career, and it was an extended indictment of the Johnson administration for "pulling our best punches in Vietnam." Ford had become a spokesman for a coordinated Republican effort to challenge Johnson on the war in the 1968 election. He argued that there was "no justification for sending *one* more American over there" unless the president was going to make "maximum use of American conventional air and sea power" to put pressure directly on North Vietnam.[5]

With Nixon's election in 1968, Ford's public rhetoric on Vietnam changed to fit new political and public-opinion realities. With a Republican in the White House who had campaigned on a pledge to end the war, Ford fully endorsed his president's policies. As his party's leader in the House of Representatives, he received regular White House briefings on Indochina, including information on the highly secret air war in Cambodia and Laos. Recognizing the war weariness of the American people, the administration pledged U.S. troop withdrawals and increased material aid to South Vietnam to enable it to fight its own war. As the nature of the U.S. involvement changed, so did the stated objective of that intervention. Gone was the no-substitute-for-victory rhetoric, and Ford joined the administration chorus proclaiming the much less absolute goal of "peace with honor."

Ford's loyal support of Nixon's Indochina policies never wavered, and it was a factor in Nixon's selection of Ford to be his vice-president after Spiro Agnew's resignation in 1973. One scholar has even compared Ford's praise of Nixon's efforts to "fealty to a medieval lord."[6] When public outrage erupted after Nixon ordered U.S. troops into Cambodia in 1970, Ford resolutely insisted that this "decision *does not* make this Mr. Nixon's war." On the contrary, he asserted, Nixon "*is bringing Americans home*" and "is determined that the South Vietnamese assume the major responsibility for their own defense and welfare."[7] In Congress, Ford opposed the Cooper-Church amendment and other efforts to cut off funds for U.S. military operations in Indochina.

Nixon was doubtlessly grateful for the support, but Ford's actions were not simple partisanship. They were consistent with his long-held convictions that U.S. involvement in Vietnam was correct and that U.S. goals could be achieved not by ground troops but by extending material resources to the beleaguered South Vietnamese and Cambodian governments. Hence, when Ford succeeded Nixon in the Oval Office, the new president was not simply attempting to implement his predecessor's design but was pursuing a policy that was in fact his own.

When Ford took the presidential oath on August 9, 1974, he faced very limited choices in Southeast Asia. He still clung to the fig leaf of "peace with honor" but was well aware of public and congressional sentiment against any reinsertion of U.S. forces into the region. The final withdrawal of the few remaining U.S. troops and the release of U.S. prisoners of war in the weeks after the January 1973 signing of the Paris Peace Accords had marked the finish of the war as far as most Americans were concerned. Fighting continued within Vietnam and Cambodia and questions lingered about Americans missing in action (MIA), but these problems moved few citizens to approve of further U.S. military risks. To guarantee noninvolvement, Congress tied appropriation for further military aid to South Vietnam and Cambodia to an absolute prohibition against any U.S. combat activity of any type anywhere in Southeast Asia. It enacted, over Nixon's veto, a War Powers Resolution that explicitly prohibited presidents from sending forces into combat anywhere without a declaration of war, other statutory authority, or direct attack on the United States. The act also required the chief executive to report promptly to Congress and consult with legislative leaders on any orders that risked combat. Furthermore, only days before his resignation, Nixon had signed a congressional authorization bill for military aid to Vietnam that set a ceiling of $1 billion, $600 million less than the administration had sought.[8] Ford's challenge as president was to find a way to reconcile these limits with his own conviction that continued U.S. support of the regimes in Saigon and Phnom Penh was justified.

Aware of the tightrope he would be walking, Ford immediately made a private and a public move to address, respectively, the international and domestic aspects of his difficulty. He signed a personal letter to South Vietnam's president Nguyen Van Thieu on August 10, affirming that "existing commitments this nation has made in the past are still valid and will be fully honored in my administration."[9] Thieu was thrilled, but this message was just one of several Ford signed in the early hours of his administration to assure U.S. allies that there would be no change in U.S. foreign policy as a result of Nixon's unprecedented resignation. Kissinger and the National Security Council (NSC) staff prepared these letters. Graham Martin, the U.S. ambassador to the Republic of Vietnam (RVN), participated in drafting the Thieu letter. Ford provided the signature.

The president's readiness to endorse continued support of South Vietnam was genuine and not surprising, but he did not fully comprehend what he was pledging. Thieu already had a thick file of similar private letters from Nixon containing a host of promises, including one to "respond with full force should the [Paris] settlement be violated by North Vietnam."[10] Nixon and Kissinger had not divulged the content of these letters to Congress or to other administration officials. It appears from available sources that Ford never read the Nixon letters until April 1975, when copies of some of them were sent to him by an RVN official. Regardless of what the president knew about the substance of the correspondence, he was in full agreement with the need to bolster Thieu's morale with firm assurances. After discussions with Kissinger and Martin, he sent additional messages to Thieu in September and October, repeating that "my administration will remain steadfast and strong in its support of Viet-Nam."[11]

While privately stroking Thieu, Ford moved publicly to assuage some of the domestic pains of the Vietnam experience. He chose to announce in an address to the national convention of the Veterans of Foreign Wars (VFW) on August 19 a program of conditional amnesty, or "earned reentry" as he called it, for draft evaders and military deserters. According to Ford, Secretary of Defense James Schlesinger first suggested the idea to him as a gesture to distinguish the new administration from Nixon's—to convey openness and toleration in place of suspicion and recrimination. Antiwar spokesmen attacked the failure to grant unconditional amnesty to those who, as civilians or soldiers, had followed their consciences; MIA families and other defenders of military service opposed any leniency to those charged with shirking their patriotic duty. The program lasted twelve months and attracted only 6 percent of the eligible offenders. About 8,000 men—comprising one-third of the applicants—received formal offers of clemency. Ignorance, apathy, and especially distrust accounted for the low response rate, and most deserters and evaders obtained no relief from what were often tragic legal and economic consequences of their actions. For Ford, however, the clemency offer was deft politics. Conservative critics admired the boldness of announcing it in front of the VFW, and much of the less attentive public blithely accepted the president's assertion that he had made a just offer. It was a demonstration of personal fortitude in the face of widely diverse criticisms somewhat similar to his intrepid pardon of Nixon a month after succeeding the discredited chief executive.[12]

Ford had political nerve, and he needed it to continue to press Congress for the maintenance of significant levels of military and economic assistance to South Vietnam and Cambodia. The prevailing belief on Capitol Hill was that Washington's client regimes in Indochina had reached the limits of U.S. largess. As Ford settled into the White House, congressional committees were busily reducing the appropriations for the already lowered authorization for Southeast Asia. On October 9, Ford signed a military appropriations bill that provided only $700 million for South Vietnam for the coming year. In December, Congress passed a worldwide foreign assistance act that reconfirmed the military limits and set a ceiling of only $617 million in economic aid for South Vietnam, Cambodia, and Laos combined.[13]

As these bills worked their way through the legislative process, the president lobbied many of his former Capitol Hill colleagues for higher amounts and fewer restrictions on executive use of the funds. He and his aides argued that an appropriation below $1 billion would "seriously weaken South Vietnamese forces during a critical period when Communist forces in South Vietnam are growing stronger and more aggressive." A drop in aid would encourage enemy attacks and "demoralize the South Vietnamese who are depending on us." It was essential too "to show the world that the U.S. is standing firmly by its commitments and continues to be a reliable and steadfast ally."[14] Within the administration there was yet another reason for concern: "The fundamental rights and responsibilities of the Executive would be challenged or degraded by unacceptable controls imposed by the Legislative Branch."[15] As the Foreign Assistance Act took final form in December, the NSC staff advised Ford that several sections would "impose severe restrictions on the conduct of a logical foreign policy," create "real danger for the United States," and "make consideration of a veto a necessity."[16] "With some reservations," the president signed the law on December 30. He deemed it "clearly inadequate to meet minimum basic needs" in Cambodia and charged that it endangered "the progress we have achieved" in South Vietnam.[17]

A week later, North Vietnamese Army (NVA) and Vietcong (VC) forces captured Phuoc Long, a sparsely populated mountain province of South Vietnam on the Cambodian border. Hanoi had launched this assault in December to test the extent of U.S. response and had encountered neither U.S. intervention nor RVN reinforcement of its outnumbered forces in the province. With U.S. aid dwindling, Thieu was already husbanding his stock of ammunition, fuel, and other matériel. The fall of Phuoc Long was the first seizure of an entire province, and it set in motion the process that administration officials had argued would follow a drop in aid. It emboldened North Vietnam to push quickly for final victory, and it began to erode what confidence remained in the South for the Saigon government.[18]

During the early weeks of 1975, the Ford administration's effort to solicit more aid from Congress shifted dramatically from what might happen to what would certainly happen in Indochina without substantial U.S. support. Critical questions emerged. Direct U.S. military intervention was prohibited by law, but could military aid alone, such as ammunition and spare parts, turn the tide? Was Ford's effort to secure more aid only a gesture to improve world perception of U.S. determination, or was there some small hope of salvaging even a portion of the South? Was Ford's own view consistent or changing? Were his policies entirely at the mercy of Congress, or could he preserve some presidential discretion in the crisis?

The capture of Phuoc Long and an intensifying Khmer Rouge campaign to isolate Phnom Penh spurred the administration to action. Kissinger tried some simple posturing by leaking to the press that U.S. Navy warships were en route to the coast of Vietnam because of NVA "cease-fire violations." Although the ships' commanders never received their orders and came nowhere near Indochina, Congresswoman Bella Abzug (D-N.Y.) reacted to the press reports with a stinging telegram to Ford. She cited specific federal laws that would be violated by such actions and added: "Continuing to bolster

President Thieu prevents peace and threatens reinvolvement in this most un-popular war. Public outrage is already being expressed."[19]

A State Department memorandum described congressional opposition to further aid as "massive," but Ford decided to confront Congress immediately with a request for a supplemental appropriation for Vietnam and Cambodia. The White House strategy would be to repeat its previous arguments and increase emotional pressure on the lawmakers. A high-ranking congressional delegation would be urged to visit Indochina to put "the burden of decision on their shoulders."[20] Kissinger advised Ford to say to Senate leaders: "I do not believe America could live with itself if we let allies go under because we did not give them the additional increment of aid which is essential to their survival."[21] On January 28, the president formally requested $300 million for South Vietnam and $222 million for Cambodia. These appropriations would restore the $1 billion originally authorized for the RVN and place Cambodian aid at $497 million.[22]

Briefing the Cabinet on the proposal, Ford emphasized that "we will stand behind it 100%." To do otherwise would burden the United States with a "guilt complex" for "having withdrawn support from Vietnam."[23] NSC briefing papers for the Cabinet made it clear that "we are on the way *out*, not *in*," but they stressed the need to demonstrate to the world the "constancy of our pledges." A significant aid appropriation would assist delicate negotiations in areas such as the Middle East, where the message must be clear: "America has never abandoned a friend."[24]

Whether Ford and Kissinger personally believed that a military defense of South Vietnam and Cambodia was still feasible at this late date remains unknown because key documents are still security classified. Circumstantial evidence indicates that the top level of the administration may not yet have accepted the prevailing public and congressional presumption that further defense was hopeless. Available administration documents maintain that the only certainty of collapse would be if the aid was withheld. White House spokesmen insisted that with aid, some chance for military stability remained. "The signs are ominous," the Defense Attache's Office (DAO) in Saigon reported secretly, and it predicted that "major combat will soon be forthcoming." The intelligence survey's "worst case" scenario, however, envisioned only the loss of much of Military Region One (the four northern provinces of South Vietnam) with major attacks on Danang and Pleiku, for which the Army of the Republic of Vietnam (ARVN) was preparing "on a coordinated and innovative basis."[25] Ambassador Martin returned to Washington to lobby for the aid bill, and he too presented a grim but manageable picture of the situation. Kissinger sent the president a positive report on the ARVN's fighting ability from British Southeast Asian expert Sir Robert Thompson. Also, as of February, the NVA and VC had not followed up their January campaign with a new assault. Ford could have believed when he submitted the supplemental request that feasible military options remained for South Vietnam. Indeed, on February 14, he sent a letter to the president of the RVN senate exuding confidence "that the South Vietnamese people are able and determined to defend themselves."[26]

Of course, the rhetoric may have been only a bold front to counter the strong contention of aid opponents that the United States had already been more than generous in giving its blood and treasure to Vietnam and that the time had come to say "enough." Eighty-two members of the House and Senate signed a letter to Ford on February 6 declaring that they did not believe that aid would bring peace to Vietnam and that the United States must end its involvement there once and for all. "We are not prepared for it to continue indefinitely," they warned.[27] To try to remove this image of a never-ending cycle of aid requests, Ford floated the idea of a three-year plan to phase out gradually U.S. assistance as South Vietnam's economic potential grew on the basis of rice, sugar, and recently discovered offshore oil and natural gas fields. Martin stoutly defended the concept, and it got some support from Senators Sam Nunn (D-Ga.), Frank Church (D-Idaho), and James Pearson (R-Kans.). But with most legislators dubious about South Vietnam's survival for the next three months, let alone three years, the proposal generated no notable enthusiasm.[28]

The administration's best and riskiest ploy to secure passage of an aid package was to try to get a congressional delegation to make a favorable recommendation based on a firsthand assessment. Aided personally by the president, the State Department invited senior members of both houses to go on a "no holds barred" inspection tour of Indochina. Senate leaders Robert Byrd (D-W.Va.), Mike Mansfield (D-Mont.), and Hugh Scott (R-Pa.) and House Minority Leader John Rhodes (R-Ariz.) rebuffed the initiative and refused to sponsor it. They declared that they had all the information they needed but agreed not to oppose participation by members who decided to go. A group was finally assembled, but it lacked the prestige the White House had desired. It included only one senator, Dewey Bartlett (R-Okla.), who headed the delegation along with Congressman John Flynt, Jr. (D-Ga.). There were two other Republicans—Pete McCloskey (Calif.) and Millicent Fenwick (N.J.)—and four other Democrats—Bella Abzug, Donald Frazer (Minn.), William Chappell (Fla.), and John Murtha (Pa.).

The group was basically balanced between supporters and opponents of supplemental aid. Bartlett and McCloskey arrived in Saigon on February 24, and the others arrived three days later. They all departed on March 2.[29]

Over the years, hundreds of legislators had donned freshly starched jungle fatigues and trekked through Indochina, but this particular delegation took on special symbolic significance. Its members were not particularly powerful on Capitol Hill, and its ultimate report might not change many minds on aid, but the lengths to which the administration had gone just to arrange this visit revealed how dependent the White House was on Congress. All previous presidents from Truman through Nixon had acted first and then relied on Congress to acquiesce to their executive initiatives. Now the administration's ability to act at all seemed to stand in abeyance until Congress formally revealed its will.[30]

The inspection did not go particularly well for the administration, although White House aide Robert Wolthuis, who traveled with the group, tried to be optimistic. He thought that "the trip on balance appears to be a plus," because five or six members seemed willing to support some aid.[31] President Thieu reminded the delegation that five U.S. presidents had made a solemn commitment to support South Vietnam as long as it resisted communism, and he asked whether that commitment was to be of any value. Several of the visitors were more interested, however, in what Thieu had to say about his regime's treatment of political prisoners and journalists. After meeting with Martin in Saigon, some members were so disturbed by the ambassador's lack of objectivity about Thieu's faults that they considered recommending the diplomat's removal. McCloskey met privately with Thieu, traveled to Phnom Penh, and was, in Wolthuis's view, the most diligent and the "key" member of the delegation. McCloskey produced his own report in which he concluded that, regardless of what the United States did on aid, the North Vietnamese and Vietcong "will likely overrun the South within three years." Both Wolthuis and Martin challenged this finding and maintained that, despite its problems, South Vietnam was growing stronger. Ford met with the delegation on March 5 to hear their views and to restate his own position. A week later, the Democratic caucus in both the House and the Senate voted to oppose further aid to South Vietnam and Cambodia.[32]

The stage seemed set for an administration defeat on the supplemental appropriation when battlefield developments in Indochina dramatically shifted attention away from the halls of Congress. On the morning of March 10, NVA and VC forces opened their campaign to take the Central Highlands with a surprise attack on Ban Me Thuot. By the time the congressional

Democrats cast their caucus votes on aid, the town was in enemy hands. A South Vietnamese official recalled that the vote coinciding with the military setback was "like a kick in the groin, deep and painful."[33] In Cambodia, battlefield conditions were worse. The Khmer Rouge had cut off land and water access to Phnom Penh and left the capital's defense totally dependent on air resupply. In rural areas, Khmer Rouge soldiers were already murdering civil servants, teachers, and other "counterrevolutionaries" in a chilling prelude of what was in store for that country. Cambodian president Lon Nol, who had not impressed the members of the congressional delegation who met with him, sounded increasingly as if he were ready to resign.[34]

In the days following the fall of Ban Me Thuot, South Vietnam's military defenses fell into shambles. Thieu ordered a major redeployment of his troops out of the Central Highlands to defend more populated coastal areas and to prepare a counterattack. The movement became totally disorganized and allowed the communist forces to take Pleiku and Kontum. Hanoi then committed its reserve units to Military Region One, and by March 26 the NVA had seized Hue and was threatening Danang, which was glutted with panicked refugees and retreating ARVN soldiers desperate to flee further south.

The Ford administration moved on several fronts. The president and his aides pledged to cooperate with Congress but continued to hit hard for approval of the requested aid. Acknowledging that the curtain may have opened on the final act in Indochina, a White House "talking paper" for meetings with lawmakers declared: "The way the war ends there and the way the U.S. ends its involvement in Vietnam is of vital importance." The document asserted that throughout the world the United States' "adversaries and allies alike" viewed the extent of U.S. assistance and effort in Indochina "as a fundamental gauge of American determination to keep faith with those under attack and to oppose militant and adventurist policies."[35] Meanwhile, to encourage the reeling Thieu regime, Ford cabled the South Vietnamese president that "America shall stand firmly [behind] the RVN at this critical hour." Unable to disregard congressional resistance and White House irritation at Thieu's bungled withdrawal from the Central Highlands, the drafters of this letter inserted qualifications not found in previous Nixon and Ford messages. The president was considering unspecified "actions which the situation may require and the law permit."[36]

By late March, Ford faced a crucial decision. Should he continue to stand firm on more aid despite the military reverses and the obvious desire of Congress and the American public to be done with the agony of Vietnam and

Cambodia? He needed to know whether the current rout of RVN forces could be stopped or would continue all the way to Saigon. To get some military answers, he sent Army Chief of Staff General Frederick T. Weyand to Vietnam and Cambodia to make an evaluation. Meanwhile, the White House staff began work on a major presidential address on foreign policy to be delivered to a joint session of Congress after the Easter recess. Much to the consternation of his press secretary, Ron Nessen, Ford then departed for Palm Springs, California, for a long-planned golfing vacation. Nessen worried justifiably about how Americans would perceive television news reports of the president relaxing with Hollywood celebrities while other reports showed painful scenes of frightened and frantic South Vietnamese fleeing for their lives.[37]

While Ford vacationed, Lon Nol departed Cambodia for Indonesia, and Danang fell to the NVA onslaught. Thousands of refugees scrambled to board ships and planes leaving South Vietnam's second largest city. The president issued a statement that "a severe emergency exists" in South Vietnam and that he was ordering U.S. Navy and civilian vessels to assist in evacuating refugees. At least one member of Congress labeled the order "an impeachable offense" because it violated legal prohibitions against U.S. personnel participating in hostilities in Indochina.[38] Ford began steering a carefully calculated middle course between cooperating with and pressuring Congress. On the one hand, he strove to observe the letter of the War Powers Resolution by formally notifying Congress that the Danang evacuation was part of an international humanitarian effort. He also sent notification that U.S. military transportation with Marine security units was being used to fly Americans, some Cambodians, and some others out of Phnom Penh. Jack Marsh, Ford's legislative aide, advised the president that Senator Clifford Case (R-N.J.), a coauthor of the War Powers Resolution, did not believe that rescue efforts required congressional approval but fell within the president's authority as commander in chief. Still, the notifications were made to try to minimize legal friction with Capitol Hill.[39]

While keeping an eye on war powers statutes, the administration also began a careful but pointed plan to place some blame on Congress for the suffering then occurring in Indochina. At a news conference in San Diego on April 3, Ford insisted that he would not assess fault and that he wanted to work with Congress, but he then recited the precise amounts that the legislature had cut from administration requests. "These are the facts," he added; "I think it is up to the American people to pass judgment on who was at fault or where the blame may rest."[40] This answer had been carefully prepared in staff discussions. Kissinger had argued that Congress should not be allowed to escape blame, but Marsh had demurred and suggested that the president's upcoming address would be a better forum in which to challenge Congress "in a Churchillian sense."[41]

While still in Palm Springs, Ford received Weyand's report. On April 5, the president and secretary of state conferred with the general and his team, two CIA officers and a Defense Department aid specialist. Notably missing was Weyand's superior, Secretary of Defense Schlesinger. The secretary was not enthusiastic about fighting for more aid and did not enjoy the same close relationship with Ford that Kissinger had. Weyand essentially told Ford what the administration was already telling Congress. With additional ammunition, fuel, and supplies, the RVN military could still "rebuild their capabilities," and, the general advised, "we owe them that support." He itemized specific needs and arrived at a price tag of $722 million. Weyand noted in passing that there was "sound military justification" for B-52 attacks against exposed enemy units, but he recognized "the significant legal and political implications for such a point of view." He added that prudence suggested consideration of a plan for a military evacuation of Americans, Vietnamese, and others. Weyand's basic thesis, however, was that the RVN might make it with adequate aid and that the United States had an obligation to give the Saigon regime that chance. It was strikingly similar to his final report as the last U.S. military commander in South Vietnam in 1973.[42]

Even before Weyand reported to Ford, the president's speech writers had prepared a first draft for the address to Congress that renewed the call for aid. As Ford and his aides worked on the speech, the mood was truculent. They would lay out once again the arguments they had been using and let Congress bear the onus of letting an ally go under if it refused to vote for the assistance. Staffers carefully polled opinion on Capitol Hill and advised the president that many members would oppose or not support him. Ford's friend and former House colleague, Donald Riegle (R-Mich.), cautioned that "the American people and the elected Congress had decided to close the book" on Southeast Asia and nothing the president "can say or do will change that." If Ford proposed aid again, Riegle predicted, the president would lose "mainstreet America." Congressman Bob Michel (R-Ill.) put his advice in a more positive form. He thought that Ford could make "a clean break with Vietnam" and feel no "sense of guilt over Vietnam and Cambodia during his stewardship because he is in an altogether new ball game since Nixon and Watergate."[43]

Although not "Churchillian" in literary elegance, Ford's address to Congress and a national television audience on April 10 was blunt in its recommendations and unapologetic in its defense of presidential conduct of foreign policy. Beginning with a theme he had often expressed during his own career in the House, he heralded "the five Presidents before me" who, with the partnership of Congress, had "sustained and advanced" the collective security of millions of people around the world since World War II. He quoted from Truman's address to Congress in March 1947—the famous Truman Doctrine—declaring that U.S. leadership was vital to "the peace of the world." Turning quickly to the subject at hand, he began again with Truman: "Under five Presidents and 12 Congresses, the United States was engaged in Indochina." He noted that Congress had appropriated over $150 billion over the years for that effort and that the result was a settlement—the Paris Accords—that, if adhered to, would have enabled South Vietnam to survive and rebuild. This line was an explicit defense of Kissinger's work on the 1973 agreement and a reflection of the secretary's influence on the drafting of the speech. Charging that North Vietnam had flagrantly and systematically violated the agreements, Ford then laid the problem in the lap of Congress: "We deprived ourselves by law of the ability to enforce the agreement, thus giving North Vietnam assurance that it could violate that agreement with impunity." The reductions in economic and arms aid, he claimed, "signalled our increasing reluctance to give any support to that nation struggling for its survival." The Saigon government's disastrous attempt at a strategic withdrawal came because of the "uncertainty of further American assistance." Having thus chastised his Capitol audience, he announced that he would not assess blame and would "start afresh" working with Congress.

His specific requests to Congress were (1) to appropriate $722 million for military assistance and $250 million for economic and humanitarian aid for South Vietnam, (2) to clarify his authority to use U.S. forces to evacuate and protect Americans, and (3) to revise the law to allow evacuation of Vietnamese endangered by close association with the United States. The military figure was more than double his January request. The additional $250 million was primarily for refugee relief. The other two parts were standby authority "should the worst come to pass." There was no explicit dollar amount sought for Cambodia, but Ford read a plea from the acting president of Cambodia for food and ammunition. Ford recalled his January request for Cambodia and added that "as of this evening, it may soon be too late." He spoke for several more minutes about U.S. policies elsewhere in the world and then closed with a pointed reminder. The Constitution places "primary responsibility for the conduct of foreign affairs" in the presidency, he observed, and he asked Congress to help him "keep America's word good throughout the world."⁴⁴

It was a bravura performance, but the speech changed few minds. Ford was not interrupted once by applause. The members listened in silence, and two even walked out. The next day, four committees began consideration of the legislation. A bill in the Senate Armed Services Committee would have provided about a third of the military request, and other bills contained humanitarian funds, but all the proposals incorporated numerous restrictions on presidential authority. Although the president received a few congratulatory telegrams after the speech from old Indochina hands such as General William Westmoreland and Ambassador Elbridge Durbrow, the overall tally of telephone calls and telegrams to the White House on April 11 was 1,033 pro and 2,436 con.⁴⁵

Much of the public and many in Congress were opposed to any further expenditures in Vietnam for emotional reasons—they were simply weary of the burden—but pragmatists both in and out of the Capitol knew that money was only symbolic. Kissinger conceded to reporters that Weyand's judgment on the military effect of the $722 million might not be correct, but he quickly added that "other purposes that America has would still be best served by the granting of this sum."⁴⁶ One of these was the genuine, if also tiresome, concern about credibility. The reaction of other countries to U.S. conduct in this crisis was a prominent part of the agenda when Ford met privately on April 14 in an extraordinary session with the Senate Foreign Relations Committee (something that had not occurred since the Wilson administration). The State Department and CIA had compiled some sharply critical, private comments from "top foreign officials" (whose identities remain classified), including one that said the "soft Americans lack the spirit to openly confront Communism" and another that asserted "the current developments in South Vietnam are a good indication of the fate in store for those who rely too heavily on the U.S."⁴⁷

Another of the purposes to which Kissinger alluded was the rapidly mounting possibility of an evacuation of Americans and of South Vietnamese who had worked closely with Americans. The administration's dilemma had to do with timing: moving too quickly would create panic and precipitate a collapse of South Vietnamese morale, but moving too slowly would leave large numbers trapped. Ford's longtime aide Robert Hartmann later described the problem bluntly: "It [the $722 million] was high-stakes poker in an effort to buy a little time to ransom the remaining Americans and as many blacklisted South Vietnamese as we could get out." Congress would not pay for it, Hartmann recalled, and added bitterly: "They knew Ford's unspoken reason, but they were chicken. Let Ford take the blame."[48]

While Congress pondered and procrastinated, events throughout Indochina continued with their own momentum toward a total collapse in Phnom Penh and Saigon. With the Phnom Penh airport closed by Khmer Rouge bombardment, U.S. ambassador John Gunther Dean and his staff and a small number of Cambodians were lifted by marine helicopters out of the Cambodian capital on April 12. Five days later, the Khmer Rouge controlled the city and the government. As the end came in Cambodia, it was coming nearer in Vietnam. Saigon was not yet under attack, but NVA units continued to score victories throughout the country. After defending Thieu for so long, Martin finally came to the conclusion that the RVN president would have to go if there was to be any hope of a negotiated truce. It was already too late for talks, but Thieu faced the reality of his discredited leadership and resigned on April 21. At the same time the Politburo in Hanoi authorized the final assault on Saigon.[49]

With the noose tightening in Southeast Asia, the tension between the president and Congress intensified. Ford told the Cabinet on April 16 that "Congress has shown no cooperation in a meaningful way." He called the $200 million emergency fund in the current Senate bill "as bad as getting nothing at all."[50] In a brief public statement the following day, he expressed sadness about the fall of the Cambodian government and goaded Congress with praise for the Cambodian defenders "who fought valiantly with their remaining supplies."[51] In a lengthy interview with CBS News on April 21, Ford reviewed again the White House brief of how Congress had made enforcement of the Paris Accords impossible. He insisted that he had to be frank about the historical record but repeated that he was ready to move forward without recrimination.[52] Two days later he stunned a mostly student audience at Tulane University and received a thunderous ovation when he asserted that the nation's lost pride "cannot be achieved by refighting a war that is finished as far as America is concerned."[53] The carefully prepared remark placing the war in the past tense provoked a flurry of favorable reporting in the press. Kissinger was miffed that the president's speech writers and press aides had not cleared the phrase with him but only with the president. Ford, on the other hand, was delighted with the public's reaction and with this reminder to Kissinger of who was in charge of policy.[54]

Lawmakers responded to the president's complaints against them with the charge that administration rhetoric threatened to reignite domestic divisions over Vietnam. Some sought to put the White House on the defensive by demanding that Ford release any secret correspondence between Nixon and Thieu. Ford refused on the grounds that there were no secret agreements in the letters, that publicizing private messages was a bad precedent for chief executives, and that nothing in the letters was relevant to current decisions. Another more discreet but more pertinent point of congressional pressure was on the need to evacuate Americans from Saigon. A steady stream of messages flowed into the White House from Capitol Hill urging quick action and threatening public pressure through a congressional resolution.[55]

The White House had been acutely aware of the evacuation dilemma all month. Part of the administration's slow response was attributable to Ambassador Martin. Despite DAO and CIA estimates that an evacuation was likely soon, he had resisted even preliminary planning for fear that it would destroy the already low morale in Saigon and render truce talks impossible. In addition, a massive evacuation of over a thousand Americans and possibly tens of thousands of Vietnamese friends would likely involve U.S. ground and air units in combat, even if for a very brief period. Without explicit enabling legislation, which was tied to the still pending aid request, any fighting or even risk of armed conflict could be deemed a violation of federal statutes.

On April 28, the evacuation and the aid legislation reached a simultaneous moment of decision. On that day, the Senate passed a conference report on H.R. 6096, a bill that provided $327 million for humanitarian and evacuation purposes and that authorized, albeit with a host of limitations, the president to evacuate Americans and Vietnamese using U.S. military forces. A House vote was scheduled for the next day with approval expected. On the same day, Ford received word from Saigon that Ton Son Nhut airport was under attack and flight operations were impossible. After more reports of the panic and chaos in the South Vietnamese capital, the president sent orders to Martin to begin Operation FREQUENT WIND, a helicopter evacuation of the U.S. embassy.[56]

Throughout the day on April 29, a fleet of eighty-one helicopters transported about 1,000 Americans and 5,500 Vietnamese to U.S. Navy ships off the coast. Ford telephoned Speaker of the House Carl Albert in the morning and asked that the vote on H.R. 6096 be pulled from the day's calendar. Concerned that congressional action might fuel the panic in the streets of Saigon, the president argued that a delay could help save American and South Vietnamese lives. Albert complied. Ford then met with the Cabinet. He and Kissinger confirmed that over the last two weeks the public fight for aid had been "to prevent panic in South Vietnam which would endanger

American evacuation, deter North Vietnamese activity, and stabilize the situation so that a successful evacuation could take place." Secretary of Transportation William T. Coleman, Jr., mentioned that the president's April 10 speech "had been aimed in large part toward ensuring stability during evacuation," and neither Ford nor Kissinger challenged that observation.[57]

On April 30, communist troops took over the presidential palace in Saigon, which would be renamed Ho Chi Minh City, and the war was over. Back in Washington, Ford sent formal notification to Congress, as required by the War Powers Resolution, of his use of U.S. forces on April 29, citing as his authority his constitutional powers as commander in chief. When Albert withdrew H.R. 6096, he had in effect allowed the president to act without the explicit approval of Congress. Another vote on the measure was scheduled for May 1, and Ford sent a letter to Albert urging passage, although events had overtaken many of the provisions. Before April 28, the president might have vetoed the bill because of the limitations it contained on executive prerogatives, but now White House thinking had changed. Ford's letter argued that passage would be the most expedient way to make funds available immediately for the 70,000 Vietnamese evacuees who had fled the South. To allay suspicion about the military authority in the bill, the president pledged that "I do not intend to send armed forces of the United States back into Vietnamese territory."[58]

On May 1, the House defeated H.R. 6096. Liberals who opposed the troop provisions and conservatives who feared that U.S. funds might go to communists voted against the bill. Ford and his aides were outraged at what they viewed as the House's blatant disregard for the fate of the refugees. The White House submitted a request on May 5 for $507 million for refugee assistance and obtained passage on May 21. A refugee resettlement program continued for the rest of the year. Since the president got the refugee assistance he desired in a separate measure, the defeat of H.R. 6096 in effect gave the executive a significant victory. The House had left undefined the president's authority to protect Americans overseas. Ford's unilateral action of April 29 under his claim of constitutional authority went unchallenged by legislative action.[59]

A test of this executive power came only two weeks after the Saigon evacuation, when a Cambodian gunboat stopped and removed the crew from a U.S. merchant ship, the *Mayaguez*. As the events unfolded on May 12 and 13, the White House worked to gather information on the fate of the crew, maneuvered U.S. Navy vessels into place for a possible rescue attempt, tried to make diplomatic contact with Cambodia through the Chinese, and assessed an array of options. On May 14, protected by tactical air strikes, marines landed on the ship and a neighboring island. They found no crew members, but while the operation was under way, the crew was released.[60]

Mindful of the War Powers Resolution, the White House notified congressional leaders immediately as each military decision was made. The administration did not feel compelled by statute to share with Congress all options under consideration, such as one proposed and rejected for B-52 raids on Cambodia. Thinking of the North Korean capture of the USS *Pueblo* in 1968, which left American sailors in captivity for a year, the president and his staff also moved quickly to find and extract the crew before they were hidden or harmed. Some lawmakers charged that Congress was not properly consulted about this military action, which cost forty-one U.S. Marines their lives. "The President's resort to force in this case appears to have been illegal and unconstitutional," Congresswoman Elizabeth Holtzman (D-N.Y.) charged.[61] Ford's legal advisers and many members of Congress believed, however, that the war powers provisions had been satisfied. Whatever the legalities, the public strongly endorsed the rescue effort. By the morning of May 16, the White House had received 8,130 telephone calls and telegrams favoring the president's decision and only 528 opposed. Ford's overall job-approval rating in public opinion polls went up eleven points.[62]

The president's assertive response to the *Mayaguez* seizure provided a coda to policies he had pursued during the final months of the Indochina war. In this incident, he continued the effort to stabilize military conditions to provide protection for Americans, preserve the global credibility of U.S. power and determination, and guard presidential authority from congressional usurpation. After the fall of Saigon, Senate Majority Leader Mansfield praised executive-legislative cooperation in the final days of the war, but he also asserted that the end "came finally because Congress was unwilling to give the Executive Branch a blank check in providing the close-out funds."[63] Ford disagreed and believed that Congress had only hampered his management of an orderly withdrawal. When Mansfield joined Holtzman and other Democrats in publicly assailing the abuse of war powers authority in the *Mayaguez* crisis, Ford labeled their reaction "hopelessly naive."[64]

In his memoirs, Ford affirmed his belief that the Vietnam War could have been won. He recalled his "pulling our punches" critique of Johnson and implied that it was under Johnson's policies that the United States went wrong. After the *Mayaguez* incident, a reporter asked Ford about his feelings on the use of force, and Ford replied: "I have always been on the side of stronger rather than weaker action, and I think my comments, for example, during the early stages of the Vietnam War reflect that."[65] Ford's postmortems are an example of what scholars have since labeled the "win thesis," namely, that with more power and determination the United States could have prevailed over the armed forces of North Vietnam and the South Vietnamese and Cambodian insurgents. Many of these scholars also add that the win thesis disregards historical realities in Indochina that no amount of outside force could have changed.[66] Despite his own frustrations in trying to end the war satisfactorily, Ford maintained the conviction that all his predecessors since Truman had shared—that U.S. intervention in Vietnam was merited and could be successful.

Notes

Research for this chapter was supported in part by a grant from the Gerald R. Ford Foundation.

1. Gerald R. Ford, *A Time to Heal: The Autobiography of Gerald R. Ford* (New York: Harper & Row, 1979), 128–29; Robert D. Schulzinger, *Henry Kissinger: Doctor of Diplomacy* (New York: Columbia University Press, 1989), 5–6; Charles E. Goodell, "Decision-Making in the Ford Presidency," in Kenneth W. Thompson, ed., *The Ford Presidency* (Lanham, Md.: University Press of America; Charlottesville, Va.: Miller Center of the University of Virginia, 1988), 265–66.

2. Ford to Donald K. Blackie, June 17, 1965, box B30, Gerald R. Ford Congressional Papers, Gerald R. Ford Library, Ann Arbor, Mich.

3. Ford, "Your Washington Review," January 26, 1966, box D2, Ford Congressional Papers. For analyses of Ford's congressional record on the Vietnam War, see United States House of Representatives, Committee on the Judiciary, *Nomination of Gerald R. Ford to Be the Vice President of the United States: Hearings*, 93d Cong., 1st sess., November 15-16, 19-21, 26, 1973, pp. 743–45; Jeff Charnley, "Power Apprenticeship: Congressman Gerald R. Ford and the Vietnam War, 1964-1973," paper presented at the Gerald Ford Conference, Hofstra University, 1989, copy in Ford Library; and Edward L. Schapsmeier and Frederick H. Schapsmeier, *Gerald R. Ford's Date with Destiny: A Political Biography* (New York: Peter Lang, 1989), 95–97, 103–14.

4. Ford News Release, January 26, 1966, box D2, Ford Congressional Papers.

5. Ford, "Your Washington Review," August 16, 1967, box D3, ibid. (emphasis is Ford's). See also Ford, *A Time to Heal*, 80–83; Charnley, "Power Apprenticeship," 6–10; and *New York Times*, October 1, 1966.

6. Charnley, "Power Apprenticeship," 18–22. See also Richard Reeves, *A Ford, Not a Lincoln* (New York: Harcourt Brace Jovanovich, 1975), 28; and A. James

Reichley, *Conservatives in an Age of Change: The Nixon and Ford Administrations* (Washington, D.C.: Brookings Institution, 1981), 282–84.

7. Ford, "Your Washington Review," May 18, 1970, box D3, Ford Congressional Papers (emphasis is Ford's).

8. P. Edward Haley, *Congress and the Fall of South Vietnam and Cambodia* (Rutherford, N.J.: Fairleigh Dickinson University Press; London: Associated University Presses, 1982), 41–45.

9. Ford to Thieu, August 10, 1974, in Nguyen Tien Hung and Jerrold L. Schecter, *The Palace File* (New York: Harper & Row, 1986), 240. See also Frank Snepp, *Decent Interval: An Insider's Account of Saigon's Indecent End* (New York: Vintage, 1978), 113.

10. Nixon to Thieu, January 5, 1973, in Hung and Schecter, *Palace File*, 392.

11. Ford to Thieu, September 14, 1974, CO165-2 Vietnam (South), White House Central Files Subject File, box 59, Ford Library (hereafter cited as WHCF). See also Kissinger memorandum on meeting with Martin, September 13, 1974, and Ford to Thieu, October 24, 1974, ibid.; Kathy Troia to General [Brent Scowcroft?], April 8, 1975, Vietnam—Correspondence from Richard Nixon to Nguyen Van Thieu, Richard B. Cheney Files, box 13, Ford Library; and Hung and Schecter, *Palace File*, 306–9.

12. *Public Papers of the Presidents of the United States: Gerald R. Ford, 1974* (Washington, D.C.: GPO, 1975), 22–28; *Public Papers: Ford, 1975* (Washington, D.C.: GPO, 1977), 1445; Ford, *A Time to Heal*, 141–42; Robert T. Hartmann, *Palace Politics: An Inside Account of the Ford Years* (New York: McGraw-Hill, 1980), 209–12; Charles DeBenedetti with Charles Chatfield, *An American Ordeal: The Antiwar Movement of the Vietnam Era* (Syracuse, N.Y.: Syracuse University Press, 1990), 370; Lawrence M. Baskir and William A. Strauss, *Chance and Circumstance: The Draft, the War and the Vietnam Generation* (New York: Vintage, 1978), 215–24.

13. *Public Papers: Ford, 1974*, 244; Haley, *Congress*, 45–46; Arnold R. Isaacs, *Without Honor: Defeat in Vietnam and Cambodia* (New York: Vintage, 1984), 314.

14. William E. Timmons to Ford, August 12, 1974, Foreign Aid Legislation, William E. Timmons Files, box 3, Ford Library. See also Timmons memorandum on meeting with bipartisan leaders, September 10, 1974, FO3-2, President's Handwriting File, box 21, Ford Library. This file contains documents that Ford initialed, annotated, or drafted.

15. Richard T. Kennedy to Timmons, August 19, 1974, Legislative Interdepartmental Group Meetings, Timmons Files, box 4.

16. Kissinger to Ford, draft memorandum, attached to Kennedy to Scowcroft, December 19, 1974, FO3-2, WHCF, box 15.

17. *Public Papers: Ford, 1974*, 778–79.

18. Isaacs, *Without Honor*, 330–35.

19. Abzug to Ford, January 7, 1975, ND18/CO165-2 Wars/South Vietnam, WHCF, box 36. See also Snepp, *Decent Interval*, 142; and Isaacs, *Without Honor*, 242.

20. Linwood Holton to Kissinger, January 21, 1975, Vietnam: Visit by Members of Congress, Robert K. Wolthuis Files, box 5, Ford Library.

21. Kissinger memorandum on meeting with Senators Strom Thurmond and William Scott, January 27, 1975, FO8, WHCF, box 35.

22. Roy L. Ash to Ford, January 27, 1975, FI4-2/1975/1-10, ibid., box 15; *Public Papers: Ford, 1975*, 119-23.

23. Notes of the Cabinet Meeting, January 29, 1975, James E. Connor Files, box 4, Ford Library.

24. Scowcroft to Connor, February 3, 1975, FO3-2/CO165-2, WHCF, box 25 (emphasis is Scowcroft's).

25. USDAO Saigon Monthly Intelligence Summary and Threat Analysis for January 1975, Vietnam: Fact Sheets, Wolthuis Files, box 5. See also William L. Stearman to Scowcroft, February 19, 1975, FO3-2/CO165-2(1), WHCF, box 25.

26. Ford to Tran Van Lam, February 14, 1975, ND18/CO165 Wars/Vietnam, WHCF, box 36. See also Kissinger memorandum on meeting with Thompson, [February 1975], Brent Scowcroft Files, box 3, Ford Library; and Snepp, *Decent Interval*, 148, 153.

27. Members of Congress for Peace through Law to Ford, February 6, 1975, FO3-2/CO165(3), WHCF, box 25.

28. Sam Nunn, *Vietnam Aid—The Painful Options: Report to the Senate Committee on Armed Services*, February 12, 1975, Scowcroft Files, box 2; Kissinger memorandum on meeting with Senators Church and Pearson, March 4, 1975, FO3-2, WHCF, box 15; William T. Kendall to Max L. Friedersdorf, March 12, 1975, Indochina—U.S. Involvement, Max L. Friedersdorf Files, box 13, Ford Library.

29. Friedersdorf to Ford, February 10, 1975, and Friedersdorf to Ford, February 13, 1975, CO165-2, President's Handwriting File, box 7; Saigon Embassy to Secretary of State, March 3, 1975, Vietnam: Visit by Members of Congress, Wolthuis Files, box 5.

30. Haley, *Congress*, 15-39.

31. Wolthuis to Friedersdorf, March 3, 1975, Vietnam—Congressional Trip, John O. Marsh Files, box 43, Ford Library.

32. Paul N. McCloskey, Jr., "Report, Vietnam Fact-Finding Trip, Feb. 24–March 3, 1975," March 14, 1975, Vietnam: Report by Congressman McCloskey, Wolthuis Files, box 5. See also Wolthuis to McCloskey, March 19, 1975, and Stearman to Wolthuis, March 12, 1975, ibid.; CODEL meeting with President Thieu, February 27, 1975, and Thieu address to CODEL, March 1, 1975, Vietnam: Visit by Members of Congress, ibid.; Kissinger memorandum on meeting with members of Congress, March 5, 1975, FO3-2, WHCF, box 15; Isaacs, *Without Honor*, 310, 337; and Haley, *Congress*, 67-68.

33. Hung quoted in Hung and Schecter, *Palace File*, 270. See also Isaacs, *Without Honor*, 345-46.

34. Isaacs, *Without Honor*, 260-62.

35. "Talking Points: Supplemental Assistance for South Vietnam," April 1975, Vietnam: Supplemental Military Assistance (2), Marsh Files, box 43.

36. Ford to Thieu, March 22, 1975, in Hung and Schecter, *Palace File*, 284-85.

37. Ron Nessen, *It Sure Looks Different from the Inside* (Chicago: Playboy Press, 1978), 95-96.

38. Robert L. Leggett to Ford, April 1, 1975, ND18/CO165, WHCF, box 36. See also *Public Papers: Ford, 1975*, 163; and Isaacs, *Without Honor*, 265–67.

39. Marsh to Rumsfeld, April 3, 1975, Vietnam—General, Marsh Files, box 42; Marsh to Ford, April 4, 1975, National Security—Refugees, Vietnam, President's Handwriting File, box 32.

40. *Public Papers: Ford, 1975*, 420–21.

41. Marsh to Rumsfeld, April 3, 1975, Vietnam—General, Marsh Files, box 43. See also Kissinger press conference, April 5, 1975, Vietnam & Cambodia (2), Vernon Loen and Charles Leppert Files, box 26, Ford Library.

42. Weyand memorandum for the president, April 4, 1975, CO165-2, WHCF, box 59. See also Snepp, *Decent Interval*, 280–81; and Jeffrey J. Clarke, *The United States Army and Vietnam: Advice and Support: The Final Years, 1965–1973* (Washington, D.C.: GPO, 1988), 493–95.

43. Loen, Leppert, and Doug Bennett to Friedersdorf, April 7, 1975, National Security—Wars—Vietnam (1), President's Handwriting File, box 33. See also Jeanne W. Davis to Scowcroft, April 2, 1975, and Don Riegle, "Ford's Future Rides on Vietnam Decision," April 9, 1975, SP2-3-36, WHCF, box 11; and Wolthuis to Marsh, April 2, 1975, Vietnam—Supplemental Military Assistance (2), Marsh Files, box 43.

44. *Public Papers: Ford, 1975*, 459–73.

45. Phone call and telegram update on 4/10/75 speech as of 4:00 P.M., 4/11/75, Foreign Policy Address 4/10/75, box 11, Nessen Papers. Congratulatory telegrams in SP2-3-36 4/10/75 (4), WHCF, box 12. See also Friedersdorf to Ford, April 15, 1975, ND18/CO165, ibid., box 36; McCloskey to Kissinger, April 16, 1975, Vietnam: General, Wolthuis Files, box 5; Friedersdorf to Ford, April 21 and April 23, 1975, Vietnam—General, Marsh Files, box 43; and Isaacs, *Without Honor*, 407–8.

46. Kissinger background briefing of press on president's speech, April 10, 1975, Foreign Policy Address 4-10-75 (1), box 11, Nessen Papers.

47. Meeting with Senate Foreign Relations Committee, April 14, 1975, Presidential Meetings with Senate Members, Friedersdorf Files, box 7.

48. Hartmann, *Palace Politics*, 318.

49. Isaacs, *Without Honor*, 276–85, 418–23; Snepp, *Decent Interval*, 346.

50. Notes of the Cabinet Meeting, April 16, 1975, Connor Files, box 4.

51. *Public Papers: Ford, 1975*, 507.

52. Ibid., 539–46.

53. Quoted in Nessen, *It Sure Looks Different from the Inside*, 108.

54. Ibid., 107–9; Hartmann, *Palace Politics*, 322; Schulzinger, *Henry Kissinger*, 200–201.

55. Thomas E. Morgan to Ford, April 17, 1975, Friedersdorf to Berkley Bedell, April 18, 1975, Norman Y. Mineta to Ford, April 22, 1975, and Ford to John Sparkman, April 25, 1975, ND18/CO165, WHCF, box 36; Jack Brooks to Ford, April 17, 1975, CO165-2, ibid.

56. Ford, *A Time to Heal*, 256; Hartmann, *Palace Politics*, 320; Haley, *Congress*, 145–47; Snepp, *Decent Interval*, 292–99.

57. Notes of the Cabinet Meeting, April 29, 1975, Connor Files, box 4. See also *Public Papers: Ford, 1975*, 605; and Haley, *Congress*, 147.

58. Ford to Albert, April 30, 1975, Vietnam: General, Wolthuis Files, box 5. See

also Kissinger to Ford, April 30, 1975, ibid.; and Ford to James O. Eastland, April 30, 1975, ND18/CO165, WHCF, box 36.

59. *Public Papers: Ford, 1975*, 619; Ford, *A Time to Heal*, 256–57; Haley, *Congress*, 147–49; Kendell to Friedersdorf, May 3, 1975, Vietnam (2), William T. Kendall Files, box 5, Ford Library.

60. Stearman to Kissinger, July 23, 1975, Mayaguez Situation—GAO Report, Philip W. Buchen Files, box 25, Ford Library.

61. Friedersdorf to Ford, May 16, 1975, ND18/CO26, WHCF, box 32. See also Marsh to Buchen, May 13, 1975, Mayaguez Crisis, Marsh Files, box 20; Buchen to Marsh, May 14, 1975, Mayaguez Situation General (1), Buchen Files, box 25; and *Public Papers: Ford, 1975*, 668–70.

62. Updated reaction to Mayaguez, May 16, 1975, Mayaguez—Telephone Calls and Telegram Tallies, box 14, Nessen Papers; Ford, *A Time to Heal*, 284.

63. Mansfield statement, April 30, 1975, attached to Friedersdorf to Ford, May 2, 1975, ND18/CO165, President's Handwriting File, box 33.

64. Ford, *A Time to Heal*, 283.

65. Ford interview by Hugh Sidey, May 16, 1975, box 50, Nessen Papers. See also Ford, *A Time to Heal*, 249.

66. George C. Herring, "America and Vietnam: The Debate Continues," *American Historical Review* 92 (April 1987): 350–62; Thomas G. Paterson, "Historical Memory and Illusive Victories: Vietnam and Central America," *Diplomatic History* 12 (Winter 1988): 1–18.

10
Conclusion

David L. Anderson

Harry Truman initially authorized direct U.S. involvement in Indochina among a host of presidential actions to meet a perceived threat from global communism. The extension of U.S. aid to the French war effort in Southeast Asia was a seemingly small step compared to his momentous decisions to drop atomic bombs on Japan, to commit millions of dollars to the rehabilitation of Europe and Japan, and to obligate the United States to the defense of Europe through NATO. Although dangers to U.S. ideals and well-being seemed to abound everywhere in the world, the president's foreign policy initiatives—both big and small—appeared achievable in the surge of moral rectitude and physical strength that flowed from victory over fascist tyranny in World War II. Truman did not personally design what came to be known as the American containment of communism, but he readily employed what Theodore Roosevelt termed the "bully pulpit" of the presidency to promote the strategy with Congress and the American people. His manifesto was the Truman Doctrine, and in that pivotal address to Congress in 1947 he declared that "the free people of the world look to us for support in maintaining their freedoms."[1] In the context of the world contest with communism, this concept of freedom encompassed free enterprise as well as other free institutions. Truman's rhetoric recognized no limits to U.S. responsibility and was as easily applicable to Vietnam as to Germany, Korea, or any other Cold War battleground.

The means for realizing U.S. purposes in Southeast Asia were as cloudy to Truman and his advisers as the goal of preserving freedom was clear. Despite the presumption that communist success anywhere was a setback for the United States, some areas of the world—especially Western Europe and Japan—were of greater strategic value than Indochina. In fact, much of the region's importance was its historical and economic connection with Western Europe and Japan. Consequently, Truman and Dwight Eisenhower initially shaped their tactics in Vietnam with as much regard for the interests of other U.S. allies as for the people of Southeast Asia. This approach brought the United States into an uneasy partnership with France, which intended to retain its old colonial dominion in Indochina.

After Eisenhower entered the White House, the option of relying on France to defend Western interests in Southeast Asia became untenable. U.S. officials had never approved of French colonialism and had tolerated it only as a temporary expedient to contain the spread of communist ideology and political control. By 1954, Eisenhower and his aides had recognized that the French would neither defeat the communist-led Vietminh nor extend self-rule to those Vietnamese battling the Vietminh. Experienced in the politics of warfare, the president made the decision to separate the United States from the collapsing French effort. Unable to abandon the belief that Vietnam was a vital outpost of containment, however, Eisenhower set the United States on a unilateral course to deny at least part of Indochina to the communists. The soldier-politician rejected the need for or wisdom of U.S. forces fighting in Vietnam and turned instead to a plan to build a new nation in the South to serve as the bulwark against the Democratic Republic of Vietnam (DRV) in the North. Despite bold assertions of miraculous development in South Vietnam under the leadership of Ngo Dinh Diem, Eisenhower left office with Diem's regime under pressure from both the northern regime and southern opponents and totally dependent on the United States for survival.

When the youthful John Kennedy succeeded the elderly Eisenhower, there was an appearance of vigor and innovation in the White House and in U.S. policies around the world. The new president and his team of "New Frontiersmen" possessed genuine confidence in the nation's ability to fulfill Truman's and Eisenhower's commitment to global freedom despite a host of obstacles, such as the resilience of the Vietnamese communists, the Castro revolution in Cuba, and the building of the Berlin Wall. In Vietnam, the Kennedy administration introduced counterinsurgency warfare to combat the DRV and Vietcong war of national liberation. This shift in U.S. thinking brought more military advisers and economic specialists to South Vietnam, but it did not address the historical and social roots of Diem's weakness or his opponents' durability. When Diem and Kennedy died in November 1963, U.S. policy was still intent upon finding an American solution to Vietnam's problems.

Lyndon Johnson made the Americanization of the Vietnam War virtually complete with his massive escalation of U.S. air and ground forces in the conflict. As he faced these momentous decisions, however, he was no more able than his intelligent and energetic predecessor to answer the hard questions about the origins and nature of the war. A master of domestic politics, Johnson knew little of the world or world affairs. He was narrowly provincial, especially for a leader of a modern nation, and his awkward efforts to intimidate Vietnamese enemies and cajole Vietnamese friends in ways that worked in U.S. politics proved to be disastrous for U.S. friends and foes alike. Moreover, his great talent for persuasion and consensus building, which had made him a dominant force in the U.S. Senate and enabled him to craft the Great Society as president, failed him in Vietnam. His doomed effort to juggle the requirements of major domestic reform and limited war abroad was beyond the magic of even his practiced political skills. Although he was able to exploit his role as commander in chief to launch and sustain one of the largest foreign military operations in U.S. history, he was never fully in charge of the war's management. He often avoided deciding among conflicting recommendations or blurred points of debate and, thus, created a stalemate in U.S. policy that was neither a strategy for victory nor a plan for retreat. Both Johnson and the idea of executive leadership in foreign policy became political casualties of the military maelstrom he had unleashed.

It remained for Richard Nixon to break the Vietnam stalemate left by Johnson. Nixon was a belligerent foe of world communism. His career virtually symbolized the purposes that Truman and Eisenhower had first articulated for post–World War II U.S. foreign policy. It was Nixon's intention to defend those long-held goals and to protect the presidency from the debilitating damage that a perceived defeat in Vietnam would inflict upon the office. The original commitment of U.S. wealth and power to Vietnam and the escalation of the hostilities there had been made by a series of presidents with only minimally explicit sanction from Congress or the public. For that reason, the war's long shadow lay on the White House, and responsibility for failure would fall squarely on the Oval Office and its current occupant.

To construct an exit from the war both for himself and for the executive branch, Nixon battled on two fronts: (1) against the DRV and Vietcong and (2) against the war's domestic critics. At home he devised tactics to manage media coverage of the war, and he worked to undermine the youthful antiwar movement through his appeal to the silent majority and the reduction of the military draft. Despite his disdain for peaceniks, his elaborate schemes to limit their activities were grudging recognition of the limits they set on his presidential power to fight the war. As for the battlefront itself, Nixon subtly redefined the war's objective from the limitless defense of freedom to the equally abstract notion of "peace with honor." The settlement he sought was one that would allow U.S. forces to withdraw and leave the government of Nguyen Van Thieu in place in Saigon.

Through Vietnamization of the ground war and an extensive and largely secret bombardment of targets throughout Indochina, Nixon gained his desired peace in January 1973. He had brought an end to the U.S. military intervention in Vietnam and had, the preceding November, won reelection over an obstreperous critic of the war, Senator George McGovern (D-S.Dak.). Neither Nixon nor the presidency escaped the consequences, however, of a war that had grown so unpopular with and, indeed, indefensible to many citizens. Even as the peace accord was being signed in Paris, the first criminal convictions were being handed down in the case of the Watergate break-in of June 17, 1972. In the months and weeks following, persistent investigators unearthed a massive conspiracy that included even the president in illegal activity. Much of this criminal conduct flowed from the efforts of Nixon and his aides to manage the flow of war information and to silence critics. One of the articles of impeachment considered by the House Judiciary Committee against Nixon charged him with conducting the air war against Cambodia without the knowledge or consent of Congress. Furthermore, when Nixon resigned in disgrace and left the presidency humbled in 1974, fighting still raged among the people of Indochina, and no peace had come to that troubled region.

Gerald Ford's frustration with Southeast Asian problems contrasted starkly with the confidence (outwardly, at least) and conviction that characterized the Vietnam decisions of previous presidents. Public and congressional wariness in the wake of Vietnam and Watergate had incapacitated the once imperial presidency but had not rendered it impotent.

Since the fall of South Vietnam in 1975, presidents have sent U.S. forces into battle or risked potential warfare in Lebanon, the Persian Gulf, Grenada, Panama, Saudi Arabia, Iraq, and elsewhere without first securing congressional sanction. The failure of U.S. military intervention in Vietnam to achieve U.S. global objectives has not deterred presidents from making war, but, since the Vietnam debacle, congressional and public oversight of the executive's war-making ability has increased. The Vietnam War was part of the rise and decline, but not fall, of executive power in foreign affairs.

Notes

1. *Public Papers of the Presidents of the United States: Harry S. Truman, 1947* (Washington, D.C.: GPO, 1963), 176–80.

Suggestions for Further Reading

The number of books on the presidency and on the Vietnam War is enormous and continually increasing. The following are only a small portion of that massive literature and are offered as simply a place to begin exploring in detail the themes addressed by this book. Many of the works cited here have excellent bibliographies that provide further guidance.

On the presidency, some standard works are James David Barber, *The Presidential Character*, 3d ed. (Englewood Cliffs, N.J.: Prentice-Hall, 1985); Richard E. Neustadt, *Presidential Power and the Modern Presidents*, rev. ed. (New York: Free Press, 1990); Clinton Rossiter, *The American Presidency*, 2d ed. (New York: Harcourt, Brace & World, 1960); and Arthur M. Schlesinger, Jr., *The Imperial Presidency* (Boston: Houghton Mifflin, 1973). For other general assessments of the post–World War II presidency, see Fred I. Greenstein, ed., *Leadership in the Modern Presidency* (Cambridge, Mass.: Harvard University Press, 1988); Hugh Heclo and Lester M. Salamon, eds., *The Illusion of Presidential Government* (Boulder, Colo.: Westview, 1981); George E. Reedy, *The Twilight of the Presidency* (New York: New American Library, 1970); and Aaron Wildavsky, ed., *Perspectives on the Presidency* (Boston: Little, Brown, 1975).

Books that address the role of the president in the making of foreign policy include Alexander L. George, *Presidential Decisionmaking in Foreign Policy* (Boulder, Colo.: Westview, 1980); Cecil V. Crabb and Pat M. Holt, *Invitation to Struggle: Congress, the President and Foreign Policy*, 2d ed. (Washington, D.C.: Congressional Quarterly, 1984); Louis Henkin, *Foreign Affairs and the Constitution* (New York: Norton, 1975); Edmund S. Muskie, Kenneth Rush, and Kenneth W. Thompson, *The President, the Congress and Foreign Policy* (Lanham, Md.: University Press of America, 1986); John Spanier and Joseph R. Nogee, eds., *Congress, the President and American Foreign Policy* (New York: Pergamon, 1981); and Robert A. Strong, *Decisions and Dilemmas: Case Studies in Presidential Foreign Policy Making* (Englewood Cliffs, N.J.: Prentice-Hall, 1992). Three books that help provide the context in which modern presidents acted are William E. Leuchtenburg, *In the*

Shadow of FDR: From Harry Truman to Ronald Reagan (Ithaca, N.Y.: Cornell University Press, 1983); John Lewis Gaddis, *Strategies of Containment: A Critical Appraisal of Postwar American National Security Policy* (New York: Oxford University Press, 1982); and Alonzo L. Hamby, *Liberalism and Its Challengers: From F.D.R. to Bush*, 2d ed. (New York: Oxford University Press, 1992).

For good general histories of the U.S. role in the Vietnam War, see George C. Herring, *America's Longest War: The United States and Vietnam, 1950-1975*, 2d ed. (New York: Knopf, 1986); Gary R. Hess, *Vietnam and the United States* (Boston: Twayne, 1990); Stanley Karnow, *Vietnam: A History* (New York: Viking, 1983); Gabriel Kolko, *Anatomy of a War: Vietnam, the United States, and the Modern Historical Experience* (New York: Pantheon, 1985); and Marilyn B. Young, *The Vietnam Wars* (New York: HarperCollins, 1991). Important readings on the war are collected in Jeffrey P. Kimball, ed., *To Reason Why: The Debate about the Causes of U.S. Involvement in the Vietnam War* (New York: McGraw-Hill; Philadelphia: Temple University Press, 1990); Robert J. McMahon, ed., *Major Problems in the History of the Vietnam War* (Lexington, Mass.: Heath, 1990); and Andrew J. Rotter, ed., *Light at the End of the Tunnel: A Vietnam War Anthology* (New York: St. Martin's Press, 1991). Three textbooks with good coverage are Thomas D. Boettcher, *Vietnam: The Valor and the Sorrow* (Boston: Little, Brown, 1985); George Donelson Moss, *Vietnam: An American Ordeal* (Englewood Cliffs, N.J.: Prentice-Hall, 1990); and James S. Olson and Randy Roberts, *Where the Domino Fell: America and Vietnam, 1945-1990* (New York: St. Martin's Press, 1991). Valuable document compilations are William Appleman Williams, et al., eds., *America in Vietnam: A Documentary History* (New York: Doubleday, 1985); and United States Department of Defense, *The Pentagon Papers: The Senator Gravel Edition*, 4 vols. (Boston: Beacon, 1971). Other standard works on the war are William J. Duiker, *The Communist Road to Power in Vietnam* (Boulder, Colo.: Westview, 1981); Frances FitzGerald, *Fire in the Lake: The Vietnamese and the Americans in Vietnam* (Boston: Atlantic–Little, Brown, 1972); David Halberstam, *The Best and the Brightest* (New York: Random House, 1972); and Charles DeBenedetti with Charles Chatfield, *An American Ordeal: The Antiwar Movement of the Vietnam War* (Syracuse, N.Y.: Syracuse University Press, 1990).

Two former foreign service officers have produced thoughtful analyses of presidential decisions on Vietnam. These are Paul M. Kattenburg, *The Vietnam Trauma in American Foreign Policy, 1945-75* (New Brunswick, N.J.: Transaction, 1980); and Peter A. Poole, *Eight Presidents and Indochina* (Huntington, N.Y.: Krieger, 1978). A study of congressional-executive relations during the Vietnam era is William Conrad Gibbons, *The U.S. Government and the Vietnam War: Executive and Legislative Roles and Relationships*, 3 parts (Princeton, N.J.: Princeton University Press, 1986–1989). John P. Burke and Fred I. Greenstein with Larry Berman and Richard Immerman, *How Presidents Test Reality: Decisions on Vietnam, 1954 and 1965* (New York: Russell Sage Foundation, 1989), compares the advisory systems in the Eisenhower and Johnson administrations. John E. Mueller, *Wars, Presidents and Public Opinion* (New York: Wiley, 1973), offers another perspective on the presidency and Vietnam through public-opinion polling data.

For Harry S. Truman's policies, Gary R. Hess, *The United States' Emergence as a*

Southeast Asian Power, 1940–1950 (New York: Columbia University Press, 1987), offers a detailed account of the U.S. approach to the Southeast Asian region, and Melvyn P. Leffler, *A Preponderance of Power: National Security, the Truman Administration, and the Cold War* (Stanford, Calif.: Stanford University Press, 1991), places Indochina policy in the context of the global strategic response to the perceived Soviet threat. Robert M. Blum, *Drawing the Line: The Origin of the American Containment Policy in East Asia* (New York: Norton, 1982), emphasizes the domestic politics involved in Truman's decisions. Three studies that trace the Truman administration's linkage of Vietnam to other areas deemed vital to U.S. interests are Lloyd C. Gardner, *Approaching Vietnam: From World War II through Dienbienphu* (New York: Norton, 1988); Andrew J. Rotter, *The Path to Vietnam: Origins of the American Commitment to Southeast Asia* (Ithaca, N.Y.: Cornell University Press, 1987); and Michael Schaller, *The American Occupation of Japan: The Origins of the Cold War in Asia* (New York: Oxford University Press, 1985).

Dwight D. Eisenhower's policies are covered in detail in David L. Anderson, *Trapped by Success: The Eisenhower Administration and Vietnam, 1953–1961* (New York: Columbia University Press, 1991). Much of Gardner, *Approaching Vietnam* (cited above), is devoted to Eisenhower's first term. For in-depth analyses of critical decisions in 1954, see Melanie Billings-Yun, *Decision against War: Eisenhower and Dien Bien Phu, 1954* (New York: Columbia University Press, 1988); and Lawrence S. Kaplan, Denise Artaud, and Mark R. Rubin, eds., *Dien Bien Phu and the Crisis of Franco-American Relations, 1954–1955* (Wilmington, Del.: Scholarly Resources, 1990). Useful general studies of Eisenhower's presidency are Stephen E. Ambrose, *Eisenhower: The President* (New York: Simon & Schuster, 1984); Robert A. Divine, *Eisenhower and the Cold War* (New York: Oxford University Press, 1981); and Chester J. Pach, Jr., and Elmo Richardson, *The Presidency of Dwight D. Eisenhower*, rev. ed. (Lawrence: University Press of Kansas, 1991). Also of value is the first volume of Eisenhower's memoirs, *Mandate for Change* (Garden City, N.Y.: Doubleday, 1963).

On John F. Kennedy, sympathetic accounts such as Arthur M. Schlesinger, Jr., *A Thousand Days: John F. Kennedy in the White House* (Boston: Houghton Mifflin, 1965); and Herbert Parmet, *JFK: The Presidency of John F. Kennedy* (New York: Dial, 1983), are balanced by more critical assessments such as Thomas G. Paterson, ed., *Kennedy's Quest for Victory: American Foreign Policy, 1961–1963* (New York: Oxford University Press, 1989); and Michael R. Beschloss, *The Crisis Years: Kennedy and Khrushchev, 1960–1963* (New York: HarperCollins, 1991). James N. Giglio, *The Presidency of John F. Kennedy* (Lawrence: University Press of Kansas, 1991), provides a dispassionate analysis. Books that focus more specifically on Kennedy and Vietnam are David L. Di Leo, *George Ball, Vietnam, and the Rethinking of Containment* (Chapel Hill: University of North Carolina Press, 1991); Ellen J. Hammer, *A Death in November: America in Vietnam, 1963* (New York: Oxford University Press, 1988); Roger Hilsman, *To Move a Nation: The Politics of Foreign Policy in the Administration of John F. Kennedy* (Garden City, N.Y.: Doubleday, 1967); John M. Newman, *JFK and Vietnam: Deception, Intrigue and the Struggle for Power* (New York: Warner Books, 1992); and William J. Rust, *Kennedy and Vietnam* (New York: Scribners, 1985).

A general history of Lyndon B. Johnson's war policies is found in two books by Larry Berman: *Planning a Tragedy: The Americanization of the War in Vietnam* (New York: Norton, 1982); and *Lyndon Johnson's War: The Road to Stalemate in Vietnam* (New York: Norton, 1989). Analyses of Johnson's escalation of the war include George McT. Kahin, *Intervention: How America Became Involved in Vietnam* (New York: Knopf, 1986); and Brian VanDeMark, *Into the Quagmire: Lyndon Johnson and the Escalation of the Vietnam War* (New York: Oxford University Press, 1991). Some good specialized studies of Johnson's actions are Melvin Small, *Johnson, Nixon, and the Doves* (New Brunswick, N.J.: Rutgers University Press, 1988); Herbert Y. Schandler, *The Unmaking of a President: Lyndon Johnson and Vietnam* (Princeton, N.J.: Princeton University Press, 1977); Kathleen J. Turner, *Lyndon Johnson's Dual War: Vietnam and the Press* (Chicago: University of Chicago Press, 1985); and Larry Cable, *Unholy Grail: The US and the Wars in Vietnam, 1965–8* (London: Routledge, 1991). Biographical studies are Vaughn Davis Bornet, *The Presidency of Lyndon B. Johnson* (Lawrence: University Press of Kansas, 1983); Doris Kearns, *Lyndon Johnson and the American Dream* (New York: Harper & Row, 1976); and the multivolume works of Robert A. Caro and Robert Dallek, which are still in preparation. Caro has published *The Years of Lyndon Johnson: The Path to Power* (New York: Knopf, 1982), and *The Years of Lyndon Johnson: Means of Ascent* (New York: Knopf, 1990). Dallek has published *Lone Star Rising: Lyndon Johnson and His Times, 1908–1960* (New York: Oxford University Press, 1991). Also useful is Lyndon Baines Johnson, *The Vantage Point: Perspectives on the Presidency, 1963–1969* (New York: Holt, Rinehart and Winston, 1971).

Richard M. Nixon's conduct of the war and of the peace negotiations is described in Richard Nixon, *RN: The Memoirs of Richard Nixon* (New York: Grosset & Dunlap, 1978); and Henry Kissinger, *White House Years* (Boston: Little, Brown, 1979). Biographies of Nixon include Stephen E. Ambrose, *Nixon*, 3 vols. (New York: Simon & Schuster, 1987–1991); and Herbert Parmet, *Richard Nixon and His America* (Boston: Little, Brown, 1990). For analyses of Nixon's Vietnam policies, see Small, *Johnson, Nixon, and the Doves* (cited above); Allen E. Goodman, *The Lost Peace: America's Search for a Negotiated Settlement of the Vietnam War* (Stanford, Calif.: Hoover Institution Press, 1978); Seymour M. Hersh, *The Price of Power: Kissinger in the Nixon White House* (New York: Summit, 1983); Stanley I. Kutler, *The Wars of Watergate: The Last Crisis of Richard Nixon* (New York: Knopf, 1990); Nguyen Tien Hung and Jerrold L. Schecter, *The Palace File* (New York: Harper & Row, 1986); Gareth Porter, *A Peace Denied: The United States, Vietnam, and the Paris Agreement* (Bloomington: Indiana University Press, 1975); Robert D. Schulzinger, *Henry Kissinger: Doctor of Diplomacy* (New York: Columbia University Press, 1989); and Joseph Spear, *Presidents and the Press: The Nixon Legacy* (Cambridge, Mass.: MIT Press, 1984).

Gerald R. Ford's Vietnam decisions are discussed in Gerald R. Ford, *A Time to Heal: The Autobiography of Gerald R. Ford* (New York: Harper & Row, 1979); Robert T. Hartmann, *Palace Politics: An Inside Account of the Ford Years* (New York: McGraw-Hill, 1980); Hung and Schecter, *The Palace File* (cited above); Arnold Isaacs, *Without Honor: Defeat in Vietnam and Cambodia* (Baltimore: Johns Hopkins University Press, 1983); Ron Nessen, *It Sure Looks Different from the In-*

side (Chicago: Playboy Press, 1978); and Frank Snepp, *Decent Interval* (New York: Random House, 1977). Also useful is P. Edward Haley, *Congress and the Fall of South Vietnam and Cambodia* (Rutherford, N.J.: Fairleigh Dickinson University Press; London: Associated University Presses, 1982).

About the Contributors

DAVID L. ANDERSON is professor of history and chair of the Department of History and Political Science at the University of Indianapolis. He is the author of *Trapped by Success: The Eisenhower Administration and Vietnam, 1953-1961* (1991), which was a co-winner of the Robert H. Ferrell Book Prize awarded by the Society for Historians of American Foreign Relations, and of *Imperialism and Idealism: American Diplomats in China, 1861-1898* (1985).

GEORGE C. HERRING is Alumni Professor of History at the University of Kentucky. A specialist in the history of U.S. foreign relations, his recent work has focused on the Vietnam War and includes *America's Longest War: The United States and Vietnam, 1950-1975* (rev. ed., 1986) and *The Secret Diplomacy of the Vietnam War: The "Negotiating Volumes" of the Pentagon Papers* (1983). His chapter in this book draws on work for his forthcoming study of Johnson's management of the war. During 1991, he was Visiting Fulbright Scholar at the University of Otago, Dunedin, New Zealand. He was president of the Society for Historians of American Foreign Relations in 1989.

GARY R. HESS is Distinguished Research Professor at Bowling Green State University. His research interests have focused on U.S. policy in South and Southeast Asia, and his most recent books are *The United States' Emergence as a Southeast Asian Power, 1940-1950* (1987) and *Vietnam and the United States: Origins and Legacy of War* (1990). He is past president of the Society for Historians of American Foreign Relations.

JEFFREY P. KIMBALL is professor of history at Miami University. He is author of *To Reason Why: The Debate about the Causes of U.S. Involvement in the Vietnam War* (1990) and is currently working on a book about Richard Nixon's policies during the Vietnam War. He is secretary-treasurer of the Council on Peace Research in History.

ROBERT J. McMAHON is professor of history at the University of Florida. He is the author of *Colonialism and Cold War: The United States and the Struggle for Indonesian Independence, 1945–1949* (1981), editor of *Major Problems in the History of the Vietnam War* (1990), and coeditor of *The Origins of the Cold War* (3d ed., 1991). He has recently completed a book manuscript entitled *The Cold War on the Periphery: The United States, India, and Pakistan, 1947–1965*.

MELVIN SMALL is a professor of history at Wayne State University and president of the Council on Peace Research in History. He wrote *Was War Necessary?* (1980) and *Johnson, Nixon, and the Doves* (1988); coauthored *The Wages of War* (1972) and *Resort to Arms* (1982); edited *Public Opinion and Historians* (1970); and coedited *International War* (1985), *Appeasing Fascism* (1991), and *Give Peace a Chance* (1992). He is currently working on a study of the antiwar movement and the media.

SANDRA C. TAYLOR is professor of history at the University of Utah. She has published several review articles on the Vietnam War in *Reviews in American History* and an article on the war in Laos in E. J. Errington and B. J. C. McKercher, eds., *The Vietnam War as History* (1990). Her book on Japanese internment during World War II will be published in 1993. She is continuing her research on Laos and is pursuing a project on relations between the United States and Vietnam since 1975.

Index